ADVANCE PRAISE

Carl Jung, the Swiss psychiatrist and psychoanalyst, wrote, "Life is a short pause between two great mysteries." Jung did not mean to devalue the "short pause" but rather heighten the importance of it; to encourage us to grab ahold of it with an unquenchable curiosity, an insurmountable courage, and a clear-eyed soberness, and to reflect as transparently as possible on what this "short pause" might mean so as to better understand the "two great mysteries." Reverend Dr. Jean Milliken does exactly this through her memoir, *The Holy Spirit and the Honey Bee.*

Milliken takes the reader on a journey that scales mountains and plumbs the valleys of a life well-lived. Along the way, we are given the efficacious gift of seeing life through her eyes as she fiercely and unflinchingly wrestles with questions about God, the role of women in both the church and society, family and profession, and the ever-present reality of trauma that shadows so many of our stories. The poet Christian Wiman wrote, "Memories mercies mostly aren't. But there are days, I swear, that are veined with grace." Through Milliken's wonderfully candid prose, *The Holy Spirit and the Honey Bee* offers a hand that leads us to see these graces as arresting and artful, challenging and comforting, and insightful and inclusive. This is an important book written by a marvelous human being that will bless all who engage with it.

–**Dave Hillis**,
Shoemaker Senior Fellow at the Leadership Foundations
Colangelo Carpenter Innovation Center and author of
A Complicated Grace and *Cities: Playgrounds or Battlegrounds?*

This rich, reflective, theologically informed memoir not only recounts a faith journey but invites readers to explore the forces at work in ourselves as we come to terms with our social and spiritual formation. Jean offers engaging, practical direction from her training as a priest and therapist toward ways of healing from buried traumas, finding our voices, and learning to trust. She speaks with the voice of a wise elder whose backward glance has been clear-eyed and filled with gratitude, who has made her peace with mortality, and who has lived into a joy that becomes a gift to her readers.

–**Marilyn McEntyre**,
author of *Caring for Words in a Culture of Lies* and
other books and writings available at marilynmcentyre.com

It's rare to know someone who lives their life to the absolute fullest. Jean Milliken is a great example. This is a deeply honest story of her great courage, insightfulness, and dedication at many forms and levels—asking the hard internal questions, taking responsibility, breaking inherited negative patterns, connecting with God, identifying as a spiritual being, creating as an individual, co-creating as a wife, nurturing as a mother, collaborating with friends. This is a life well lived, a story well told.

–**Gerry Eitner**, Spiritual Coach,
President, Communities of Peace

In *The Holy Spirit and the Honey Bee*, Jean Milliken offers a gracious gift—the story of her remarkable journey of faith lived with courage, conviction, and wisdom. Her disarming honesty in facing personal and justice challenges, from family wounds to forging an egalitarian marriage, is matched only by her openness to God's transforming love at every turn. Milliken's deep knowledge of Scripture and theology enlivens every page, yet it is her immense heart for God and others that most powerfully moves the reader. As she recounts listening for the Holy Spirit through seasons of growth as a mother, priest, counselor, and contemplative, one feels in the presence of a true spiritual master.

Ultimately, this memoir is a testament to a life wholly given over to Christ, in tender love for family and fierce advocacy for justice. *The Holy Spirit and the Honey Bee* is a rare and exquisite treasure.

–**Dan Cardinelli**,
Board Chair of the Fetzer Institute

Daughter, Sister, Wife, Mother, Grandmother: these are the lenses through which Jean Milliken reflects on her life and the commitments she has made to her family and to the Church she has faithfully served. Many readers will identify with the challenges and the joys she has experienced in her 45 years as a priest, pastoral counselor, and friend to many of us who have had the good fortune to know Jean and to work with her.

–**The Very Reverend Martha Horne**, Dean and President of Virginia Theological Seminary, 1994-2007

Jean Milliken offers us a welcome gift from her heart, mind, and soul—a personal story well told of life, learning, and love. Through the warmth of her writing, we quickly discover resonance and insight invaluable to our own still unfolding stories. Reverend Milliken dives deep into the "givens" of family and circumstances that shape each of us from before we are born, the power of the freedom of choice and what we do with it, the heartbreak and joy of marriage that might stretch to the breaking point and then, through commitment and work, bring us back together with a more understanding and powerful love. Faced with the profound challenges of a life well-lived, Milliken draws upon influences ranging from her mother and grandparents to psychologist Carl Jung, theologian Paul Tillich, Episcopal priest Cynthia Bourgault, and Franciscan teacher Richard Rohr. These teachers join with the power of the Holy Spirit, pollinating our hearts with unconditional love, to create a powerful Wisdom that Jean Milliken brings to each of us.

–**Susan L. Marquis**, author, *I Am Not a Tractor: How Florida Farmworkers Took on the Fast-Food Giants and Won!*, Charles and Marie Robertson Chair, Princeton University

THE
HOLY SPIRIT
and the
HONEY BEE

*A Wise Elder's Journey of Discovery
as a Partner, Mother, Friend,
and Priest*

JEAN LOUISE MILLIKEN

The Holy Spirit and the Honey Bee

ISBN: 979-8-9928630-6-2

Book Design by Transcendent Publishing
Cover Image Art by Suren Nersisyan
Editing by Mary Rembert

Printed in the United States of America.

To my husband, Bill, who has "walked his talk" to be faithful
to his life's purpose, serving at-risk young people and
providing resources for them to stay in school and have a vision
for a healthy, successful life. His enduring love for me,
our children, and our grandchildren has, in many ways,
been the "wind beneath our wings."

TABLE OF CONTENTS

"Out beyond the ideas of wrongdoing and rightdoing, there is a field. I will meet you there."

–Rumi, a 13th-century poet,
first published in Persian in
The Collected Poems of Shams of Tabriz,
translated into English

INTRODUCTION

You might think this is a book for women, but, in fact, it is a book for both men and women who are creating a vision to become whole human beings, to build healthy families, partnerships, and communities that call forth and use everyone's gifts—a vision that invites cross-pollination and yields new life.

In my mind's eye, I imagine a honey bee leaving the hive she is tasked with protecting and keeping clean, fluttering her wings, and using her ability to see ultraviolet light to discern the scent, color, and nectar of plants and flowers.

This mysterious light guides her to flowers ready to provide nectar, which will ultimately produce honey. Her legs and stomach will carry pollen from the male part of the plant to the female part of the next flower she visits, allowing the plant to produce seeds that have the potential to create new plant life.

Like the honey bee, it is a bit mysterious whose heart the Holy Spirit will enter to pollinate, yielding the seeds for new life and bearing the fruit of God's love in the world. Does the Spirit have a kind of ultraviolet light that guides the pollination of the soul to those who are in need of hope, discernment, and/or new life to emerge out of loss and suffering?

I periodically get mailings warning about the extinction of honey bees, resulting in the lack of pollinators for fruits and flowers that bring us food and beauty. I wonder if the Holy Spirit is in danger of becoming extinct in our lives due to our busyness and fear of committing to the internal growth needed to sustain long-term committed relationships with others and with God.

How can we talk about spiritual life and faith in the One who "makes all things new" while using language that often feels like we are putting "new wine into old wineskins?" It is so difficult that sometimes it feels like we have given up trying.

As a young woman, I desperately needed language to communicate my reality. My need for new words to describe my reality deepened as my social situation changed. Moving from a homogeneous community in suburban Pittsburgh to a diverse community in New York City gave me a whole new perspective, as for the first time, I was a minority, both racially and religiously.

While serving as a chaplain and pastoral psychotherapist resident at Georgia Baptist Hospital in Atlanta, where I was trained to interpret faith experiences in psychological terms, I learned a second language, the language of psychology. Reading updated translations of scripture that offered gender-inclusive language was transformative.

As I began to understand the connection between the character of Wisdom expressed in feminine terms in both the Hebrew and Christian scriptures and captured in the third person of the Trinity, the Holy Spirit, I embraced the truth that I was truly created in the Image of God.

Weaving these three strands together in this memoir, I have attempted to communicate a holistic and contemporary understanding of faith that includes the theological, that is, our language about God, Jesus, and the Holy Spirit; the psychological, be it psychoanalytic, Jungian, or Family Systems; and the social/political/cultural forces at work among and within us. I have woven my family story throughout this memoir, too, because as I once heard Peter Buffett, son of financier Warren Buffett, say, "We are all born into someone else's story."

It is true that we all have givens—things we had no choice about; the families we were born into, stories that were told about us and to us as children that shaped our sense of ourselves—our DNA, our dispositions, and the core selves we came into the world with which are ours to discover, develop, and express.

Then, too, there are the decisions we make as we exercise our free will. Certainly, we are influenced by extended family, community friends, education, who we marry, if we do, and the work in which we are engaged. These are all things we have chosen. Ultimately, no one can take away our freedom of choice. None of us lives this life without doing harm and/or having harm done to us. Who we become cannot be legislated by the government or earned by following the rules of the church or believing certain doctrines; it is shaped by our choices.

Our earliest sense of security and attachment to a nurturing caregiver comes from growing in the knowledge that we belong to those who care for us, our people—our tribe. Knowing you belong to a tribe is a good thing for a child. The tribe, extended family, or close multigenerational community can provide safety, security, shelter, love, and an identity upon which one can grow a life with deep roots to weather the strong winds of change.

The questions, "Who is my family?" "Where do I belong?" and "Am I safe here among these people?" began for me as early as I can remember. It was a shaky foundation on which to build. The first time I drew a family map, I was shocked to see broken lines on both sides representing the divorces of both my paternal and maternal grandparents, my mother and father, and the broken marriage relationship of my mother's only brother.

The overuse of alcohol by the men in my family also created an environment that lacked safety, predictability, emotional connection, and helpful discipline. The trauma of The Great Depression, beginning in 1929, caused by the stock market crash, bank failures, high tariffs affecting international trade, and wealth being concentrated at the top still loomed large in the lives of those who had lived through it.

As I think about World War II and the years following, which also shaped my grandparents and parents' lives, I can appreciate the challenges both men and women faced to rebuild their marriages and families. Most women were unqualified to find meaningful work outside the home that provided a livable wage. Men who had served in the military were struggling as they tried to regain their places at home with work and family while processing the trauma of war.

The story I was born into of multi-generational divorce, adults numbing emotions with tobacco and alcohol, and moving from place to place with my mother prepared me to fit in wherever I found myself. In large part, these things prepared me to marry Bill, move from a homogeneous suburb to live in New York City, and find my way amidst people of many cultures. Watching my mother clip coupons to save money on groceries, sew my school clothes, and manage our family finances, I learned how to provide for our family with limited financial resources since my husband had to raise his own salary working as a youth worker, and we often came up short at the end of each month.

Our marriage has provided fertile ground for healing from the past. By grace and hard work, we have helped each other grow up, have survived the growing pains, and have learned what "reality love" is. I thought I had chosen a man who wouldn't abandon me, but abandonment comes in many forms. Bill traveled weekly to build Cities in Schools (now Communities in Schools) around the country. The opportunity to face my abandonment fears came with painful regularity.

This memoir is intended to honor my forebears, particularly my mother, whose contribution to raising children, cooking healthy meals, and creating a home was often taken for granted. I have written it so that my mother's children, my brother and sister, Linda and Kurt; her grandchildren, Sean, Lani, Kathryn, David, Margaret, Jennifer, and Mariel; and great-grandchildren, Alexandra, Jack, Shiloh, and Jonah, can know her better through my experience of her. And, too, I am grateful for my stepfather and maternal grandparents, who worked to provide a home and love for my mother and me.

While being stunted in my life of faith by culture-bound preaching, theology, and practices in institutional religion, I appreciate the worship, outreach, and compassionate actions for those in need practiced by many religious communities. As I look back and into the future, viewing the world our children and grandchildren are facing presently, I have unwavering support and gratitude for faith communities that teach children who God is and how Jesus, The Cosmic Christ, embodies God's nature of love for all of humanity and all of God's creation and teaches how to discern wrongdoing when you fail to live up to what you know is right, and how to confess it and move forward in relationship to Unconditional Love. Faith communities can lay the foundation for children to trust in a loving God and for the Holy Spirit to be a lifelong companion and guide for children as they use their unique gifts and creative imaginations to engage in life's challenges.

I have served as an Episcopal priest and pastoral counselor for most of my adult life. My long marriage to Bill and the challenge of parenting two very different children, now adults, in a multi-ethnic and racially mixed neighborhood, has stretched me thin—at times almost to the breaking point. I know from long experience that light shines in the darkness, even in periods of depression, anxiety, and loss.

Carl Jung and Paul Tillich, two great twentieth-century voices in psychology and theology, encouraged me to explore and befriend both my masculine and feminine nature and suggested a new name for God, "the Ground of Being." Richard Rohr, a Franciscan priest and teacher who finds creative expression of universal truth, and Cynthia Bourgault, an Episcopal priest and scholar of the Wisdom tradition, set the wisdom tradition in a new context for me. Jungian analysts Irene Claremont de Castillejo and Marian Woodman have been beacons of light and breathed fresh air into my relationship with the Creator.

My years serving as pastor to the staff and visitors of the Washington National Cathedral introduced me to the values of many faith traditions and those who practice them in a spirit of love and service. Serving on the staff and board of Faith at Work (now Lumunos), founded by The Reverend Sam Shoemaker, spiritual advisor to the men who developed the 12 Steps practiced by AA, I learned to share honestly about my life's challenges and receive love and encouragement from others that came without advice or judgment.

The wisdom of these teachers is threaded through my story as it has informed the various questions and seasons of my life. Sometimes, I give them credit when I quote them. Other times, I have not been sure where their thinking ends and mine begins, as I have shared musings from my journals. Please forgive me if I have not given credit where it is due. I offer immense gratitude to all of you for what you have given me; may it bear fruit.

Someone once said that the most valuable possession any of us has to share is our life story. "When an old person dies who hasn't shared their story, it is like a library has burned down." Everyone has at least one story to tell. I have written mine; I hope you will write yours.

Jean Louise Moore Kondas Milliken

IN THE BEGINNING:
CHILDHOOD

My Mother's Candles

When my mother died, my sister and I went through the house to sort her household items. Opening the side door of the buffet in the dining room, my sister exclaimed, "There are boxes and boxes of unburned candles in here!" Some were bent from melting, and others were drab and colorless from years of being boxed up and kept in the dark—candles saved and preserved to be used for something special in the future, which never fulfilled their purpose in her lifetime.

The memory of my mother's candles, faded, misshapen, and never used, has motivated me not to wait to celebrate in the present or to fulfill my dreams beginning now.

Today, I am lighting a smoky vanilla candle I have had for several years. It will burn clean because it is made from soy wax and nontoxic essential oils. Like my mother, I have been saving this candle for something special.

Today is a day to put pen to paper to honor my life story and put a match to this special candle. Why haven't I lit the candle before now? I know it often takes years to get ready to do something you have wanted to do for a long time. I'm also aware of Maya Angelou's words, "There is no greater agony than bearing an untold story inside you."[1] Perhaps I have had to wait until the agony within became so great that I had to

---

[1] Maya Angelou, *I Know Why the Caged Bird Sings* (New York: Random House, 1969), 31.

tell it so I could release the negative thoughts and experiences of the past and live in freedom in the present.

Today is the right time to light the candle, pray for the flame to light my memory, and offer my life experience to my family and friends, known and unknown. I trust that the memories I have preserved and reflected upon will be brought to light and enriched by time, reflection, and experience. I offer them to do my part to light the way for the next generation.

I found the courage to continue to write my story when I read the following words from therapist Terry Real, "Family dysfunction rolls down from generation to generation, like fire in the woods, taking down everything in its path until one person in one generation has the courage to turn and face the flames. That person brings peace to their ancestors and spares the children that follow."[2] To claim that I have the courage of a firefighter facing the flames seems a little grandiose, yet it is a daunting task to look honestly at one's life choices, celebrating the ones that were life-giving and making amends for self-centered ones that hurt others.

I want to be brave and hope that I have the courage to "face the flames" of my childhood and adulthood and break the cycle of the ways my life has been shaped by divorce and the misuse of alcohol by those who have come before me. At the same time, I am sure that I have passed things on to my children that I am responsible for that have hurt them and will be their "flames" to face.

One thing I know is that the fear of rejection and abandonment has been a constant companion throughout my life. It still can grab me by the throat and keep me from speaking the truth as I see it. My need to belong has caused me to abandon myself to please others.

These are my memories; each person who is a part of my story will likely have remembered events differently or given them different meanings. I value and respect their experiences as I honor my own. I am encouraged in my reflections by the words of the ancient philosopher

---

[2] Terry Real, *The New Rules of Marriage: What You Need to Know to Make Love Work* (2007).

Socrates, recorded in Plato's *Apology*, who said, "The unexamined life is not worth living."

My mother, Lois, was born in 1919 on the north side of Pittsburgh, Pennsylvania, in the wake of World War I. Like her mother, she was small in stature. Sitting behind the wheel of her black Plymouth, you could barely see her head above the steering wheel. When she was behind the wheel, my grandfather Vogel called her "Leadfoot Lodie." She drove fast with energy and determination.

During her life, my mother went by four last names: two from her mother's marriages and two from her own. She died in 1983 at 63 of breast cancer that had metastasized to her bones and brain. In photos taken over the two years she lived following the cancer diagnosis, I can see her decline. On visits home to Pittsburgh during the early phase of her cancer treatment, I saw her stand in front of the bathroom mirror, expressing her distress about the clumps of hair falling out each time she combed her hair. The wig she wore to replace the hair she lost due to the chemotherapy was blond and didn't look like the permed, gray, curly hair she had washed, dried, and styled at the beauty shop every week. She pushed herself to keep caring for her home and family, but the spark had left her eyes.

Although healthy as a child and young woman before her cancer diagnosis, Mom also developed heart problems as an adult that caused her to have a blocked artery cleaned out in her neck and to take nitroglycerin pills to control the symptoms. She was exhausted by five or six in the evening and often fell asleep sitting on the couch, chin resting on her chest as the television played on with no one watching.

Readying myself to leave for home after our visits, I tried to hide my tears. I could see the pain she was in and knew there was nothing I could do to ease it. I felt torn. I wanted to stay in Pittsburgh and help with her care, but Bill and our two children were at home in Atlanta. They needed my care as well. I found myself wishing she could be more assertive with her doctors about treatment, but for her generation, the doctors were the authority, and it was uncommon to question them. And the options for the treatment of breast cancer were limited in the early 1980s.

As the cancer continued to spread, Mom asked me to pray that she would get well, but I knew I couldn't honestly offer a prayer for physical health. I could pray for her healing in mind and spirit. Sometimes miracles do happen, and physical healing can occur through medical treatment, prayer, faith, and God's grace. It seemed to me, however, that her healing would happen at the level of mind and spirit if she could accept that her death was inevitable.

I prayed to find the strength within me to affirm her desire to live, at the same time knowing that her time would most likely end soon. I was hoping that she might want to say some things to friends and family that were important for her to say and for us to hear about the joys and sorrows of her life. It was painful not to be able to have those honest conversations since she hung on so tenaciously to the belief that somehow she would be able to live. I couldn't find a way to initiate those conversations. I, too, was in partial denial; I believed in healing prayer and hoped for a miracle. She was so young and wanted so much to see Sean and Lani grow up and to know the grandchildren she expected Linda and Kurt and their spouses to have in the future. But all the physical signs showed she was close to the end of her life.

In her childhood, Mom was her brother Bobby's big sister, and she watched out for him. Though she never grew beyond five feet, she wasn't afraid of the neighborhood boys and protected Bobby from bullies in the Northside neighborhood where they lived with their mother, Louise, and her three brothers following her divorce.

I discovered several letters Mom had saved from her father that he had written after he and Grandma divorced. They were tender and loving. I sensed she was also close to her father's mother, who made beautiful quilts, some of which I now use, but Mom never spoke of her grandmother. It led me to believe she lost that relationship, too, when her parents divorced.

Although Mom dated a number of young men after high school during her two years of college, my father kept coming back into the picture, trying to convince her to marry him before he left for military service abroad. I don't know what he said to convince her to give up her dream of finishing college and becoming a teacher, but I imagine the fear of loss during wartime was a powerful factor.

She and I never talked about her brief marriage to my father, though I was 40 when she died, and there were opportunities when we could have. I never asked. I never heard her speak of him at all and somehow got the message early on that the subject was taboo—too painful to talk about. I am convinced that the trauma she suffered from her father's leaving the family and later her husband's abandonment lodged in her heart and mind like a tumor and contributed to her failing health and early death.

Even during hard times, Mom was optimistic about life's challenges and opportunities. After she remarried when I was nine, I don't remember a night when she didn't have dinner on the table at 5:30 when my stepfather came home. We could count on meat, often chicken, hamburger, or meatloaf, mashed potatoes, a vegetable, and salad at every meal. The only exception was on Fridays when we had Mrs. Paul's fish sticks to honor my father's Catholic traditions.

Once my brother, sister, and I became more independent, she began pursuing some of her own interests. She loved growing flowers in her backyard garden, creating and submitting flower arrangements to the Garden Club for their yearly show. One 4th of July, her flower arrangement was presented on a tablecloth of stars and stripes bordered by a ball fringe with napkins to match, which she had sewn. I saved it for many years and then passed it on to my sister, who I believe has occasions to use it now.

Mom had a beautiful singing voice and loved dressing up in formal attire and singing with a Sweet Adelines singing group. She looked so beautiful in her long dresses, and the fragrance of her Chanel #5, replaced each year by our dad at Christmas, indicated that she was feeling beautiful and ready to meet the singing group to perform.

As a young woman, I looked back on my mother's life and saw her as powerless. I saw her submitting and adapting, choosing to respond to the wishes of the family members on whom she was financially dependent. I saw her surrounded by men who drank every night to deal with their pain and unresolved trauma from war, abuse in school, and childhood trauma at home. Husbands and fathers sometimes bottled up unexplored emotions until they exploded in rage, often at the dinner table, displacing their emotions onto wives and children by focusing on things like table manners.

It seems to me that she was left in an emotional desert, taking care of others while ignoring the need to care for herself. The letters she left behind when she died have given me a deeper insight into how few choices she had about many things. I now see that what I once judged as passivity can be seen through a different lens as strength. She used that strength to nurture our family's health and well-being through service and personal sacrifice.

One might say Mom died of a broken heart. She kept silent about the grief and shame of my father's abandonment, rejection, and unfaithfulness. She suffered the abusive treatment of his father, who did not approve of their marriage. He demanded that she carry heavy buckets of hot water up the farmhouse stairs for his bath while she was pregnant. His father tried in every way he could think of to undermine their marriage, treating her like a household servant and driving a wedge between the young couple.

Mom was a feisty young woman. I imagine she fought for her relationship with my father, but she was one young woman standing against a 6-foot-4-inch giant of a father-in-law who was an alcoholic, deeply enmeshed with his son, and on whom she depended for housing and food when my father was home on leave as well as when he was away serving in the Army. The deck was stacked against her. My father's loyalty to his father won out.

Her ability to care for herself, speak up for herself, and fulfill her dream to become a teacher was limited by many factors: her decision to drop out of college after two years to marry, my father's absence during the war and his unwillingness to offer any financial support for us to live on or for her to continue her education, the cultural and religiously defined roles of women and men in marriage, and the legacy of divorce. Nevertheless, her faithfulness, prayers, presence, and guidance made it possible for me to find my voice and my calling as a priest, pastoral therapist, marriage partner, and mother. I am deeply grateful.

My Grandmother's Gifts

My grandmother's name was Louise, my middle name. It has been a family name for generations, starting with my grandmother's grandmother, and it continues beyond me to the next generation. Before she died at age 94, I interviewed my maternal grandmother, whom I lovingly called Gram, for a class assignment about foremothers. Although at the outset she seemed apologetic about what the women in our family had accomplished, it didn't take long before she was excited and pleased to tell as much as she could remember about them.

Although life was hard for my mother and grandmother, who were single parents with limited financial support, they found ways to provide for themselves and their children with the help of extended family. They were gentle women with high moral standards. Both were bright, courageous, and good businesswomen. They were good cooks and could sew. They loved children and competently managed their households, including the family finances.

Gram gave up school to go to work when her mother died young. She worked in an office, a bank, and a department store, and cleaned houses to support her children after her husband left. She loved to read and was self-educated. She was a kind, generous woman with a strong faith in God.

When she remarried, she chose a man who loved her deeply and provided for her financially. Because he was well-established in several businesses, they had the resources to travel. When their daughter arrived unexpectedly, he had the time to help raise her and was engaged with all her grandchildren, including me. She described the women of the family as strong, determined, and courageous. Those terms certainly described her.

Gram was born a twin in 1900. Her twin sister died at birth. She had three older brothers, John (Jack), Edward, and William (Bill), with whom she was very close. When her husband, Ralph, became involved with a woman at the office, Gram took a stand and asked him to leave. She had left school in eighth grade to go to work. Although she was smart, an avid reader, and a hard worker, she had no marketable skills to support her and her children as a single mother. Her three brothers lived with her, helped her survive financially, and provided male guidance for my mother and her brother, Bobby.

After my mother and Uncle Bobby grew up and became independent, Gram and Norbert (Pop) Vogel, five years her senior, fell in love and wanted to marry. Because she was a divorced woman and Pop's family was Catholic, they were sure his mother would never approve.

They married secretly and lived separately for the first year of their marriage. Gram unexpectedly became pregnant at age 41. In time, his family embraced her and their daughter, Karen. It often felt as if Grandma was my mother and my mother was my grown-up sister, since we lived with Gram and Pop until I was five and were financially dependent on them.

I spent every summer at their cottage at Conneaut Lake while my mother stayed home in Pittsburgh and worked. Gram was in charge of running the household. Pop helped her, provided protection and security, and served as my surrogate father.

My mother called me once after I was married and had children of my own, somewhat distraught, to ask me who I thought raised me. She and Gram were disagreeing about it. I felt put on the spot and answered, "You are my mother," which was the truth and didn't devalue what Grandma had given me or my mother's unwavering commitment to my well-being.

I can only imagine how difficult it must have been for these two women to share homemaking and childrearing for so many years—competing, cooperating, and loving at the same time—but they did it, as many other women of their generation did. And their love for each other remained strong.

Gram was my source of information and stories about my father until I entered high school and chose to meet him myself. The story she told me about my father leaving Mom and me captured a snapshot of both my strong connection to my father by age two and a half and the deep sadness I felt when he left us at Gram and Pop's.

My mother established contact with my father's mother when he left. Mother Anna, as she preferred to be called, was kind and supportive of my mother and was glad to have me as her granddaughter. The story my grandmother Louise told me was that Clyde Sr., my father's father, was a womanizer and a heavy drinker. Anna feared for her life.

One day, she picked up and ran away. Without a job and with limited savings, she headed to New Jersey, leaving the children with their father since she knew he would provide for them. She planned to reconnect and provide for them when she got on her feet. What she didn't know was that their father would poison their minds against her.

Sadly, my father and his mother never spoke again. Helen, her daughter, did establish contact with her mother later in life. The environment Helen lived in with her father and his much younger second wife and their two boys did not seem to be a healthy one for her; over time, she became emotionally unstable and alienated from her mother. After finding her way to Absecon, New Jersey, Anna met and married Arthur Scott, a cigar salesman many years her senior, and established herself as a tutor/teacher of children.

My mother and I visited Mother Anna once or twice a year. On one visit, I saw a picture of her dressed in a nurse's uniform. Puzzled because I hadn't heard that she was a nurse, too, I asked, "It looks like you were a nurse in this picture. Were you?" She replied, "When your father wouldn't answer any of my attempts to communicate with him, and I knew he was serving in the Army, I volunteered as a Grey Lady to support the war effort. I thought if I took care of young men who were injured for their families, maybe someone would take care of my son, wherever he might be if he was injured."

I'll never forget the picture she had framed on her fireplace mantel of an unknown child, which took the place of her own children, of whom she had no photographs. When I inquired who the child was, she matter-of-factly responded, "I have no pictures of my children, so I cut it out of a magazine."

My heart filled with a pool of sadness at that simple explanation. Mother Anna had to leave her children behind, yet coped with her loss by giving unceasingly to the children of others through her teaching and tutoring. Her life always seemed tragic to me because she felt she had no options but to leave her children behind when she left an abusive relationship with my grandfather, Clyde, to save herself. My father was eight, and his sister, Helen, was six.

I have letters Mother Anna wrote to my father and aunt, inviting them to come for a visit and offering to pay their way once she got on her feet. I found the letters among my mother's papers after she died, which had been returned to Mother Anna unread. I am sure she carried a boatload of grief about the loss of her relationship with her children, but like my mother and maternal grandmother, she never expressed her feelings about these losses, at least not to me. I don't know if she felt regret. She seemed resolved to build a new life for herself despite the excruciating loss of her children and the people and things she had left behind.

Longing for Fatherly Love

My Grandmother Louise painted a vivid picture for me when she told me the story of my father leaving us. "Daddy, Daddy, don't go," I cried as I tried to run toward the car.

"Get that kid out of my way," my father shouted as he rolled up his window and pulled away, tires screeching as he sped down the long driveway to the street below. My grandmother and mother stood in stony silence, my mother frozen in place, holding tightly to my hand.

When his father broke his neck from falling into a hole while under the influence of alcohol and died unexpectedly, my father, Clyde Jr., was released early from the Army to come home and take over the family business, the Moore-Flesher Hauling Company.

Over the years, I heard bits and pieces about my father from family members and business associates. He married the secretary with whom he became involved while still married to my mother. Together, they had five children who were unknown to me growing up.

For as long as I can remember, when we traveled on a major highway or the Pennsylvania Turnpike, I would read the signs on the truck doors, looking for the Moore-Flesher logo, hoping my father would be driving, and I could catch a glimpse of him.

Throughout childhood, adolescence, and young adulthood, an underlying theme was wondering if my father knew about my various accomplishments. Did he know I was the tallest girl in my fifth-grade class or that I was chosen to go to the city-wide art class downtown at the museum? Did he know I had a lead in the high school play? Did he know I was an A student? Miss Debutante and on the precision drill team in high school? College May Queen? Homecoming Queen? President of my college sorority? Maybe he saw my picture in the paper of the Homecoming Queens in the colleges surrounding Westminster. My drive to be visible and popular was doubtless motivated in part by my need to be seen by him and receive his blessing.

After my mother's death, I found and read letters my father had written to my mother while he was stationed in Europe, stating that he wanted her to agree to a divorce so he could honor the promise he had made to his father to seek a divorce. The following is a passage from one of those letters.

> "Well, kid, now that Dad is gone, it looks like my life is all laid out. He asked me to do certain things for him in case anything happened to him. It happened. Lois, would you give me a divorce while I am over here or when I get back? It's a thing neither of us can help, and you would be a lot better off if you could see things my way. I don't want to do this, but you'll find that I am right.
>
> "About Jean, I would like to have her, but you will want her too. Let me know what you think is best."

It was written on March 13, 1944. I was one year old.

Soon after my father arrived home, having been released early from the army, we packed up our belongings at the Moore farm, where we had lived off and on during his absence. He dropped us off in the driveway of Gram and Pop's home and drove away. In the space of a few minutes, my heart was broken. I no longer trusted in a loving father.

My mother wanted to return to college to finish her teaching degree. Among the papers she saved were two letters with the return address of Absecon, New Jersey, drafted in the handwriting of Grandmother Anna. The draft letters were copied by my mother and sent to the Registrar at Indiana State Teachers' College, requesting the information my mother needed to return to college to finish her degree.

> *Dear Sir,*
>
> *I am interested in completing my college work and earning my degree. In order to do so, I will need a transcript of my grades and credit earned at Indiana State Teachers College beginning in January of 1939 until June of 1941 …*

After receiving her transcript, my mother wrote to Penn State College in State College, Pennsylvania.

> *Dear Sir,*
>
> *I am interested in getting my Bachelor of Science degree. I attended Indiana State Teachers College … for two and one-half years and earned 83 credits. How many additional credits do I need in order to receive my degree from your college?*
>
> *Does your campus provide facilities for the housing and care of children? I have a little girl, age four, whom I would like to keep with me while I work for my degree. Is it possible for me to live on campus with my child, or would it be necessary for me to rent a room off campus?*
>
> *Your reply will be appreciated.*
>
> *Yours very truly,*
> *Lois Moore*

I don't know what response my mother received, but she was not able to follow through, at least in part because my father refused to support us financially. Even while he was in the Army, he refused to send any child support. After he was released from the Army and was running the trucking company, he claimed he had no money, evidenced by a handwritten note she had written in June of 1947 in response to a phone call from my father:

> *Clyde called and asked, "When are you going through with the divorce?" I responded, "I would like a settlement of $20,000." His response was, "I will never have any money." "Then I will wait to get the divorce," I replied. He said, "I'll talk to you about it later."*

She never finished her teaching degree. Women could take short courses in shorthand and train to be secretaries. This is what she chose to do to support us. Her first job was as secretary to Bill's father at the Milliken Brick Company. In retrospect, it seems providential that when Bill Milliken introduced himself to us the day I first met him many years later, Mom was a little more open than she might have been to the man I would eventually marry.

Am I Catholic or Protestant?

Although my mother and birth father lived apart for many years, my mother refused to give him a divorce. She didn't want to end the marriage. However, my father found a way to get her to agree. One day, a Catholic priest appeared at the door of our apartment to convince my mother to sign papers agreeing to a divorce so that my father could remarry. My father's intended second wife was Catholic and wanted to be married in the Catholic Church.

I don't know what the priest said to my mother to convince her to agree to a divorce. I do know, having read a letter the priest wrote to my mother, that he tried to use the power of his office to persuade her to divorce. He said that although their marriage wasn't official in the

Catholic Church since they had been married by a justice of the peace in Winchester, Virginia, if she ever married again and the man was Catholic, it would make it possible for him to continue in the Church. Maybe she remembered Pop Vogel's sadness in being denied the sacraments by the Catholic Church, having married my divorced grandmother, Louise, or maybe she just realized that reconciling was hopeless and was ready to let go and move on.

Reading these old letters after my mother's death, I felt angry and disowned, having carried my father's surname until I married. How could the Catholic Church justify pronouncing my parents' marriage invalid? Did that mean that I was illegitimate in the eyes of the Catholic Church? What kind of a church was this that would invalidate a six-year marriage that had resulted in the birth of a then five-year-old child?

Even though Grandmother Louise and my mother were Protestants, the Catholic Church was ever-present in the lives of the women in my family. My grandmother Anna had two aunts who became Catholic nuns. She was a committed Catholic, and Clyde Sr. converted to Catholicism when they married. My father, Clyde Jr., was Catholic in name only. My stepfather, Andrew (Andy) Kondas, was Catholic. My step-grandfather, Norb (Pop) Vogel, was Catholic.

My mother took instruction in the Catholic Church in preparation for her marriage to my stepfather, Andrew, and agreed to raise any future children Catholic, though she herself never converted. Andy treated me like a daughter, but biologically, I was not his, and I didn't carry his name. Mother refused his offer to adopt me since I'd already started school as Jean Moore. On Sunday mornings, after she remarried, Gram, Karen, Mom, and I went to the Presbyterian Church, and the men stayed home.

In my childhood family, Catholics were considered different from us Protestants. Grandmother Louise communicated a subtle suspicion of Catholics, which made sense, given her mother-in-law's attitude toward her and the church's exclusion of my step-grandfather from the sacraments for marrying her.

By osmosis, I took on her attitude toward Catholics. As I grew in my understanding of the Christian faith, I wondered why she and my mother had married Catholic men. I wish I had asked her before she died.

As an adult, after I learned more about Roman Catholicism, I wondered if my grandmother and mother were unconsciously attracted to the fun-loving, hard-drinking men whose attitudes were so at odds with their morally based faith and puritan lifestyle. Could they be searching for something the Catholic Church offered through the ritual, drama, and beauty of the liturgy, I wondered. The worship space of Catholic Churches was so different from the clear glass windows, black-robed clergy, and moral sermons of our Presbyterian Church. It appealed to all of the senses.

Did the forgiveness of sin offered by the Catholic Church in weekly confession offer my grandfather Vogel freedom from carrying guilt and shame of any wrongdoing and serve as the basis for playfulness and fun rather than the serious way my mother and grandmother approached life? Did weekly confession supply the basis for starting anew each week? He regularly played with us, eliciting light-hearted laughter and delight from Karen and me when Pop flexed his bicep, pretending there was a bug in his arm. He never tired of letting us try to press it down and squash the "bug."

As I considered the doctrines and practices of the Catholic Church, even though the statues of saints were considered to be idols by Protestants, the prominence of Mary in the Catholic Church at least gave those who worshiped there some awareness of the contribution of a woman to the Christian Church. Mary survived the all-male hierarchy of the Church, though she was primarily honored as the mother of God and mostly limited to that understanding and role.

The "Magnificat" in the Gospel of Luke 1:52-53 paints a fuller picture of Mary as one who is passionate about justice and the poor. "He has brought down the powerful from their thrones and lifted up the lowly. He has filled the hungry with good things and sent the rich away empty" (NRSV with Apocrypha).

Clearly, there is more to Mary than motherhood. Her wisdom in the ways of the world remained mostly hidden and unspoken in Sunday morning sermons. Still, the Catholic Church recognized her as a valuable expression of the nurturing feminine to whom one could pray and be understood. In the Presbyterian Church, there was no female figure to associate with God, and praying to Mary or any of the saints was considered to be idolatry.

Given the history of my family's complicated relationship with the Protestant and Catholic Churches, my relationship with the church was complicated as well. It was something I needed to sort out as I grew and became responsible for my choices. This was key in defining my sense of belonging in the worshiping communities I entered after that.

The church, through its largely male translation and interpretation of the scripture and teaching, gave my mother and grandmother no sense of how the power of the feminine and the wisdom gained through their life experience and prayers could serve the common good or be acknowledged as an expression of the Holy Spirit of God speaking wisdom through them.

Whenever I hear the passage from 2 Timothy 1:5-7, it reminds me of my mother's and grandmother's faithfulness in prayer. The author tells Timothy, "I am reminded of your sincere faith, a faith that lived first in your grandmother, Lois, and your mother, Eunice, and now, I am sure, lives in you. For this reason, I remind you to rekindle the gift of God that is within you through the laying on of my hands; for God did not give us a spirit of cowardice, but rather a spirit of power and of love and of self-discipline" (NRSV with Apocrypha).

Powerless as they were in the world outside their homes and voiceless in the preaching and interpreting of scripture, the women in my family affected change through faithfulness to their marriage partners and self-sacrificial love for their children and grandchildren, teaching us values that would guide us in making healthy choices for our lives.

Their faithfulness to marriage and motherhood and their prayers helped us to gain an education and develop the ego strength to stand up for the rights of women to be equal partners at home and in the world if we chose to do so. I am reminded of one of the Ten Commandments to "honor your father and your mother." I believe I am doing this as I sort through these memories, honoring what they gave me, choosing what is true for me in the time in which I live, and letting go of what isn't.

The Big Stone House on the Hill

A tall, graceful, weeping willow tree filled a corner of my grandparents' front yard, protecting their house and offering the privacy they valued. I loved that tree. Its branches arched and then fell almost to the ground. For the first five years of my life, that tree provided a leafy green secret place of protection where I could be alone. Under her protective branches, a sense of safety enveloped me. It was as though the tree was weeping with me, releasing my pent-up fear that my mother might not return from work one day. It seemed to hold the wisdom of the ages and be able to calm my fears.

My father was gone. Grandma spent most of her days cooking, cleaning, doing laundry, and caring for her daughter, Karen, and me. Since Pop was a partner in several small businesses, he could manage his own time and chose to spend a lot of it at home, playing with Karen and me, helping Gram, and caring for the lawn, garden, and chickens out back.

When my mother left for work each day, it felt as if I had lost both my parents. When the door closed behind her, I wanted to run to her and say, "Please stay home. I miss you when you're gone. I'm afraid you won't come back." I felt sad and misunderstood by my grandmother. She rarely took time to answer my questions with more than a token word or two and a suggestion that Karen and I go out and play.

Much later, she opened up a treasure trove of family stories. Now I realize that when she was 45, it must have been hard to take care of me, age three, and her daughter Karen, age four, and manage the big home she shared with Pop, Karen, her reclusive bachelor brother, Uncle Bill, my mom, and me. I can still see her in the basement laundry room, hair hanging in her face and sweat dripping from her brow, boiling the sheets and sending them through the hand wringer to ready them to hang out on the backyard line to dry. She did the meal planning and cooking. Now, I see clearly that she had little time or energy to take in a three-year-old's sadness and sense of loss or to answer her questions. The love she could offer then came through providing a home for all of us and caring for it and us, care that cost her many hours of hard physical labor.

I had an adventurous spirit and wanted to explore the neighboring fields, but was constrained by my grandmother's need to keep me close to home and safe. Whether I was angry or afraid, I imagined the tree wrapping her branches around me and offering silent comfort. Her roots reached deep into the ground, and I nestled into her wide embrace.

I have wondered why it seemed important to include a whole chapter on the house where my life began and where I lived most of the time with my mother and extended family until I was five. Esther de Waal, in her little book, *The White Stone: The Art of Letting Go*, put words to it for me. In her first chapter, she quotes Leonard Woolf, who wrote in his autobiography *Beginning Again*, "What cuts the deepest channels in our lives are the different houses in which we live." De Waal goes on to say, "... houses shape people, and in return, people shape their houses. For houses have a life force. They offer more than shelter: they offer security, stability, a sense of sanctuary."[3]

It has been over 70 years since I lived in the Big Stone House on the hill in Penn Hills, Pennsylvania. At times, memories of my childhood still appear and flood me with mystery, stroking my imagination and making me long to remember more. Those who could answer my questions are now long gone, except for Karen.

Karen, my senior by nine months, and I were raised like sisters in The Big House during those early years by my mother, Gram, and Pop Vogel, and yet we were actually niece and aunt. There is no question that the house and my extended family who lived in it shaped my life.

---

[3] Esther de Waal, *The White Stone: The Art of Letting Go* (Liturgical Press, 2022), 2.

One day, I decided to call Karen to reminisce about our childhood. My questions were many since our lives had gone in different directions. After high school, she married a Marine, loved tennis, was an artist, and lived in the country with her husband and three children before retiring to a golf community in Florida.

On the other hand, I went to college, married my high school sweetheart, and joined him in New York City following graduation to work with young people. Karen and I didn't see much of each other for many years, except for large extended family gatherings during the holidays in Pittsburgh, and we had never talked about our growing up until I called.

I asked, "How did you feel about me living in this house built by your parents?"

"Well," she responded tentatively, "It was good to have someone my age to play with; we did fight a lot, though."

"Did you think you were rich?" I asked.

"Yes," she answered. "My parents were older. Mother was in her 40s, and Dad was a well-established businessman. We had homes in Delray Beach, Florida, and at Conneaut Lake, Pennsylvania. In addition to the big house in Penn Hills, my dad was a founding member of the Churchill Country Club, so I had access to places and resources my peers in school didn't have."

My experience was very different from Karen's. Although I was loved and don't remember ever being treated as though I didn't belong, I still felt like a stepchild, unsure of my belonging, and had no room of my own until I was an adult. My paternal identity was a big, dark hole.

I was curious: "Do you remember when my mother and I moved into The Big House permanently when you were three and a half and I was two and a half?"

Hesitantly, she answered, "I thought you always lived there; I don't remember a time when you weren't there."

To me, it seemed as if the house had a personality of its own, fused with our family memories and secrets. My grandparents decided to sell the house when I was five, move to a town house next door, and then move to Florida for the winter months and to their cottage at the lake in northeastern Pennsylvania for the summer. Karen and I made a childhood promise that we would buy the house back one day and live there again. It felt as though its castle-like stone walls were arms of love that bound us together and gave us roots.

This grand stone house on the hill was set apart from the noise of the street below and other homes. Surrounded by formal gardens in the front and on one side, it was private and quiet. A long, winding driveway provided access to the house that was largely invisible from the road below. In the back, Smokey, the German shepherd, sat watch. His domain included a dog house and a wire run that allowed him to both be free and yet limited to the perimeter of the backyard. His job was to keep us safe from unexpected intruders by barking a warning signal that we had a visitor. Further back was the chicken coop and fenced-in yard that housed chickens and a rooster. Thanks to them, we had fresh eggs and protein for many of our meals.

I can still picture my grandmother coming out of the back door in her printed flower bib apron and signaling to my grandfather, who was working in the chicken yard, "Norb, I am ready to cook dinner." My grandfather stopped what he was doing, chose a fat hen, held it up for my grandmother's inspection with a smile, and asked, "How's this one?" After receiving her nod of approval, he turned the hen upside down, fit her neck into a tin funnel nailed to a tree, and chopped off her head. I felt a little scared and sick as the body flew out of the funnel and was scooped up and placed into my grandmother's hands. She drained the blood and plucked the body clean of feathers, making it ready to enter the cooking pot.

The Big House had three stories with lots of nooks and crannies to explore. During our phone call, Karen and I took a several-hour stroll down memory lane, reflecting on the house and our memories of living there. Volleying back and forth, the question we served to each other over and over was, "Do you remember ...?"

Most of our daily living took place on the middle floor. The kitchen, with its sunny bay window, contained a round table in a breakfast nook that looked out on the back of the house. A dumbwaiter sent food and drinks to the floor above and below. I loved the warm feeling of the kitchen and the fragrant, spicy smells of my grandmother's cooking, influenced by her German, French, and English roots.

Many times, I dreamed about how the dumbwaiter worked, and once, I whispered to Karen, "Do you think we could take a ride to the basement in the dumbwaiter? Could we do it without Grandma knowing? If I get in after dinner when she has left the kitchen and you press the button to send me downstairs, you could walk down and let me out. And then I could close you in and push the button for you to come up. Wouldn't that be fun?" The thought of getting stuck inside and Grandma finding out made us shake in our boots. A ride in the dumbwaiter remained an unfulfilled dream.

A sparkling crystal chandelier hung heavily over the formal dining room table, where we ate dinner almost every night and were expected to be on our best behavior. A deep wine-red wall-to-wall carpet covered the dining room floor and spilled down the two steps into the front entrance hall and sitting room. The carpet continued down the main hallway, branching off to the side halfway down, creating a path that led to the bedroom wing.

My earliest memory came back when I participated in regression therapy. I was in a crib in my mother's bedroom. My father, Clyde, was home from the military on leave, and they were in the bed next to me, arguing, engaged in a heated power struggle. My body memory was one of fear.

When I grew older, I moved into Karen's bedroom across the hall, which had twin beds and white distressed wood furniture. I don't know whether she wanted to share her room with me. I am guessing she wasn't given a choice. The third bedroom at the end of the hall was my grandparents' room. It was a large, sunny room with walnut furniture accented with gold. The gold and multicolored oriental rug covering their floor was passed on to my mother when Gram, then a widow, moved into an apartment built onto my mother and stepfather's home. Many years later, it came to rest in mine. The rug has provided a sense of stability and connection for me.

During the first few years my mother and I lived in The Big House, my grandmother was paralyzed for a period of time. I didn't understand why she stayed in bed. The doctors had no medical explanation for her paralysis.

Later, in therapy, I explored why, as a hospital chaplain, certain patients with whom I visited triggered the feeling that I was going to be sick or faint if I stayed with them. I remembered passing out when the doctor visited my grandmother to lance a huge carbuncle full of pus while I quietly sat in the corner of the room unnoticed by anyone.

After that memory surfaced and I could talk about it in therapy, the nausea of visiting sick people in their hospital rooms lessened and ultimately disappeared. Perhaps if I could have talked about how scared I was that Grandma was going to die, that emotion would not have been embedded in my unconscious mind, heart, and body, becoming a hindrance to my work as a chaplain.

Continuing down memory lane, walking out of the bedroom wing and turning left, the wine-colored carpet came to an end at a white marble staircase winding to the formal living room and library upstairs. In her sternest voice, Grandma warned Karen and me, "Do not go up the stairs. The marble steps are dangerous, and you could fall and hurt yourselves. Also, it is not a place for children to play." After that warning, nothing would stop us from finding times to sneak up there.

A naked lady carved out of marble stood at the landing halfway up and held a torch to light the stairs. The marble temptress beckoned Karen and me to continue to climb the stairs and explore the forbidden rooms beyond. The formal living room, with its blue and rose-patterned oriental rug and baby grand piano, led to a tiled deck that opened to the outside and offered a luscious view of the trees and gardens below. The room was beautifully decorated with figurines and vases collected by my grandparents when they traveled to Cuba and other exotic places. Venturing into the library next to it for the first time, I felt like the girl detective Nancy Drew. "Look, Karen, there is a safe hidden behind this picture on the wall. I wonder what is in there?"

Beside the steps at the end of the main entrance hall leading upstairs were steps leading to the basement, where a shuffleboard court built into the hall floor promised fun and recreation. Uncle Bill, Gram's bachelor brother, lived in a room across the hall from the laundry room where my grandmother spent a lot of her time washing and hanging sheets and clothes to dry.

Pop had created a lounge with a fireplace, sofa, and chairs at the end of the hall. In the next room was a bar with several booths to sit in. Food and drinks were sent down from the kitchen via the dumbwaiter for him and his "cronies," Grandmother's name for Pop's friends, when they gathered to play cards.

Since no extended family lives in Pittsburgh anymore, I haven't kept up with how the beloved "Big House" has fared over the ensuing 70 years. Karen has gone back a number of times, though, and last year said the house looked well cared for. Planters filled with bright flowers were visible on the upstairs deck.

It is said that "You can't go home again," but I just did. Memories of life in the much-loved Big Stone House on the hill remain vivid in my imagination to this day, even though the house was sold when I was five. Designing and building it was, for my grandparents, a dream fulfilled. For me, it was "home," a safe, secure place of beauty inside and out, that formed my identity and image of home. I carry that sense of safety and belonging with me to draw on when insecurity and chaos threaten to pull me under. The memory of the Big Stone House and its gardens has provided a vision for making my own home a place of beauty in the years that have followed.

The Opal and the Sapphire

Bill wanted to give me a gift I would enjoy for my 80th birthday. Since he dislikes shopping for anything except groceries, his proposal came as a surprise: "Let's go to the jewelry store and see if we can find earrings to match the necklace Sean and Jill gave you for your birthday." That sounded like a great idea to me. Though I mostly wear silver jewelry, I loved the dainty gold chain with a small blue stone pendant they had given me. I had begun to wear it every day with a second gold chain for good measure.

As we entered the store lined on both sides with cases of sparkling diamonds and other precious stones, my attention was drawn to a gold ring with a shimmering milky white opal in the center. Seeing it transported me back to my fifth birthday and the backyard of my grandparents' home, where chickens roamed in a fenced-in area.

One of Pop Vogel's businesses was a jewelry store. For my fifth birthday, Grandma and Pop gave me an opal ring. It was my first piece of jewelry. I fell in love with it the moment I opened the red velvet box. Every day when I woke up, I checked to see if it was still on my finger and gazed at it with pride. Every day, that is, until one fateful day in the chicken yard.

I enjoyed teasing the chickens by sticking my fingers in the fence to see if they would come to me looking for food. One day, the big fat rooster, which I named "Red," strutted over to the fence, showing off his striking red comb and flaps under his beak. In the blink of an eye, Red pecked my opal right out of my ring and swallowed it whole. I couldn't believe my eyes.

"Oh, no, what just happened? That rooster just ate my opal!" I cried. "Can we get it back?"

Even though Red had been a favorite of mine, at that point, I hoped he would be chosen for Sunday dinner, and we could retrieve the opal. I held out hope for weeks, but it never came to pass.

My grandmother was very unhappy with me. She had warned me not to tease the chickens and certainly not to stick my finger inside the fence. I felt ashamed for causing the rooster to peck out my opal stone. From then on, I never wanted another opal. Childhood grief gets stuck in places many of us don't stumble upon until years later.

Bill and I didn't find gold earrings with blue sapphires we felt we could afford, so we looked for an alternative. Before making a decision, I took time at home the next day to look through the jewelry I had collected over the years.

To my surprise, I saw a single tiny gold earring with a blue stone. I assumed our daughter had bought it as a third pierced earring and left it behind when she moved. When I asked her, though, she said it wasn't hers. Then I saw a matching one. I had no idea where they had come from. They were a perfect match for my necklace.

The jeweler looked at them the next day and pronounced, "Yes, the earrings are gold, and the stone is a light blue sapphire called an aquamarine." I felt such joy. It was as though the opal that rooster pecked out 75 years ago had reappeared, transformed into two tiny aquamarines, set in gold, free of charge, made into a gift of love from my husband of 58 years.

My 80th birthday felt like a big one. My extended family of 17 people gathered at dinner for the occasion, having traveled from Michigan, Virginia Beach, and Florida to Alexandria to celebrate. Finally, I could embrace my family's shared love and sense of belonging.

I flashed back to the image of my grandmother at 94, sitting in her bed in the hospital. She had refused surgery for an obstruction in her stomach, knowing she wouldn't recover if she made that choice. It wasn't until then that she realized, as one by one we came to visit her, that she was loved for being herself, not just for what she could do for the family.

I remembered the disbelief and sadness I felt when, surrounded by several of her grandchildren, she turned to me and said, "I really am loved, aren't I, Jeannie?" *How could she not know how loved she was?*

Sitting in a private room of a local restaurant surrounded by Bill, our children, grandchildren, and my brother and sister and their children, her realization flashed through my mind. I could now take in the love they were offering by coming to celebrate my 80th birthday. Tears filled my eyes, and my heart burst wide open with love and gratitude. I knew I was loved, but I was surprised by the experience of it in my heart.

I wanted to hear birthday stories from everyone there, so I asked the family to share their favorite birthday memory. The sharing began as each one recalled their favorite birthday, but shortly, people began to share their memories of me. That really undid me as I listened to the memories of my siblings, my husband, our children, grandchildren, and my nieces and nephews.

Of course, there have been moments in my lifetime when I felt I was loved and belonged in the family, but it was at my 80th birthday, as they all gathered for the weekend, that my childhood sadness of feeling as though I didn't belong to a family was transformed. I let go of the loneliness of that only child under the weeping willow, who alone carried the name of the birth father she didn't know and who felt like a stepchild most of her life.

At dinner, as each one shared memories and messages of loving kindness into my "Roger Pen," a device that carried their voices directly to my hearing aids, I knew I was no longer a stepchild, half-sister, or a not-good-enough wife and mother but an ordinary person who fully belonged to a family created out of a mother's care and love and the love and faithfulness of the father who was the biological father to my brother and sister and raised me as his own.

I have been a part of many church communities and families of choice, which have contributed to my healing and sense of belonging. A primary vehicle of healing the lonely child within me has been the years of love and commitment of my brother, sister, their spouses and children, Bill, our children and grandchildren, and the time and energy they invested to nurture family ties over many years.

It is not a perfect family, and we are not perfect people. Sometimes, we hurt each other by words or actions born out of childhood needs that didn't get met and remain unconscious, or perhaps loyalty to beliefs of our family of origin, which have yet to be explored in our current life in light of what it means to follow the way of love. But our solidarity is empowered and sustained by the Spirit of Love and the choice to suspend judgment and be curious about what motivates each of us to choose what we choose and do what we do.

Would Cinderella Find Her Prince?

When Pop and Gram Vogel decided to sell The Big House, they first moved to one of the town houses next door. Mom and I moved into a smaller town house in the same complex. A year later, they moved to Florida for the winters, and Mom and I moved into a second-floor apartment that was more affordable several miles away but still in Penn Hills.

"When you get home from school, lock the door and don't open it to anyone until I get home," my mother warned. I wasn't sure what I should fear, but it was clear from my mother's stern tone that I should be afraid of something or someone. I felt safe in school. I was a good student and secure in my first-grade class, but it seemed that dangers lurked in our apartment building.

So I walked home with Jimmy, a boy who lived nearby. I hurried upstairs to let myself into the apartment and locked the door, whispering to myself, "Whew, I made it!" I could hear the neighborhood kids' shrieks outside and imagine them swinging high on the swings. I heard someone's foot connect with the kickball as their team cheered them to first base. I yearned to be out there with them.

Once in a while, a knock came at the door. I held my breath until I heard Jimmy's voice. He would come by to say hello and sometimes slide a piece of chewing gum under the door. He and I would talk for a few minutes through the door. I so wanted to unlock it and go out and play, but I was afraid. Instead, I quietly thanked him: I didn't want to disobey my mother. I felt lonely. I missed my grandparents and Karen, my constant companion, who had moved with them to Florida for the winters.

After a snack, I would reluctantly settle down to listen to records until my mother arrived home from work several hours later. I played two records over and over again: "Are My Ears on Straight?" and "Cinderella." The first was a song about a doll that was broken when she was dropped, so she was sent out for repair and was to be returned to her owner at Christmas.

When it was time to be picked up, the doll was anxious about how she looked and if she would still be loved by the little girl now that she had been broken. It expressed emotions I felt but hadn't put into my own words.

As I sang along, the words and melody sank deeply into my heart. I worried that if I wasn't well-behaved and cute, my mother and I wouldn't meet the approval of my grandparents, and somehow, we'd be "rejected on Christmas Day," so to speak. And it would be my fault. As I recall these scenes through the lenses of marriage, motherhood, and training as a therapist and priest, I have compassion for the child I was and for the many children who live with feelings like these. I also have a deep appreciation for my mother, who needed to work to support us and did her best to control her fears and keep me safe while she was gone.

The summers I spent at Conneaut Lake with my grandparents and Karen were filled with adventure. I felt free to explore, ride horses, swim in the lake, and play badminton with friends in the lot next to the cottage after dinner. Still, a subtle awareness was always with me that I was their grandchild, not their child. I had no father, and my mother was at home in Pittsburgh working. When it was time for school at summer's end, and I rejoined my mother at home wherever we were living, the feelings of fun and freedom would recede, and worries about money and safety would return.

At times, I felt jealous of Karen. She had two parents who were able to provide whatever she needed or wanted. Although just nine months older than I, it seemed to me that she got all the privileges. She was allowed to drive the boat and was taught to drive the car when she turned 16. She got new outfits at the end of the summer when we went into Meadville to shop for school clothes. I remember the anxiety I felt standing in the children's department of the clothing store, hoping Grandma would offer to buy me a new matching skirt and sweater, an outfit my mother could neither create for me at the sewing machine nor afford to buy.

Although Grandma and Karen weren't mean to me, Karen and I fought a lot: our competition lay just below the surface. I felt like Cinderella. I read my favorite book and played the record, *Cinderella*, often and dreamed that, like Cinderella, I would find my prince. Together, we would create a family, and he would provide safety, freedom, adventure, and belonging.

CREATING MY OWN STORY

A Surprise Encounter

In 1965, before "the sixties" became code for war protests, sexual freedom, and political upheaval, most of my female friends and college classmates aspired to marriage and motherhood. Building our resumes and developing our professional lives would, at best, be a secondary pursuit that might follow alongside maintaining a household, raising children, and supporting our husbands' work.

We were trained by culture and religion to be our husbands' helpmates, which meant adapting to their needs. Most of us at our small Presbyterian college in Amish country were virgins or trying to be. The expectation was that you wouldn't have sex with your boyfriend or girlfriend or live together until you were married. If you did, you kept it a secret.

That year, I chose to marry a man who took major risks. Bill had moved to Harlem and later to the Lower East Side of Manhattan to do street work with young people. He introduced them to a life of faith in God and hope for a future that would motivate them to complete their education, get a job, and provide for themselves and their future family. Many young men his age were fighting a war overseas in Vietnam; he was fighting a different kind of war on the streets of the Lower East Side of Manhattan. Bill waded feet first into a culture different from the one in which he was raised and depended on people with financial resources who believed in what he was doing to pay his living expenses.

I was willing to take risks if I believed in the direction he was going, and so I would follow his lead. Marrying Bill started me on a path of self-discovery and gradual willingness to take my own risks that I couldn't have imagined when I said, "I do," on November 6, 1965. It opened a way to reclaim in our relationship the adventurous part of me that I had cut off in childhood to survive.

Our relationship began in a suburb of Pittsburgh on a Sunday morning at Hebron United Presbyterian Church. I was 16, and he was 19. I was sitting quietly, waiting for the worship service to begin, when out of the corner of my eye, I noticed a handsome young man I had never seen before. The next thing I knew, he was coming down the center aisle, passing the collection plate. Hesitating at my pew, he shifted the collection plate to one hand and, with the other, quickly plucked the white usher's carnation from his lapel. Carefully placing it in the shiny gold collection plate, he pointed to the flower and then to me, indicating he was offering it to me.

My mother and grandmother, who flanked me on either side, looked puzzled and then surprised as I reached in, deposited my offering in the plate filled with pledge envelopes, checks, and cash, and removed the flower in one smooth motion. It may have been the most risky, improper thing I had ever done.

After the service, the young man was waiting on the church steps to introduce himself. Reaching his hand to shake mine, he said, "My name is Bill. The minute I saw you, I knew I wanted to meet you. I hope I didn't embarrass you by sending my carnation in the collection plate; it was a spontaneous gesture. I am new to this church, and to be truthful, any church, and I am unfamiliar with the protocol." I had no idea what to say.

With a wide grin, he continued, "Given that it's youth Sunday and there weren't many youths here, they tapped me to usher." His grin grew into a broad smile. "They took a big chance asking me to handle the money." Quickly changing the subject, he said somewhat shyly, "I was wondering if I might call you sometime?"

At that point, my mother joined the conversation and asked him for his last name. After hearing it, she indicated she was acquainted with Bill's family. In fact, as I've mentioned, her first position out of secretarial school had been working for his family's brick company. She respected and liked his father, so I could see he was getting a stamp of approval. My grandmother, too, recognized the name. Although she didn't like to go to the Churchill Country Club, where my grandfather Vogel was a founding member and played cards each week, she knew Bill's parents, who were also long-time members of the Club.

There was a significant problem with all of this, however. I was already going steady with another young man who attended the same high school Bill had attended. In fact, looking down, I was painfully aware that I was wearing my boyfriend's high school class ring on my finger at that very moment. One couldn't miss that ring. Wilkinsburg High School was stamped around a huge blue stone. It was clearly a man's size, wrapped with a mound of first aid tape so it would stay on. If Bill had noticed it, it didn't seem to deter him in the least. I was so charmed by Bill's approach that I gave him my number. I would figure out later what to do if he called.

It took me several days to decide what I wanted to do. Finally, I called Ronnie and asked if we could get together to talk. A few days later, I was no longer wearing the ring, affectionately named "the blue blob" by my family. I returned the ring with a halting, tearful, and confusing explanation of why I no longer wanted to go steady.

When the call came from Bill inviting me to a double date a few days later, a roller coaster relationship filled with risk, joy, growth, and adventure began that led to our wedding at that same church six years later.

The minister's voice rang out into the full congregation, "I now pronounce you man and wife." There it was; my fate was sealed. I was no longer a woman equal to the man I stood beside. According to the church, he was a man; I was a wife. I wasn't aware enough at that point to question the language and wonder why we weren't pronounced husband and wife. I am a woman, not just a role in this marriage. It took years to fully realize the ways the language of the church did not recognize women as equals.

As the marriage service drew to a close, Bill and I stood facing the minister, holding hands, waiting for the final pronouncement, at which time the mother and father of the bride and groom would normally wipe away tears of sadness and joy that their daughter and son were now married and leaving home to begin their own family.

"You may now kiss the bride," the minister concluded, and we shyly shared a quick kiss and turned to face the congregation. At that moment, there was a commotion in the second-story balcony at the back of the church. A black cloth sign was unfurled and suspended from the balcony rail, proclaiming both disbelief and joy in large white letters that read, "Can you believe it?"

We broke into smiles. Turning to see what was happening in the balcony that had caused our smiles, the congregation burst into laughter and applause. Most of the people present knew the history of our rocky romance. Now 22 and 25, I had finished college, and Bill had gone to New York City to live and work with young people living in the Harlem housing projects and on the Lower East Side of Manhattan.

Our life-long covenant began that day, as well as the power struggles. Standing at the altar, saying, "I do," each of us believed that the two of us would become one. I naively believed that I was "the one" we would become, meaning Bill would eventually see things my way, and we would live happily ever after.

Marriage: Why Commit?

How would it go for the two of us, starting a life together in a city not only unfamiliar but more than a little scary to me? I would be living in a culture that was alien in many ways while grounded in a faith tradition that was troublingly hierarchical. Like most of our suburban friends, our marriage began traditionally—white dress, flowers, bridesmaids, and well-defined roles. He would take out the garbage. I would make dinner. He would provide for us financially, and if I worked at all, I would teach and have the summers off to care for the children we planned to have.

The circumstances of our life together presented us with major challenges I didn't even know to anticipate. We faced racism and sexism and did not embrace many of the traditional expectations of our families and faith communities as we entered a new era and a complicated social environment.

Could we create a marriage that would honor the vows we had made—a covenant to love and cherish each other until we were parted by death—and also create a respectful marriage partnership as we adapted to a new set of social pressures? Would our faith journeys lead us down separate paths? Would both of our families' patterns of alcohol use, divorce, and threatening to leave when things got tough be ones to which we would gravitate? Or would we be able to visualize a new way to share power that would keep us connected, intimate, and cooperative as we cared for our children? Could our partnership survive my growing independence, disagreement, and even some competition?

Years later, as I helped prepare young people for weddings I would officiate, I encouraged those who wanted the time-honored ceremony of lighting one candle with two to leave their individual candles burning rather than blowing them out to signify not only the unity in marriage but the individuation needed for each one to fulfill their unique purpose.

Following the wedding, we left Penn Hills, our Pittsburgh suburb, and began the drive to New York City, stopping to spend the first night of our three-day honeymoon at a friend's guest cottage, then two nights at a country inn.

Before leaving Pittsburgh, we learned that the photographer's camera had a broken spring, so there were no wedding pictures! I was devastated. Bill attempted to lighten my sadness by saying, "So I guess there is no proof that we are married, then?" I didn't think his attempt at humor was very funny.

As we drew closer to our 21st-floor condo on the Lower East Side of Manhattan, Bill and I noticed street lights flickering. "Something is wrong with the lights, Bill." We pulled up in front of our building, wedding gifts piled in the back seat and trunk, in a city that had suddenly gone dark. Our car radio announced that we were in the midst of a blackout that stretched from Ontario, Canada, down the east coast to New York City.

"What are we going to do? There is no elevator service. We can't carry our wedding gifts up 21 flights of stairs in the dark!" The excitement and anticipation of seeing our new home for the first time drained out of me, and the fantasy of being carried over the threshold as a new bride evaporated into the blackness of the night.

My hero husband came up with a creative solution. We didn't own a credit card, but we did have cash gifts from our wedding. We would spend $65 of that money, extend our honeymoon another day, and drive to the Hilton in midtown, where they had a backup generator. We'd spend the last night of our honeymoon there. Our wedding gifts would be safely ensconced in the underground parking garage at the hotel, and, hopefully, electricity would be restored by morning. When the news report the following day announced that after thirteen hours of darkness, the electricity was back on, we happily headed downtown to set up housekeeping.

Marriage and motherhood were central to my vision for myself after college. I had prayed for a man who loved God, who would be faithful, and whom I could trust to keep the life-long covenant we would make to each other in the presence of God, family, and friends. The career path I chose in college to be an elementary school teacher could be integrated into the roles of wife and mother if I needed to contribute to the family income.

Still, I entered marriage without any clear sense of what my career path would actually be. I had a teaching degree in elementary education, but no experience or skill in classroom management. I hadn't developed the essential qualities of a good teacher who could set boundaries, enforce discipline, and teach a classroom of children from different backgrounds and ability levels.

Someone described the teaching profession as one that requires the skill of a brain surgeon, a creative artist, a comedian, and a trauma therapist. I had no idea how to engage the children in curiosity and develop a passion for learning. I was completely unprepared to find my place in a multiracial public school on the Lower East Side of Manhattan while at the same time adjusting to a new culture and marriage.

Bill was already established as a youth worker and had a community of supportive colleagues. I was warmly welcomed into his community, but didn't know how I might contribute to the good of the community or our family income. I had a lot to learn and unlearn. We weren't in suburban Penn Hills or rural Amish country anymore.

Decades later, having read the morning newspaper's style section and watched the morning news on TV, the question "Why get married?" loomed before me. I saw role models for young people, including sports heroes and Hollywood stars, who were not married, had children, were idolized, and couples announcing their marriage breakups and showing pictures of their next romantic relationship, which had already begun.

What about the children of these various relationships? How were they faring? What were they learning about commitment, I wondered. Did they even know what a marriage covenant was? Two people making a commitment to the covenant of marriage after falling in love and promising to raise their children together no longer seemed to be a culture-wide value or norm.

"Why get married?" is an important question for women to ask today, given that at least half of marriages end in divorce. If there are children, and if only one parent takes responsibility for caring for them following a divorce, it is usually the mother who struggles to make enough money to make ends meet and provide childcare while she is at work.

At home, she is expected to provide both the nurture and discipline required to meet each child's needs, do the grocery shopping, cook nutritious meals, keep a clean, organized home, wash and iron, pay the bills, and be a friendly neighbor. If both parents choose to take responsibility for raising the children following a divorce, they commit to supporting two households and a complicated schedule with children moving back and forth between two homes. It is a stressful, unstable solution for everyone.

The first time I made arrangements to meet my birth father, I was in high school. He explained his reason for dropping out of my life. "I was sure your mother would remarry, and I didn't want you to deal with the complications of two fathers and two families."

He didn't speak to the abandonment fear created in me by his choice to leave, the shame my mother experienced in the community, or the hardship resulting from his unwillingness to provide financial support for us for nine years. His explanation for abandoning my mother and me and leaving us unprotected did not help me understand or gain appreciation or respect for his choices.

Marriage, I was learning in increasingly complex ways, requires considering another person in all decisions about time, energy, and money. "The marriage" becomes a third entity to nurture and consider alongside what each individual needs and wants. Adding children to the mix adds additional levels of consideration about what each child needs.

I concluded that consciously entering a marriage covenant into which children are born can be a hero's (or heroine's) journey, in which Joseph Campbell, in his books *The Power of Myth* and *The Hero With a Thousand Faces*, explores the hero's/heroine's journey. Such a journey often involves self-sacrifice. The hero or heroine is one whose life is defined as a person who has given his or her life to something bigger than oneself.

As children grow, sound parenting also involves providing opportunities to expose them to an awareness of a transcendent guiding reality and presence that surrounds them, is in them, and is good. That transcendent reality has a moral and ethical structure that supports life and has consequences when violated. Inherent in coming to grips with the wrong that was done is the option to forgive and be forgiven by a loving Creator.

Divorced parents who choose to co-parent, even though they are no longer married, will continue to have to make decisions regarding their children's welfare. That requires good communication skills to engage with each other to prevent the children from being pulled into a triangle of disagreements and conflicts and forced to take sides. I respected the parents I knew who, having come to the decision that their marriage was no longer viable, chose to work on their communication to attune to the needs of their children.

Bill and I have had a bumpy and rewarding marriage. Having explored much of my burden of unconscious sadness and resentment about my parents' divorce, I found that once I faced these emotions and released them, I was able to move forward with the help of therapy and prayer.

I have a friend who speaks of the process of forgiveness like this: "I set my intention to forgive, aware that I feel the burden of unforgiveness in my body as well as in my mind and heart. Then, I regularly lay the situation I have been unable to let go of in my mind's eye, place it on God's altar, and ask the Holy Spirit to release me from the burden I am carrying. Over time, I notice that it begins to lessen, and then one day, I have a sense of freedom that the pain is gone from my heart, mind, and body."

The key to the process is to set an intention to suspend judgment of oneself and others. From then on, it is a matter of grace and mystery when we are released from the pain we carry. Listening to her reminded me of Dr. Bessel van der Kolk's important book, *The Body Keeps Score*. It surely does.

At times over the years, my family pattern of using divorce as an exit looked like a viable option for me—a better one than the misery and loneliness I was feeling in marriage. But over and over again, I saw that once I faced the old anger and pain lodged in my mind, body, and heart, and the fear of abandonment and judgment, those emotions were transformed into a passion to walk with others through difficult times in their marriage and were used for good. I couldn't do this without Bill's willingness to face the effects of alcoholism in his family and his own relationship deficits. He needed to work on developing the ability to contain his defensiveness, listen to my feelings, and do what he could to help me heal.

Once we understood how each other's buried painful childhood emotions had affected our relationship, we began an inner journey to move toward letting go of judgment of each other and ourselves. My personal history, once consciously faced, prepared me to respond to a future calling, yet unknown, to coach couples largely without judgment regarding the decision either to recommit to the marriage or to move toward divorce. To be nonjudgmental, I had to dive deep and process my lingering sorrow, anger, and bewilderment about the brokenness in my history.

When I felt judgment, I sought help to understand it so I could accompany couples as they made decisions about their relationship in a safe space. Although I certainly had my own values about the covenant of marriage and hoped for couples to reinvest in the love they once had for each other, I respected the choices they were making for themselves and their families to either "get in" to their marriages in a way that would be life-giving or "get out" in the least harmful way.

Young men and women considering marriage today are facing different challenges than the ones I faced or my mother and grandmothers confronted. Young women who have educational credentials and job skills in their chosen careers no longer think of themselves as needing to be taken care of financially; they can get well-paying jobs and support themselves. And, too, many young women want to experience life on their own, build their careers, and perhaps engage in multiple romantic relationships before they commit to a lifetime covenant relationship with one person. There is no longer a social taboo regarding serial monogamy or living together before marriage.

Young men face new challenges, too. The traditional role of sole provider for the family is now more commonly shared, and there is an expectation that men will learn to care for the daily needs of their children and the home as well as have a job that requires long hours of work to generate a good income.

They are exposed to online sites that are seductive and can become addictive. Pornographic sites that create an expectation of a perfect woman's body and a passionate sex life that is often unrealistic to achieve in a relationship with any real-life person are easy to find. Online gambling holds out a carrot to get rich quickly. Models of manhood are set forth that diminish women, and pictures of fun and the good life flood social media, normalizing vaping, alcohol, and drug abuse. The decision to seek therapy is more difficult for young men who might see it as a weakness rather than part of a hero's journey intended to build a strong emotional foundation for their future relationships.

Many young people I have talked with are unsure if they want to marry or bring children into a chaotic world and give up well-paying, satisfying careers that offer personal fulfillment and purpose and allow for expensive trips, cars, and homes. Some choose to adopt a dog or cat, which offers uncritical love and companionship and requires less time, energy, and money. If young people don't feel called to create a family, invest in learning to listen, learn, and grow in a marriage, and don't want to invest time and money raising children, it makes sense to make a conscious decision not to have children or marry but rather create a family of choice from trusted friends and loving animals.

It never occurred to Bill and me not to have children. It was the cultural norm, but we also wanted to be happily married and to be parents. The traditional marriage service Bill and I participated in at Hebron United Presbyterian Church, surrounded by family and friends who were present to witness our marriage vows, included a busload of young people who came from the Lower East Side, stopping in a gas station to change their clothes so they could be properly dressed to witness and support our marriage. It was a foretaste of our future of living between worlds and cultures, confronting our prejudices, and receiving love from a diverse community of people.

Community support, extended family, and creating a family of choice during our years of communal living in New York and Atlanta contributed significantly to the survival and health of our marriage. Our parents offered financial help and emotional support when we shared our need for it. Living communally made it possible for Bill and me to follow our passion and "call" to work in the world while sharing household duties with others and having help caring for our children.

In the past, when most people lived in small towns, aunts and uncles, grandparents, and friends filled in when things got strained in a marriage or family. Those who committed to us at the marriage ceremony no longer lived nearby to support us. Often, family and friends were tempted to take sides, hearing only one side of an argument by phone rather than holding the space for us to work through the power struggles to become conscious of our particular "relationship dance," so we limited how much we shared. After years of fighting and holding on by a string of hope, we began to learn communication skills that offered a way forward.

Communal living was part of the way forward for us. This extended family of choice became our "village" and held the space for us to seek the help we needed. They shouldered some of the burden of Bill's and my attempt to change from a traditional marriage where roles were fixed to one in which roles were flexible and worked for the two of us.

Bill and I had a common cultural orientation; we grew up in suburban Pittsburgh and knew each other's schools, neighborhoods, families, and friends. We were both raised Presbyterian, and our families knew each other. By the time we met when I was a junior in high school, we had each made a faith commitment to follow the way of Jesus. So we had those things in common. We didn't understand then that power struggles are normal between two people. In the stage of romantic love, when oxytocin naturally flows from the hypothalamus into the bloodstream, we felt there were no differences that would be insurmountable. After all, we were head over heels in love!

After a while, as differences emerged and the first blush of romantic love wore off, it felt unsafe to speak our wants, feelings, needs, and opinions because the response of the other was almost always misunderstanding and defensiveness.

So we stayed connected by fighting. Neither of us wanted to give up on our marriage, and we tried to work things through, but mostly, we just had the same arguments over and over. Each argument ended in frustration, but at least we expressed our concern, letting enough steam off to avoid a full-on war.

Unable to communicate in a way that led to understanding, our disagreements went underground and festered even as we continued to disagree. This pattern also affected our parenting. Because the orientation and training in our families were so different, the correct way to parent our children was also different.

Bill's boundaries with the children were loose, while mine were tight. For example, I didn't want them to watch TV shows for mature people. He felt they would be exposed to them in the homes of friends, no matter how hard we tried to limit their exposure, so why make that an issue? Both positions had merit, but who would win the power struggle?

I depended on Bill to support our family and was threatened by the many relationships he had in the community that consumed his time, energy, and passion in a world that was foreign to me. Our dance went something like this: "You are always late for dinner. I am caring for the children while making dinner, and you don't have the courtesy of being here when you said you would be, or at least call. The dinner is cold, and we are all cranky and hungry."

Bill responded, "I was engaged in a confrontation with a group of kids who were threatening each other. You don't understand what it's like out on the streets. There's no use trying to explain."

I criticized, angry; he withdrew, feeling misunderstood. Even though we both wanted our marriage to survive and were willing to invest in it, grow, and change, neither knew how to nurture that hope into existence.

My Cinderella dream of marrying my handsome prince and living happily ever after was dissolving. I realized it would take serious work to learn what it means to love and respect one another, nurture our marriage, care for our children, and pursue our work in the world, and I wasn't sure how to do it.

But a loving marriage became my primary objective and focused intention. I knew a strong marriage was the best gift we could give our children, along with following our respective paths to contribute to the good of the community. I was trying to listen to this invisible, elusive sense of my calling while at the same time honoring the commitment to our marriage and children without extended family support nearby.

At this point, I had no conscious awareness that the feminine nature of God would ground me or that the strength of the feminine in me would later give me the power and authority I needed to speak my truth to the community and church I served.

Deep down, I could feel the primal need to ascribe it not only to my mother's lifetime commitment to my well-being but also to the maternal nature of God and the archetypal human need for that maternal care. The "masculine" qualities in me—focused awareness, discipline, and boundaries, for example—were underdeveloped, not having had a father who could guide and teach me that it was okay to express my outrage at injustice and set boundaries and limits, not out of anger, but out of a desire to teach me and keep me safe.

The model I had of a fully developed woman was the woman in Proverbs 31. Although the model was unrealistic in some ways because it was a composite of ideal womanhood, she was my guide and my hope to grow into being fully alive and creative at home and in my work in the world. Up to that point, it was the only biblical picture I had to guide my efforts to be a whole person born female. Surprisingly, a composite of my two grandmothers embodied her for me.

Marriage or Mistress?

"Could Bill be having an affair?" Night after night during the early years of our marriage, I lay awake for hours, plagued by this question, paralyzed by fear, until I heard the locks on our 21st-floor New York apartment click open. I was relieved when he arrived home safely, but greeted him with rage fueled by my childhood experience of loss and my fear of being abandoned and betrayed.

My wildest fears would flare up. I wondered if I had made a mistake thinking he was trustworthy. I was sure my mother and grandmother thought their husbands were trustworthy, too, when they married, but that turned out not to be the case. I didn't think he was the kind of man who would have an affair, but he was often out until two and three in the morning. I was home with our son and couldn't go with him. He said he was going to the East Village to a coffee shop where a lot of Latin American Christians hang out to discuss faith and politics. But what was the attraction to the place? Were there young women to whom he was attracted, who shared his passion for young people looking for their purpose, while I was focused on our home and our son, Sean?

There was a real reason to fear because he was often engaged in dangerous situations and could unintentionally abandon me by getting killed.

It was impossible to have a reasonable conversation about these fears in the middle of the night. We were both tired and absolutely committed to our respective points of view. He felt misunderstood and distrusted, and I was gripped by fear. Trying to keep our voices down so as not to wake our young son, we had heated conversations, neither one listening, both defending our point of view.

Because Bill was working in the neighborhood during the day, his discretionary time was at night when he went to the East Village. He felt justified because Sean was sleeping, he was learning a lot from listening, and, from his point of view, I was free to read, watch TV, or do whatever I wanted while he was gone. Plus, it was much more fun for him to be in the Village than with an angry wife constantly criticizing him for being gone so much, always late for dinner, and preoccupied with work.

I had no sense of the strength of the rage that spewed out of me at those times. I didn't understand then that rage is often fueled by childhood fear and is different from anger, which is a self-protective attempt to set boundaries and a reasonable emotion to express. Bill had no sense of what these late nights and his absence from home to "work" were triggering in me and doing to erode our relationship.

After these confrontations, I felt terrible about myself, my lack of control, and my inability to connect emotionally with Bill. I felt despair about the future of our marriage.

At times, I considered taking Sean and going home to my parents. I felt hopeless, but a strong will and vision of a marriage partnership rooted in love and respect, and an unwillingness to admit failure to my family, kept me in New York.

Part of the challenge for me was to continue developing a vision for myself that allowed me to make peace with being married to a man who was driven by his sense of purpose while discerning my own and being a mother and homemaker. He was deeply committed to his work with young people who had no hope for their future and was fueled by his own childhood trauma—failure in school due to undiagnosed learning issues that led to his being lumped in with the "bad" kids. He met with young people who were joining gangs to replace their biological families and engaging in destructive behavior, including drug use and gun violence, because they could not succeed in school and had no vision for their future.

He came to appreciate in his childhood the strengths and vulnerabilities of the African American community through the care of his family's housekeeper, Thelma. He was, in a sense, being prepared for his future life's work. Offering a vision of hope to these young people was a mission, a "calling" for him. Could our marriage survive these pressures, as well as my unconscious fears that were driving us apart? How does one remain faithful both to a marriage commitment and to a "calling" that seems to each demand all of one's energy and time?

Later, I realized that Bill's mistress was his work at this stage of our lives. He, too, was committed to our marriage and family, but he didn't know how to balance the priorities or communicate his stress.

Finding My Voice: Discovering Wisdom

Once I began to identify my frustration of feeling trapped and dependent, I found a focus and outlet in the feminist movement. I rejected the belief system and fixed role models I had been given that perpetuated the image of a male God and interpreted scripture from a hierarchical point of view with men at the pinnacle.

I didn't know then that this change of perspective would create a feeling of being in limbo. I had moved outside the narrow cultural understanding and theology of my tribe of evangelical Christians in Pittsburgh, where I was first introduced to a living, personal faith as an adolescent and where I had found belonging. I began to seek a community with whom I could develop an understanding of faith inclusive of justice for all and respect for myself and others who differed from me in race and culture.

Later, I was led to the Episcopal Church, which, in my experience, combined the traditions of my Protestant and Catholic ancestors, encouraged me to think for myself, and now, living in a multi-racial and cultural community, both challenged and expanded my understanding of what it looked like to follow the way of Jesus.

By the time we moved from New York to Atlanta, I could see that Bill and I were in a downward spiral headed for destruction, and I began to seek help for us. I often threatened to leave, using the threat of divorce as leverage to get his attention. Bill dealt with my anger and threats to leave by overworking and getting his needs for affirmation met by colleagues and by speaking to groups.

By the grace of God, Bill was confronting his unconscious beliefs about race, gender, and white male privilege. Encounter groups in our community provided opportunities for black and white men to speak truth to each other in a safe space with a wise counselor who could hold the space for that kind of honest communication.

The feminist movement I was exposed to in New York City soon after we married helped me find my voice. Some years later, seminary gave me the grounding to know that I, too, as a woman, was created in the image of God and was beloved. The women's movement helped me become clearer about who I was, what I wanted, and the inequities embedded in our institutions, but my growing pains were very hard on our marriage and our children.

Our move to Atlanta made it possible for me to direct the outrage I felt about excluding the voices and presence of girls and women in the church into something positive. We were again living communally, and our children had other adults to help us care for them.

I began to feel a strong desire to study scripture from my point of view as a woman, so I enrolled in seminary as a special student at the Candler School of Theology at Emory University. As a part-time student, I could take a few courses without being sponsored for ordination by any particular church as I "worked out my faith with fear and trembling" as scripture advises each person to do (Philippians 2:12). To me, that meant committing to growing my faith as I experienced more of life's successes and failures. And in prayer, listening more closely to the wise, healing Spirit of the Living God.

When I identified the Wisdom tradition in the Hebrew and Christian scriptures, including the Apocrypha (the books of the Bible in between the two), I began to see that the feminine, embedded in scripture, had been there all along, though largely unacknowledged by the hierarchy of religious institutions to which I had been exposed. There she was, the character of Wisdom, named Sophia in the Greek, part of the nature of the Creator and created order.

I was developing a vision for a church that offered life-giving meaning and belonging to human beings—churches that would be places where boys and girls, as well as men and women, would have voices of equal value in interpreting scripture and where all would be welcome. My vision included equal partnership in marriage and family roles that would be fluid based on our gifts rather than fixed.

Bill was traveling around the country, expanding Communities in Schools to serve rural communities and cities. I was balancing my relationship with our children and the group of adults and children living in our communal household while going to seminary.

All that took a lot of energy; I often felt as though I was spinning plates, balancing them on a long row of sticks. As soon as I got them all spinning, some would slow down and be in danger of falling, so I needed to run to catch the ones ready to fall and send them spinning again to keep my life and my family's life afloat. I was afraid that if I allowed one plate to drop, they would all come crashing down. And worst of all, Bill would become involved with someone else and give up on our marriage.

Fueled by my recognition of the injustice of women being paid less at work while being responsible for home management and raising the children, I saw that men were free to focus on their work and provide backup support to their wives if they were free. I was exhausted and depressed, and Bill felt the weight of it in our angry interactions.

We were living in an economically blighted Atlanta neighborhood of predominantly African American neighbors. I was adjusting to a new Southern culture, struggling with being a minority in a neighborhood where robberies took place frequently.

At one point, I had a meeting with my Bishop, part of whose job was to be available for pastoral care of his clergy. He asked me how I was. As tears began to well up and stream down my face, I said, "I am totally overwhelmed. Bill is traveling every week. We are living in an unsafe neighborhood where children have gone missing and been murdered, we are living on a limited income, and the children are in poor schools. You have assigned me to serve in a church community located in a settlement house where the senior clergyperson is single and does not understand the demands of marriage or motherhood, and I don't think he respects women. I don't think I can stay there."

My Bishop became very uncomfortable and said, "I will find another placement for you in a church where you can serve while in seminary. However, you cannot cry in front of the vestry when your life at home is tough or life's demands simply stress you. I will pay for you to go to therapy to help you understand what is behind your tears." I felt both unsupported and misunderstood. At the same time, I was grateful for the financial help to explore my tears and frustration. At that point, I didn't understand the depth of these emotions myself, so I accepted his offer and said, "Yes, I am willing to explore my tears in therapy."

In therapy, it became clear that sometimes when I cry, it isn't because I am sad or overly stressed; it is because I am angry and afraid to express it directly because the well of anger is so deep and wide. My tears could be a way to soften the anger so I could speak. If I expressed it fully, I didn't trust my Bishop's ability to hear and understand what I was experiencing. I had observed that even bishops, many of whom are fairly self-aware and mature in faith, can misunderstand and be uncomfortable in the face of a woman's tears.

I also learned that pent-up feelings of betrayal from childhood can come out as rage, which is hurtful and divisive when unconsciously acted out. Rage makes it hard to reach a positive resolution. I knew what I felt was partially fueled by rage, so I contained it until I could understand it better.

Throughout our marriage, times of crisis and conflict led Bill and me to seek individual therapy and marriage counseling. Marriage counseling was essential for us to move toward personal wholeness and to forgive and embrace healing in our marriage.

Individual therapy helped, but it was also dangerous, as we were growing separately in intimate relationships with our therapists, but without the skill to communicate to each other about who we were becoming. Couples therapy was essential for a safe place to speak our truth as we grew and healed.

When we moved to Virginia in 1983, we were introduced to Imago Relationship Therapy, which helped us learn how to communicate with each other with mutual respect and make it safe to speak our truth. We developed compassion for ourselves and each other. Adopting an attitude of curiosity rather than defensiveness was a huge help in listening to each other empathically. Learning the discipline of a structured dialogue to communicate when we were stuck in a power struggle was essential to safely communicate our feelings.

John Gottman, a marriage researcher in the Pacific Northwest, determined that four patterns are generally destructive to marriage relationships. He called them "The Four Horsemen of the Apocalypse": Defensiveness, Contempt, Stonewalling, and Criticism.[4] Bill and I were practiced in all four.

When I later trained as an Imago Relationship Therapist and learned specific dialogue skills, our marriage relationship began to change. We learned how important forgiveness was and what it felt like to "love your enemy" when your enemy is your spouse and you have reached an impasse.

We now had a vision of how to move from anger, judgment, and misunderstanding to mutual respect, support, and appreciation, even as

---

[4] John Gottman, "The Four Horsemen: The Antidotes," The Gottman Institute, July 31, 2024, https://www.gottman.com/blog/the-four-horsemen-the-antidotes/.

we continued to see the world differently. We didn't have to agree; we just needed to have compassion for each other, calm our urge to defend ourselves, listen, and stay curious regarding the other's reality to find a path forward that honored both of us.

In my counseling practice with couples, I have learned that if too many unresolved disagreements go underground, they begin to erode the foundation of a marriage, even when the marriage begins with love and good intentions. After a number of years, it is hard for marriage partners to identify what produced the cracks in the foundation, so to speak, and sometimes, they are too numerous to name and repair.

It may feel as if the only way to keep from drowning in the pain, disconnection, and old resentments is to separate for a while and for some, ultimately decide to divorce. When both people still want to be married, the other option is to commit to the long haul, be willing to grow and change, surface long-held misunderstandings and resentments, and choose to forgive themselves and each other. When the marriage relationship is stressed, there often is a temptation to share one's feelings with a third party who seems more sympathetic to one's point of view and may share one's vision at work. It is important to resist that temptation and keep the energy in the marriage relationship by learning to talk to each other safely and choose to keep the emotional energy in the marriage partnership.

Our marriage was grounded in the values of self-sacrifice, emotional and physical faithfulness, a community of support, laughter, adventure, prayers, a lot of therapy and self-reflection, faith in God, and the personal commitment for each of us to fulfill our unique purpose. We examined the exits we were using to avoid the pain of disconnection and decided not to use the threat of divorce, alcohol or work, friends or colleagues, or even individual therapy to avoid talking to each other or avoid opening up Pandora's box of family life in childhood.

Most significant of all was a shared belief in a God who is love, a desire to follow the way of Jesus individually and in community, and regular time alone to listen to the wisdom of the Spirit of love to guide us in a life-giving way.

Over the years, we have continued to learn how to give and receive love and honor our differences. As I searched for a gift to give Bill on our 50th wedding anniversary, I came across a little wooden plaque with the message, "I'll keep you Safe, You keep me Wild." That pretty much describes our relationship dance over the years. Bill is a creative risk-taker who is deeply intuitive and wants to keep all options open until the last minute. I am a secondary risk-taker who wants to make decisions before the situation becomes a crisis or options are narrowed by indecision, a natural nurturer sensitive to the look and feel of my home environment, and a creator of beauty. Because of these differences, we approach life very differently.

I am beginning to step out of my comfort zone, take risks, and trust that "All will be well" even in the face of failure, suffering, and loss. Bill is becoming more sensate, noticing his environment. He has become a more conscious partner in the kitchen, for example, paying attention to where to put things so they can be easily located again and noticing if I have had my hair cut or am wearing a new dress. I am grateful for the growth challenges of this long marriage and the power of love and safety. They have helped me release the childhood fears that blocked me from expressing my care and love and kept me from offering my best self in a relationship with him, my children, grandchildren, and others in my everyday life.

My hope in honoring our lifetime covenant in marriage was and continues to be that by God's grace, with the support of a caring community and a willingness to do the inner exploration and hard work to learn to communicate and be willing to change, I will learn to trust and love more fully with an open heart.

Discovering Motherhood

On Thanksgiving Day, 1968, Bill and I were invited to join Bo and Mary Nixon at Bo's mother's apartment in the Smith Housing Projects on New York's Lower East Side for Thanksgiving dinner. Our first child was due to be born any day, which prevented us from traveling home to Pittsburgh as usual.

We sat around the dinner table laughing and telling stories about Bill and Bo's meeting in the Smith Housing Projects. Bo recalled how he hated white people and how Bill continued to pursue a friendship with him.

All of a sudden, I began to feel something strange going on in my body and asked if I could use the bathroom. When I didn't reappear in a reasonable amount of time, Ms. Nixon came to check on me. Tapping quietly on the door, she whispered, "Are you okay?"

I opened the door a crack and sheepishly confessed that I had had an accident and lost control of my bladder. When I described what had happened, she smiled knowingly and kindly said, "I am pretty sure what you have experienced is normal when you are about to deliver a baby. Your water has broken, and I think your body is telling you your baby is ready to be born." I was stunned and confused, responding, "I was expecting to experience contractions before anything else. I still have no contractions."

A quick call to the doctor ended our pleasant Thanksgiving dinner. Home we went to make sure my carefully packed suitcase had everything I needed, hoping the contractions would begin soon. By morning, I still had no contractions, so we headed to the hospital to start a protocol of medication to bring them on.

Our good friend, Sandy, was my birth coach and a nurse to my doctor. Dr. Diamond was willing to do a natural childbirth delivery using no pain medication. The nurses on the unit weren't used to assisting natural childbirth and kept entering my room to encourage me to take pain medication.

Bill hadn't felt comfortable being trained to be my labor coach, so he had no idea what to expect. Nevertheless, with my doctor's agreement, Sandy encouraged him to be present in the labor room. She stood at my side, coaching me when to breathe, rubbing my back, and generally encouraging me through the strong contractions brought on by Pitocin to induce labor.

Bill sat in a corner of the room, briefcase on his lap, ostensibly working, but instead was mesmerized by what was happening between Sandy and me. Women in surrounding rooms were yelling and screaming for help and more pain medication. Without Sandy's strength and steady coaching, I imagine I would have succumbed to the nurses' pressure to take the medication.

In the midst of this, our friend Dwight appeared in the labor room. Taken by surprise, Bill jumped up from his chair. "How did you get in here?"

It shouldn't have been a surprise to any of us how he got in. Dwight, despite being born into a prominent medical family in Boston, had spent most of his 40 years either in juvenile detention, beginning at age eight, or in prison. He was well practiced in entering places he shouldn't have had access to.

Some years before Bill and I were married, Dwight was being released from prison one more time and had nowhere to go. Bill received a call from Cardinal Cushing, Catholic Archbishop of Boston, who knew Dwight's family, and asked if he could come to New York City, live in the men's apartments, and be supervised by Bill.

Dwight was physically attractive, with light brown hair, a tall, muscular body, and an engaging manner. He was very smart, evidenced by the fact that he had cataloged one prison library with the Dewey Decimal system. But out of prison, he just couldn't fit into Boston society as his two older sisters had been able to do. Bill agreed to supervise him, and Dwight became the oldest member living in the apartments for men, which were paid for by Trinity Parish Church.

Dwight and I had become friends riding the subway to work in midtown Manhattan. He had gotten a job in the mailroom at *Guidepost Magazine*, and I was working as a receptionist at Faith at Work. Dwight would regale me with prison stories in his loud, deep voice in the crowded subway on our way to work, which turned my face beet red and caused him to tease me by saying I was "white, right, and uptight."

The problem was that it was true. I was taught to be a good girl and behave properly. My family was Republican. When I joined Bill in New York, I was the only registered Republican in our precinct on the Lower East Side of Manhattan. My skin color placed me in the minority in our neighborhood. I could change some things, but not the color of my skin.

"How are you all getting along here?" Dwight smiled as he looked around the labor room. Even though I knew he was clever, I couldn't believe he had gotten into my room without detection. I needed to stay focused on breathing to get through each contraction. They were becoming stronger and more frequent, so I ignored him. The nurse came in and pointedly ordered him out.

Finally, the time came for our baby to be born. Dr. Diamond entered the room with a flurry and announced, "Bill, if you would like, you can come and stand beside me. Be sure and let us know if you feel like you are going to faint," he quipped. Skillfully, Dr. Diamond guided our baby into the world. "It's a boy!" he announced. "Good job, everyone."

He then proceeded to do some tissue repair work, and almost as an aside, he said, "Ah, has anyone seen my watch?" It took a few minutes for us to get the humor, but slowly we each got the joke. As our son, Sean Matthew, was placed in my arms, I knew our world had changed. The two of us had become a family of three, and Bill and I were about to find out what it meant to raise a child.

Soon, the nurse took Sean to the nursery, Bill left for home, and I was taken to my room, where I fell into a deep sleep. I was awakened by a nurse who brought Sean in to teach me how to breastfeed. I had only seen him once following delivery, but when I looked at this baby, he didn't look like mine. The nurse checked his arm bracelet and found that, in fact, he wasn't our baby.

Once we got that straightened out, the nursing training began. Teaching a mother and baby how to nurse takes some serious concentration. Just as we got the knack of it, Bill appeared at the door with a young man I had never seen before. "Hi, I met Way Out Willy at our storefront in the East Village last night. He's from West Virginia. He wanted to meet you and our baby. I am so glad Sean is in the room and not in the nursery." I took one look at Way Out Willy, unkempt in his wrinkled shirt, well-worn, stained blue jeans, and a piece of straw in his sandy-colored hair, and thought, *There is no way I am going to let this person touch my newborn baby*. I politely thanked Willy for coming, and Bill got the message that this was not a good time for guests.

The challenge of parenthood had begun. Bill and I had no idea how to be parents. Three years into our marriage, we still had virtually no communication skills to help us work through basic differences, let alone different parenting styles. Even though we fought a lot, deep down, we knew we loved each other and wanted to learn how to be a happy family.

Those were hard years for Bill and me. I still didn't know what I was called to do other than make a home for us and care for our son. I had relationships in the community, but no family I could call on for help when I needed advice or a break from childcare. Nor did we have the money to hire anyone to help when Bill traveled. Racial tensions were high on the Lower East Side, and Bill, when he was home, was often working to reconcile neighboring gangs of Hispanic, Black, Chinese, and Italian teenagers during the day.

As I mentioned earlier, at night, he was at a storefront in the East Village, talking with Latin American Christians, discussing liberation theology and considering ways to respond to the inequities they saw in society.

Bill had many experiences that challenged his faith, of which I wasn't a part. I was concerned that our paths were becoming so divergent they wouldn't meet again. Some months later, a weekend meeting was arranged by one of Bill's board members, who was pivotal in the direction Bill chose to go. Only the men were invited to attend. Although I was angry that the women of the community were not included in the meeting with Baptist minister Clarence Jordan, founder of Koinonia Farms in Americus, Georgia, out of which Habitat for Humanity was eventually born, I will forever be grateful that Clarence presented a convincing argument about the New Testament's challenge to love your enemies. That weekend dialogue kept Bill from going down a path that seemed to me would dead-end in violence or, I feared, land him in prison or end our marriage.

Our last year in New York was a time of transition. It was time for Bill to move into a mentoring role and turn over the work he had begun to young leaders who had grown up there. Bill and I wanted to live more simply and share the values of the Koinonia Farms community of peace, brotherhood (sisterhood), and sharing, but we were city people not drawn to rural living.

We moved into a brownstone in Brooklyn's Cobble Hill section of New York and began an urban experiment in communal living modeled after Koinonia Farms. Good friends, with whom we planned to move to Atlanta and share a communal household following our time living in Brooklyn, had adopted two children. The year before our move to Brooklyn, they had encouraged us to consider adopting since many children in foster care needed permanent homes. I had had a miscarriage early on in a second pregnancy, and we wanted another child to join our family. Thus, just before moving into the communal house in Brooklyn, we began the adoption process.

The gender of the baby didn't matter to Bill and me. We just knew we wanted another child. In some ways, it seemed like a boy would be easier for me to raise. A girl would be subject to my unconscious projections, my unlived dreams, and my painful, confusing family history, much of which had yet to be worked through.

But at the same time, I had begun to take steps to make sense of my family history. So perhaps by the time a girl would begin to ask questions about her biological family, I could walk that path alongside her, offering support without feeling threatened. I trusted in the power of love, family, our multiracial community, and the Spirit's guidance to support our venture into this new dimension of parenting.

The adoption agency invited us to consider a two-and-a-half-month-old baby girl in foster care. Soon after arriving at the adoption agency, the social worker placed her in my arms. It seemed that her dark brown eyes radiated fear and distrust. They pierced my heart. Her thin arms pushed at my chest. Her tiny, malnourished body seemed to cry out for nurture and care.

As I held her, I asked myself, "Can I be a good mother to this child with her dark curly hair so different from mine and her almond-shaped brown eyes and light brown skin? A child who will have no family members to mirror her features and a mother with no personal experience to help her navigate her racial identity? Can I prepare her to face the challenging life of a person of color?"

I felt scared and inadequate. With Bill traveling every week to build awareness of the seriousness of the school dropout rate in our country, his presence at home would be unpredictable.

We already had one child, so I knew the challenges of caring for a child living on the 21st floor of a high-rise in Lower East Side Manhattan. Could I manage two? I wanted to be a good mother to both of our children, but I barely knew who I was. I felt powerless and out of control a lot of the time, and worked to please others rather than acknowledging my thoughts and feelings and developing my own identity. I was living in a melting pot of cultures that I had yet to figure out how to navigate.

We left the agency and went home to talk about it. I wanted my mother to know what we were considering, so I called her. In 1970, in Pittsburgh, there weren't many interracial marriages or adoptions. Growing up, I had known of none. My mother, who was loving and kind and always concerned about what people would think, responded, "Well, Jeannie, if you're outside with the baby by yourself, people will think you are married to a black man."

In her heart, I don't believe she was racist; she was a product of her limited experience and the homogeneous culture in which she lived. The reality of interracial marriage as good and acceptable was outside her generational experience, and she feared what it would mean for me.

Bill's open-hearted response to adopting this baby was an automatic "Yes." He made most decisions from intuition and instinct. I analyzed every decision to try to anticipate challenges and opportunities. He didn't have the same questions I had about whether he could be a good father to this baby girl since he had been raised by an African American housekeeper whom he loved, and she loved him. He had spent many hours in her home with her family. And, too, he had spent years working in Harlem and on the Lower East Side, where racist ideas or practices were confronted by those with whom he lived and worked. He was instinctively warm and welcoming to everyone.

I, on the other hand, had learned to be reserved until trust had time to grow. I intuitively knew that raising this baby along with our son in a culturally mixed neighborhood would likely be one of the most challenging things I would do in my life.

Nevertheless, despite my feelings of inadequacy, I embraced this baby, and Bill and I joyfully moved forward with the adoption. I knew we would always be part of a mixed-race extended community, and they would support and guide us, so I agreed. I had faith that the four of us could navigate this uncharted territory together with the much-needed support of friends and family.

I wondered what we would name this baby girl. Should we keep the name her foster family gave her or give her a new name? Because she looked Polynesian/Hawaiian and was tri-racial—black, white, and Filipino—we first considered Leilani, which means "Heavenly flower," but shortened her name to Lani. She was given a new name and a new family, and a new story began for all of us.

During the day, Lani was quiet and seemed happy, but for at least the first ten years of Lani's life, she didn't sleep through the night. Sometimes, she was awakened by hallucinations and fearful dreams. On other occasions, she just woke up crying, felt scared, and needed help to calm down and go back to sleep.

Later, when Lani searched for her birth family to learn her medical history, we wondered if these nighttime terrors were related to the medical history of her birth parents and the trauma they had both suffered before and after she was conceived.

Amid those ongoing challenges, a crisis in Sean's life thrust me into my own terror. Shortly after our move to Atlanta, before I knew much about living there, I took a drive with one of the young adults who lived with us. Sean was happy in the back seat with his arm wrapped around the much-loved red plastic motorcycle he'd been riding incessantly since his third birthday. This was before seat belts were required or even installed in many cars.

On a curve, Sean's door opened, and he fell out. The car behind us ran over him. I ran to him and began to pick him up. Then, realizing I shouldn't move him, I didn't know what to do.

The police and ambulance arrived and asked what hospital I wanted him to be taken to. The nearest hospital was Georgia Baptist. Since we didn't know what to do, the ambulance driver said, "I think it would be best to take him to Grady, where they deal with a lot of trauma cases."

We took him there. It was a hospital that served a large indigent population. I was a new volunteer in labor and delivery at Grady, so I knew an ob-gyn doctor there and called him. He came and offered Bill and me his office to sleep in.

We began a vigil, praying that Sean would survive. We weren't alone. Bill had met the rector of St. Luke's Church in his leadership Atlanta class, and Tom, the priest who later baptized Lani, came and anointed Sean. Friends started a prayer chain that extended across the country.

One night, a few days after the accident, when Bill was with Sean, he put his head into the oxygen tent and asked, "Sean, do you want me to pray that Jesus will make you well?" Sean replied, "Daddy, he already is"—a stunning response from a three-year-old.

In ten days, Sean came home, amazingly restored except for a broken collarbone and stitches in his chest where the tubes had been draining the blood from his lung and keeping it inflated. The doctor said, "I've never seen healing like that happen with that kind of trauma."

In our deep relief and thanksgiving, I had to wonder why our son had survived when the infant child of dear friends who also prayed ardently and who was surrounded by others' prayers had died. I didn't know how to think about that question. It remains the kind of mystery we don't get to penetrate fully in this life.

Lani, age two at that time, was thrilled to see Sean when he came home. She hugged him again and again. She was in a happy place. But as she grew older, we began to see signs of behaviors that concerned us. Once in school, Lani needed hours of homework support. Though the brilliance of her mind was evident as she raised questions about how the universe worked and could write creatively about her feelings, she was often strangely unable to understand homework assignments. She lamented, "I feel dumb; I can't tell time and say the months of the year like the other kids in school."

Lani sought my approval and rejected it at the same time. She wanted me to be her mother, but when she was angry, she would, like many young children, express it with a simple, painful "I hate you." If I had known better, I wouldn't have taken those words personally, but they shook my confidence that she really accepted me as her mother.

Her conflicting emotions came out in other verbal messages: "I wish I could go inside of your tummy and be born from you." "You're not my real mother." Sometimes, I could understand and not be hooked by her rejection; sometimes, I couldn't. I would feel hurt or angry and not know what to do with my feelings.

Occasionally, I wondered whether it had been in her best interest to bring her, a mixed-race child, into a white family. Were we going to be a problem for her all her life? I so wanted her. I thought love and a family who cared for her would be enough for us to bond, but now she required more.

In her adulthood, we've reflected on those times and how difficult they were, though very differently for her than for me. I was unaware, for instance, of the degree of rejection she experienced when we, her white parents, showed up at school, sharpening the social divide between her and both white and black classmates.

The adoption agency had warned that it wasn't optimal for white parents to adopt a child of color. Although we took that advice seriously, we felt it was still better for any child to have a loving family despite racial differences than to be placed in the overloaded and unpredictable foster care system.

People often thought Lani looked Polynesian, Italian, or Hispanic and were surprised to find her family was white. I didn't understand the many faces of racism, nor was I prepared for the rejection she would experience from African American children at school during a period when black pride was at its height in Atlanta. She was of mixed race, neither black, white, Hispanic, nor Italian. Most people could see she was a child of color, and some didn't treat her with respect.

I remember an incident in a department store when she was an adolescent. She went up to a counter to be waited on, and although the clerk saw her, she ignored her. I approached the counter, and the clerk said, "May I help you, ma'am?" I replied, "No, but you may help my daughter, who has been standing here waiting to make a purchase." The clerk frowned and proceeded to help Lani, but with a hostile attitude.

There were other times when I wish I had been more assertive and confronted the behavior I observed toward Lani. But racism can be subtle; I often wasn't sure if that was truly what was going on because Lani had developed a defensive attitude and behaviors that could provoke anyone to react by ignoring or rejecting her.

A lack of understanding the effect of her learning differences was also likely a factor in her acting out and internalizing a negative self-image. I was naive about the significance of early attachment between a consistent, nurturing caregiver and an infant. The natural process of attachment had been interrupted twice.

It slowly became clear that that rupture wouldn't be easy or fast to repair. Lani's preschool teachers expressed concern that she wasn't talking at her age level and suggested she might be developmentally delayed and that perhaps we would want to have her tested. I was at a loss as to what to do, so we sought testing help. Even the test results were confusing. They determined she had a learning issue called auditory memory deficit, which meant that she had trouble processing what she was hearing. She had to "see and do" before she could learn.

On the other hand, they determined that her delayed talking and inability to focus could have emotional and psychological roots. Since most of the teaching in school at that level was oral, school was a big challenge. She was bright but missed many social cues, inhibiting her ability to learn and develop friendships.

I wish I had known then to recognize the signs that Lani had some heightened sensitivities and learning difficulties that were not commonly recognized or in her control. It would have made a big difference to her and our family if we had known more about how to guide her and her teachers to respect her differences.

Over the years, I have learned to appreciate what it has taken for both Bill and Lani to live with the learning differences they were born with, find ways to compensate for them, and celebrate their gifts of creativity and compassion that have made them the people they are.

Our son developed emotional intelligence in his relationships early on and was able to navigate between people and cultures. He had an open, trusting disposition and "street smarts." He learned how to get love and approval from his teachers and the other adults in his life. Engaging in sports at the local Boys Club in Grant Park gave him a safe place to go after school and a way to release his energy.

We were grateful for the support of friends, godparents, and family to augment our inexperienced parenting. It clearly did take a village to raise our two children. There was a lot of love to go around that showed up at just the right time and held us together when we were on the verge of splitting apart.

Like Bill during his adolescence, Lani was easily influenced by children who were considered troublemakers, who were themselves struggling to find acceptance and belonging, using negative ways to get attention. I learned later that this was often a pattern among children who learn differently. In addition to Lani's being adopted and tri-racial, she needed a teaching style that drew on sight, sound, and touch rather than speech. She was also extremely sensitive to smells, clothes itching her skin, and loud sounds. I tried to help her get over her extreme sensitivities, but, in fact, she was born with heightened physical and emotional sensitivities.

I wondered what my faith in God had to offer in this situation. At the time, my relationship with God was not offering me the help I needed to live peacefully. In my naivete, I encouraged Lani to trust a world that is often racist and not trustworthy for people of color and to make her belong where she didn't want to belong.

Over the years of parenting our two children, I began to see that love invites the other to be themselves and that love can acknowledge differences and not be threatened by them.

In *This Is How It Always Is*, Laurie Frankel tells a story about a child who was gender nonconforming. His parents and four older brothers walked alongside their brother as "he" evolved into "she." Frankel concluded in the author's notes, "Parenting always involves this balance between what you know, what you guess, what you fear, and what you imagine. You're never certain, even (maybe especially), about the big deals, the huge, important ones with all of the ramifications and repercussions. But alas, no one can make these decisions or deal with their consequences but you."[5]

Sean and his family live just down the street from us now. During our regular Saturday or Sunday brunches, as we discuss current issues, I see how living in the Grant Park neighborhood in Atlanta and participating in the local Boys and Girls Club has prepared him to live in a multi-racial and multi-ethnic world.

Although he was small in stature until he reached his 6-foot-2-inch height in college, he nevertheless played football at the Boys and Girls Club and was nicknamed "The White Flash" because he was the only white boy on the team and ran really fast. He isn't subject to white liberalism in the same way as those of us who grew up in a homogenous neighborhood and who have to think through, "Am I coming from a racist attitude, or am I one human being relating to another as equal apart from the color of our skin or our socioeconomic status?"

His thoughtfulness regarding relationships and social issues, and his wisdom regarding the ways of the world, amaze me sometimes. He is a bridge builder as an adult, a quality built on the foundation of a loving, caring heart, an ongoing interest to listen to both sides of any issue to educate himself and come to his own conclusions, and a commitment to friends, family, and our larger community while often sacrificing his ego needs for the good of the whole. He has used his entrepreneurial skills

---

[5] Laurie Frankel, *This Is How It Always Is* (2018), the author's notes.

to provide for the material needs of his family in partnership with his wife, Jill.

Everyone has a birth family; we carry the genetic code of our ancestors. Our two children carry different genetic codes, and so do children who are born to the same parents. We are formed by those who raise and love us and the culture surrounding us.

Sometimes, it is those who conceive us who love and help form us, and sometimes, it is a family of choice with whom we identify and whom we embrace because they love us and can guide us to be our best selves, and we love them back. Sometimes, our birth families can't do that for a variety of reasons. Ultimately, as Lani said recently, "I am a mixture of all of that, but I am just ME."

For Lani and me, and for many others who were not raised by an intact family during their formative years and whose circumstances prevented them from receiving love and secure attachment at birth and during childhood, the process of choosing to trust love, receive love, and give it freely can take many years.

Lani and I have found belonging and unconditional love in following the Way of Jesus, the Christ, though the expression of that commitment in our daily life looks very different. Our lifestyles are also different. We both keep a clean home, but she can live with disorder, and I require order to be comfortable. We are attracted to different church traditions but are both seekers of Truth guided by the Holy Scriptures, the Holy Spirit (Sophia), and those who speak truth to us in love.

Following graduation from college with a major in psychology, Lani strongly desired to go to nursing school. This was somewhat puzzling to us since no one in our immediate family was a nurse or physician. She finished her associate degree in nursing and explored home health care, pediatric health care, and elder care before moving to the beach, where she wanted to live and transition to a nursing career in behavioral health settings.

Today, she serves a population of patients that others avoid. When she tells other registered nurses that she works in a behavioral health inpatient hospital, the consistent response is, "Oh, I could never do that!

It is too hard." Certainly, caring for mentally ill patients every day is a challenge and adventure, but she does it with compassion and care. When she began working in behavioral health, she said, "It's really hard, Mom, but I get these people."

Lani and I are baptized into the household of faith and belong to the family of God. Her baptism at age four at St. Luke's Episcopal Church in Atlanta was her entry into that spiritual ancestry. To our priest friend, Tom, as he prepared to pour the water of baptism on Lani's head after we had spent a long time fixing her hair, she said, "If you pour that water on my head, mess up my hair, and get my dress wet, I am going to kick you." This was the way Lani sometimes spoke her unfiltered truth, and Tom was able to hear it and take it in stride.

The water of baptism ritualizes our belonging in the household of faith. It provides the grounding for us to embrace our history and know that we are equally loved and worthy of offering who we are to the world, and our gifts are worthy of being received.

Sometimes, it takes a lot of years following baptism, having come into a community of faith kicking and screaming, to know in your heart that you are loved unconditionally and you belong.

As I recall Lani's story, I am reminded of two passages from the New Testament in the book of Galatians.

Galatians 3:26-29 says: "For in Christ Jesus you are all children of God through faith. As many of you who were baptized into Christ have clothed yourselves with Christ. There is no longer Jew or Greek, there is no longer slave or free, there is no longer male and female; for all of you are one in Christ Jesus. And if you belong to Christ, then you are Abraham's offspring, heirs according to the promise."

In Galatians 4:3-5, it says, "So with us; while we were minors, we were enslaved to the elemental spirits of the world. But when the fullness of time had come, God sent his son, born of a woman, born under the law, in order to redeem those who were under the law, so that we might receive adoption as children" (NRSV with Apocrypha).

Lani has been guided by the prayers and the wisdom of her African American godparents, Clarke and Edith, who know racism up close and personal. She trusts the understanding and compassion of her dad, who suffered rejection throughout his school years because, like Lani, he learned differently. And she's well aware of the steadfast love and support of our son, daughter-in-law, grandchildren, and extended family and friends. The search for a deep, stable sense of identity has taken courage and perseverance on both her part and mine.

Different as our struggles were, we both dealt with perplexing identity issues in our young lives. By now, though, we have largely come to terms with the unsettling truths of our biological parentage. This has enabled us to be more open to intimacy and, at times, share laughter at our mutual misunderstandings.

As we have grown to love and accept ourselves and internalize God's boundless love for us, we are becoming better friends with ourselves and each other. With all this help, the glacier of hurt and fear between my daughter and me continues to melt into a grace-filled pool of tenderness and respect.

What I wish for Sean and Lani, our grandchildren, Alexandra and Jack, and all children is that we, as a nation, will pull our projections back and face our unresolved issues. We will welcome diversity, conquer our fears of the "other," and be able, as one friend put it, to turn our skin inside out and see that we are all human.

On one level, race, culture, gender, and sexual orientation are defining differences and dimensions of identity. At the same time, if we could approach each other with our skin turned inside out, we would see that we are all human beings worthy of love, acceptance, and respect.

Now that Sean and Lani are adults, I want to keep learning who they are and what is important to each of them. To enjoy them rather than worry about them. To trust them to make their own decisions regarding relationships, work, and self-care, consulting whoever they believe will give them wise advice. I also want to learn from them as they have gained a lot of wisdom from their life experiences.

Not too long ago, I initiated a conversation with Sean about the bed I made for him when we moved into the communal house in Atlanta, which we painted red together. I remember it being fun for me to measure the wood and learn how to use a hammer and nails to construct the bed. He chose the red paint. He reminded me that he was only three when we did this, so it was hard for him to remember.

As a teenager, it was clear that he took an interest in architecture and real estate and was invested in helping us find our new home in Virginia. He wanted to be a part of looking at houses and choosing our new home. After a lot of looking, he spotted the one we ended up buying. He also found our current town house, which is just down the street from where he and his family live.

A number of years ago, Sean, Jill, Bill, and I were sitting at the dinner table, and the issue of our grandson's diet came up. I had mentioned the importance of feeding children healthy food. Sean reminded me of the many trips we made to McDonald's for dinner and the cans of SpaghettiOs with hot dogs I had fed him and Lani when they were little.

It was a good reminder of the early years of parenting when I was stretched thin and trying to cover all the bases; sometimes, a healthy dinner was low on the priority list. I was reminded of how I have grown in knowledge and understanding about helpful parenting and a healthy diet. I also became aware that commenting on my adult children's parenting can either come across as criticism or be a reminder of my parenting deficits and offer a chance for a good laugh.

In this stage of my life, I strive to let go of the past and set my intention to live in the present. Someone once said, "Worrying is like praying for what you don't want." I think there is truth in that statement. Worry and fear of what could possibly happen keep me from being emotionally clear, trusting God, and living in the present.

I know our children and grandchildren will make difficult choices and experience failure, fear, and losses; it is part of living. I want to protect them by anticipating possibilities based on my experience, but I have learned that giving advice is no longer my role and is often not helpful unless it is asked for.

My challenge now is to hold together the joy of life in the midst of the personal challenges of aging and the grief I feel regarding our national and global divisions and chaos. Living in the present can be hard. There are times when I find myself trying to control the uncontrollable, falling into despair when life feels out of control, or isolating and choosing to ignore suffering and live by the power of positive thinking.

The Value of Anger

By 1971, shortly after Lani's adoption, we moved our family of four from our condo on the Lower East Side into a four-story brownstone in Brooklyn with two other couples and several single friends.

The top two floors had been divided up into separate apartments. Single women lived on the top floor on one end, with one of the couples, Allan and Doris, on the other. Bill, our two children, and I shared the third-floor apartment with another couple, John and Diane. The single men shared the next floor, and our common living space was on the bottom floor, including the kitchen and living room.

John and Diane were a young, newly married couple who were recent graduates of Stanford University. John had come to do alternative service with us in lieu of going to Vietnam. Diane was employed by IBM and was working on her PhD. John and Diane converted the apartment's living room into their living space. The bathroom between their living space and ours was shared by the four adults and our two children.

Bill and I made the kitchen into a cozy but crowded bedroom by covering the cold linoleum kitchen floor with a colorful soft shag area rug made of different colored carpet remnants I stitched together. The wall at the base of our bed was lined with the kitchen sink, cabinets, and refrigerator. We squeezed our double bed, a dresser, and a rocking chair into the open space. The two small rooms at opposite ends of the hall were just big enough to accommodate a single bed and a dresser, which became our children's bedrooms.

Daily life with other men and women who had committed to peace, racial and gender equality, and sharing material goods allowed me to join with like-minded people to put into action a spiritual path of simple living that I believed followed the way of Jesus. We had a long way to go to internalize and implement the ideals and values we had sought to embrace.

We represented a diverse group racially and culturally; we were black, white, Asian, and Northern and Southern USA-born. We had many challenges ahead to learn from each other and come to a mutual understanding. Nevertheless, we made a commitment to do our best to live them out individually and collectively. We had seen the domination and racial injustice experienced by our friends who were black, Hispanic, and Asian.

Feminism also complicated the diverse perspectives each one brought, making it challenging to share life together. It was difficult for us as white women to integrate those deep concerns with our growing awareness of our own struggles to be heard and respected. Many evenings, heated conversations with the black men in our community focused on the way white feminist women were diffusing the focus on racial injustice by focusing on our own experience of injustices that were crushing our souls.

Most of us had come from evangelical Christian backgrounds that defined women and their roles in family and society in very limiting ways. I was on the verge of rejecting my Christian faith. But what would I replace it with? The majority of those who joined with us in this experiment of living out our faith in community had chosen to follow Jesus but had become disillusioned by the blindness of many Christian groups to social injustice.

Tuesday night was the night most of the men in our communal household came to dread. It was the night the women gathered in our support group to discuss what was on our minds. We were sounding boards for each other as we processed what we were hearing in the culture from feminist leaders and others and how that impacted our thinking, our faith in God, and our committed relationships.

Bill was responsible for our children on Tuesday nights, and although he had help from some of the other men, it was challenging to get a one-year-old and a two-year-old ready for bed. By the time I would arrive home, he was usually exhausted from a long day at work and taking care of the children.

This particular night, we women returned from our weekly meeting, still energetically engaged in our conversation as we walked up the stairs and said our goodnights. The single women continued to their fourth-floor rooms, as did Doris, to join her husband, Allan. Diane and I went to our rooms on the third floor to discuss with our husbands what had been stirred up.

Often, the topic of the men in our lives didn't come up in our weekly conversations as we explored our hopes and dreams for ourselves, but this particular night, it did. I approached Bill with fire in my belly.

Rocking in our rocking chair in his jeans and T-shirt, reading a magazine, Bill appeared calm, but I was pretty sure he was ambivalent and cautious about welcoming me home, and for good reason. On Tuesday nights, when I returned from these meetings, I often had a complaint regarding some form of male dominance and misuse of power. I immediately lit into him.

"You spend all your time each day and night helping find ways to free those who have been oppressed due to racial injustice and a lack of education to prepare them for real jobs, and yet, right here and now, you have a slave at home. I am responsible for caring for our children and hounding the single men living in the house to do their share of cleaning, grocery shopping, and cooking while you are free to focus on your work, not take responsibility for what needs to be done, and think you are doing your part by doing the household chores I ask you to do. I am still responsible for it all. You just help me when you're free and when I ask for help. My decision not to teach, even though I am certified, does not mean I do not want to work outside of our home and contribute to the family income. How can I, since I am with the children all day, doing laundry, cleaning, and paying bills in the evening? There is no time or energy for me to do anything else. We both live in this house, eat the food, and have a shared commitment to love and care for our children."

After he recovered from his shock, he silently resumed rocking for what seemed like an hour, though it was just minutes. Then he pounded the side of the dresser and said, "The purpose of the feminist movement and your women's meetings is not to turn the tables so that I become a slave and a victim so that you are free to dominate me."

His response shocked me. I walked away rather than defending myself and getting into our usual shouting match. I knew that what he said was true. My intention was not to dominate him. I wanted us to be partners, but neither of us had the skills to safely communicate heated differences. We needed to understand each other and find workable solutions that honored and respected our needs to fulfill our "call" to serve the wider community, receive affirmation and recognition for contributing to the common good, and co-parent our two children.

At that point, I didn't even know what was calling me, but I sensed it had to do with challenging the institutional church to recognize women and men as equals. I wanted to see if I could find the feminine aspect of God in scripture and help actualize it in the church.

As I took time and space to process what he said, his angry defense motivated me to think about how I wanted to use my voice and my power. Did I want to point out to him that his response was an admission that I was a slave in our household? All I knew for sure was that I was worn out by multitasking all day. I needed time to be quiet, focus, and listen to my heart to discern how and where I could contribute outside of our home without neglecting our children.

But how would I create the space to do that? Bill had, in fact, begun doing more household tasks than ever before. I didn't understand at that point that by pushing him to do more, I was bumping up against the unconscious maternal voice he had internalized in childhood, which was always asking for more and never seemed to be satisfied that what he did was enough.

Bill and I both wanted a marriage that honored our differences and would provide a loving environment for our children. His drive to care for young people who were locked into a system that almost guaranteed intergenerational poverty and his passion for racial justice, along with mine for partnership, psychological healing, and the inclusion of the feminine voice in religious institutions, drove us forward.

However, our lack of communication skills inhibited our efforts to hear each other and find a third way to be together, supporting each other's sense of purpose. We needed help, but from whom would it come?

I became aware of the feminist movement toward the end of the 1960s, but now, over a decade later, listening to the voices of powerful women articulating my anger at the dominance of men over women and the way cultural norms and institutions, including the church, perpetuated that dominance, that anger grew. The church was to be a place where we experienced inclusion and freedom to be who we were created to be, inclusive of race, gender, and socioeconomic status, a guide to explore life's meaning and our relationship with the Transcendent, to find and actualize our purpose.

I was at a boiling point, ready to leave my faith community and my marriage and start over to define who I was and what I believed about loving relationships with others and the Divine. Although Bill never said it was his money we lived on, nor that I had to get his permission to spend it, I wanted to contribute to the family income and experience some financial independence.

But the question remained: How would I do that while caring for two children with limited financial resources to pay for child care? Even if we had the financial resources, Bill traveled every week on different days for different periods of time. How could I arrange for consistent child care so the children would be cared for while I was at school, volunteering, or working?

I didn't want the goal of my life now to be to dominate the men in my life or to spew my ire every time it was triggered by some statement or event that devalued women. Perhaps there was a way to do this together for the good of our marriage, our children, and our community. Did I have the courage to explore my own motivations? Was my continuing anger at the structures that keep women in their place justified? Could this energy, which felt powerful and out of control, be used for good, or was it simply destructive for me and our marriage?

Years later, through Jungian psychology, I discovered a way to understand and articulate the masculine and feminine differences I was experiencing in our diverse community. This puzzle piece helped me create a new understanding of the nature of God that I could live with based on inclusion, love, and an appreciation of differences.

In her book *Knowing Woman, a Feminine Psychology*, Irene Claremont de Castillejo, a Jungian analyst, defines feminine consciousness as diffuse awareness, while masculine consciousness is more focused. Although men and women share both, research suggests that women's brains are generally better at multitasking and men's are better at focusing on one thing.

I was exhausted from "keeping all the plates spinning" in our family life. My mother's voice often popped into my mind. "Get educated and develop a profession so that you do not have to depend on a man to provide for you because they may leave." Her advice provoked distrust and fear and drove me to keep the plates spinning despite how exhausted I felt.

More help came from reading theologians like Rosemary Radford Ruether and Elisabeth Schussler Fiorenza. Their critique of the way women's history has been documented in the Christian tradition was timely and helpful. Hearing their vigorous rejection of patriarchy helped me feel as though I wasn't alone in my feelings.[6]

Although some experience it as destructive, the recognition and expression of women's anger released women and some men to seek and speak the truth. Without the force of our anger to energize those who broke down the theological and institutional barriers that kept women subordinated in the church, we would still be blind and deaf to the tremendous gifts women in ordained leadership positions could bring.

The challenge I faced was, "Did I have the courage to do the inner work to have my outrage at injustice be grounded in love and not fueled and distorted by my unconscious childhood pain, which could trigger

---

[6] My definition of patriarchy is a system that is dedicated to oppressing the poor, people of color, women, one's sexual identity to subjugate and control them, the earth, politics, and economics. Patriarchal spirituality is the extension of that system into our hearts and minds by the use of exclusively male gender names for God and the Holy Spirit, for example.

rage?" I wanted to mature in my responses so they would engender hope and bring about justice, not division.

I recognized my sentiments when I came upon Eric Fromm's words, quoted in Matthew Fox's *Original Blessing*, "The comfort of consumerism and the violence of militarism which dominate our times would suggest that we are a people with little or no hope."[7] I was seeing many who had lost hope settle for easy comforts or violence. I didn't want to spend my life walking the shopping malls looking for something to buy or sending my son or daughter off to war as a way to settle national or international disputes.

For me, many churches still represented an institution where people seeking meaning, truth, and hope would join like-minded people and be encouraged to live moral and ethical lives of loving service. They would build bridges contributing to reconciliation. I wanted to be a part of a movement in the church where men and women modeled the use of power and authority to increase hope rather than contribute to fear and despair.

I could only hope that the fragmented pieces of truth I had gleaned from a growing inner experience of God's unconditional love and grace would come together to produce some unified meaning that would guide me into the future and to find a faith community that had integrity in words and practice.

After Bill and I had been married for many years and I had been ordained a priest in the Episcopal Church and been trained and certified to work as a pastoral therapist, I came to understand that power struggles between two people committed to living together were normal. After all, we had grown up in different families and had different formative experiences. Because we were married young and hadn't done much exploration of our inner lives and family patterns, it was normal to get stuck in power struggles.

I had concluded from the many arguments Bill and I had had over the years that remained unresolved that both the one who assumed the role of the powerful and the one in the role of the powerless would

---

[7] Matthew Fox, *Original Blessing* (TarcherPerigee, 2000).

need to learn how to create a safe space to dialogue and be able to hear one another.

As feminist thinkers have matured and sought to form a new world-view based on respect for the other, I celebrate that a worldview shared by both men and women has emerged that unites rather than divides. It creates partnerships rather than hierarchies and enables power from the bottom up rather than from the top down.

It wasn't until I was trained as an Imago relationship therapist that I gained the skill to help create this new reality in my relationships and coach others to do the same. When I began to do marriage counseling, I remembered Frederick Buechner's widely quoted assurance: "The place God calls you to is the place where your deep gladness and the world's deep hunger meet."[8]

I would amend this to say: "The place God calls you is a place where your deep sadness and your deep gladness meet, offering a means to heal the deep sadness of your past and a vision to meet your own and the world's deep hunger for love and relationship."

Fueled by my own experience with divorced parents, my deepest sadness was in seeing marriages dissolve and children suffer the consequences of their parents' choice to divorce, and seeing divorced people enter into another relationship without the awareness on their part of why their previous marriage failed. I was glad when I was introduced to a way to have safe conversations with Bill using the Imago dialogue process. This approach gave Bill and me hope. With the help of a therapist coaching us, we slowly learned how to communicate with each other.

Later, having practiced using the dialogue in my relationship with Bill, I could hold the space for others to experience healing and growth in their committed relationships as they learned the skill of dialogue and adopted the attitude of curiosity rather than defensiveness. Being a witness to that happening gave me much joy.

It took years for Bill and me to learn to listen and speak our truth in a non-defensive way to each other without a coach to guide us in the

---

[8] Frederick Buechner, *Wishful Thinking: A Theological ABC* (New York: HarperOne, 1973), 119.

process. Creating a safe space to be curious rather than defensive and to use language that wasn't critical, condescending, and blaming but simply stated our reality in "I" statements took a lot of restraint.

At times, Bill would say to me, "I am not feeling safe right now to speak my feelings. You seem defensive and ready to pounce on me." I would respond through gritted teeth, "I am doing the best I can to hold back my defense." It was hard to get to a place of mutual respect and understanding when we disagreed, felt criticized, and wanted to defend ourselves. The dialogue process we learned allowed us to create a partnership that honored both our individual purposes and the needs of our family and children.

Sitting in my pastoral counseling office with couples in conflict, I was aware that the power dynamic was ever-present. With two people whose relationship is in crisis, dominating or victim energy is communicated with words, tone, controlling or helpless silence, and body language. Bill and I had danced that dance for many years; it was a very familiar pattern. The stifling stuckness of the power struggle permeates the office as a couple's power struggle dance saps the air from the room. Who in the setting of marriage counseling has the power? Do the individual partners have it? Do I, as the coach, have it? Is the power in the open sacred space between us where the Spirit of wisdom, compassion, and truth reside? Perhaps it involves all of us, each fulfilling our part in the healing dance.

My deep desire was to offer couples the tools my parents didn't have to communicate. I will always remember a conversation with one couple I had been seeing weekly for a number of years. I was challenged to hold a safe space for them to listen to each other and speak their individual truth. As they were leaving the office after a particularly difficult session, she turned and said to me, "Have you ever worked with a couple who are as difficult as we are?"

I smiled and reminded her of the good work they had done and the courage and commitment it had taken to keep coming. I thought to myself, "Have I ever worked with a couple who were so traumatized and violated by their families who weren't this difficult?"

Holding a safe space for two married people to talk who are in serious, sustained conflict is like holding two tigers in a cage with some of the bars missing. No matter how hard I work to teach containment, sometimes the fighting tigers jump through the bars and run away; sometimes, they attack each other and try to fight to the death.

As the trainer, I am secure in the skill of my faith-craft, yet sometimes I lapse into an insecure or fearful place inside myself. I fear I can't keep them safe long enough for them to connect. They fear that if they do begin to trust, it will be destroyed later. Their courage to risk hope is tentative; mine has been tested over time, and in the long run, it endures.

How can I help these tiger-people empathize with the defenseless lamb in their partner and have compassion for the helpless lamb in themselves? How do these enemies, once friends in love, become friendly lovers again? The promise and challenge of the Kingdom of God: lions and lambs, natural enemies, lying down together despite their differences; men and women, husbands and wives, natural enemies becoming friends after years of hurtful misunderstanding.

"Is there any reason to hope for safety, kindness, and intimacy after 33 years of little to none in this marriage?" she asked. "Is there any reason to hope for understanding among warring countries, angry neighbors, or different races and cultures?" I thought.

Where the first step toward trust begins, the long journey toward hopelessness begins to end. As each one speaks their truth and is listened to, heard, and validated by the other, the power struggle releases its stranglehold, and the two share a moment of unity in the space where the Spirit resides. They become co-creators with the Transcendent One whose Spirit lives in them and slowly heals and transforms times of separation and conflict into peace and intimate connection.

As a therapist and fellow traveler with couples seeking greater intimacy with each other, I have glimpsed the sacred as I have held the space for couples to talk to each other from their hearts. Holy moments emerged where the power struggle was momentarily suspended, and love in the form of empathy and compassion vibrated through the space between us to heal and challenge new growth.

Being a companion to these couples is a gift I have received for many years. Holding the space for people to become conscious of the Power that unites us in a common mission to love each other into wholeness is a sacred call I cannot engage in apart from the Wisdom of the Holy Spirit.

MY JOURNEY
TO PRIESTHOOD

The Winding Road

Since Bill and I had been raised in the Presbyterian Church, we began attending Sea and Land Presbyterian Church in our neighborhood on the Lower East Side of New York City soon after we married.

One Sunday, after a particularly long sermon peppered with sports illustrations, I declared to Bill and whomever else was close enough to hear, "I cannot sit through another sermon with football illustrations. I have to translate them into my experience as a woman. Some of the sermons seem to suggest that I should be dependent on my husband to make decisions for me as the head of the household. Sometimes, those same sermons deliver the subtle message that people of color should be praised for their endless patience in the face of injustice and discrimination."

I wanted to hear something about how my faith in God would help me with the challenges I faced living in a diverse culture as a racial minority and adapting to a new marriage—something more relevant to my experience. Little did I know at the time that this was the beginning of my call to be a part of the church's reformation and a path to priesthood.

Neither the Presbyterian Church of my mother and grandmother nor the Roman Catholic Church of the men in my family met my need for a living voice that honored the feminine. The Catholic men had been indoctrinated to believe the Catholic Church was the only true church and that their salvation depended on remaining in the fold. My stepfather, Andrew, accomplished this by sending in his yearly pledge but rarely participated in parish life except to take my brother and sister to confirmation classes to fulfill his promise to raise his children Catholic.

When my stepfather died, I was unnerved by the visit of the local parish Catholic priest who came to our home in Pittsburgh to plan the funeral. My brother, sister, and I, and our spouses, sat in our parents' living room, and the priest, whom we had never met and who had never met our dad, explained the Catholic funeral service.

Since my brother and sister had both been confirmed in the Catholic Church, though neither was a practicing Catholic at that point, they were able to take communion at the funeral. On the other hand, I, an ordained priest in the Episcopal Church, was invited to wear my vestments—clerical collar, robe, and stole, participate in leading the funeral liturgy, and give the eulogy, but was not permitted to take communion.

The priest's decision to follow the rules and exclude me from the Eucharist was hurtful and legalistic. His choice reinforced my perception that the Roman Catholic Church's leadership often followed the letter of the law rather than the Spirit of the law. The priest hadn't taken the time and care to discern what would be a loving way to meet our family's emotional and spiritual needs in planning a funeral liturgy.

At the end of my stepfather's life, because my mother had attended classes to learn Catholic doctrine and because she had agreed to raise their children Catholic, he was allowed to be buried by the Catholic Church. Most of the time, if Dad attended church at all, it was the Episcopal Church when he visited us in Atlanta or my brother and sister's protestant or Greek Orthodox churches.

My experience with the Catholic Church up to that point made me want to do something to cause change that would encourage the institutional church to be more inclusive and responsive to the spiritual needs of the people they were serving. But what?

This heritage fired my heart with the energy of reform. Theologian Paul Tillich named the drive to engage in structuring and restructuring church and society the "Protestant Principle." I felt that fire of change moving in me: I wanted to challenge how church and society excluded some members and boxed others into a belief system based on law, fear, and moral judgment rather than the Spirit of Love.

My experience of many churches of various denominations, including the Protestant and Catholic Church, was that they followed the law and stood in judgment of those who didn't conform to their cultural and religious norms. Often, the clergy lacked the compassion, loving kindness, grace, and justice born of relationship, which seemed to me the way Jesus related to anyone he met. Their legalism made it hard to imagine, let alone enter into, a living relationship with a God who loved and forgave everyone no matter what.

By the time we moved to Atlanta in 1971, Bill and I had become disillusioned with the institutional church, so we were not necessarily looking for a church community when we arrived.

I was surprised when Bill came home from his first Leadership Atlanta meeting and announced, "I was just out having a beer with the Rector of St. Luke's Episcopal Church located downtown. I like him. His faith is grounded in reality, he cares about justice, knows how to tell a good story, and is full of fun; if he can be in the church, maybe we can be, too." Bill is fond of saying of the selection process in Leadership Atlanta, "They often chose a priest, rabbi, and wacko for each class. I was the wacko, and Tom Bowers, Rector of St. Luke's, was the priest."

It was important to me that our children knew the stories of our faith so their future values and spiritual life might be shaped by an authentic, diverse Christian community. I was intrigued by Bill's description of St. Luke's. Several Sundays later, we headed into town to see for ourselves how this church worshiped and served its community.

St. Luke's Episcopal Church, founded in 1864, was designed in the late English Gothic style and built on its present site in downtown Atlanta in 1906. We expected we would be judged as outsiders and hippies, dressed in our jeans and T-shirts, but were surprised to feel at home immediately in this mammoth old church filled with stained glass and dark wood, where some members dressed to the nines and others dressed like us.

Even our children liked the folk music and the rector's children's sermons with a talking puppet named Mac, who emerged from a paper bag to say all of the "bad" things children—and adults—thought but knew they shouldn't say in church. Mac's voice sounded a bit like the rector's, but his lips didn't seem to move. How could that be?

One Sunday, as usual, the children were invited to gather on the steps in front of the altar to listen and respond to the sermon. Mac, the naughty puppet who spoke his truth no matter what, and Tom began a conversation about The Lord's Prayer. Tom said the phrase taken from the Lord's Prayer, "Give us this day our daily bread." Silence followed. Tom repeated, "Give us this day our daily bread," and all of a sudden, a loaf of Wonder Bread came flying through the air from somewhere off to the side. Tom caught the bread and responded, "See, as I told you, God does answer our prayers."

The congregation and children broke out in laughter as Tom went on to explain in simple terms how God answers our prayers. It was a simplistic message geared to the children, but it caught everyone's attention to consider how God does or doesn't answer prayer.

My mind wandered to a deeper question about prayer: Why does Jesus say, "Ask and you shall receive," yet it doesn't always happen? Is prayer a way to get God to do what I want? A way to control God or get God to change? Or could prayer be a way to speak my deepest desires to a loving, forgiving presence and then to listen for the Spirit of love and wisdom to offer me a new way of perceiving, prompting me to change and grow?

The sermons in the Episcopal Church mainly focused on the stories of Jesus and his life as told in the Gospels—Matthew, Mark, Luke, and John. Jesus said he didn't come to abolish the law but to fulfill it. But within those ordered boundaries of law, grace, truth, love, forgiveness, and justice were guiding principles that led to compassion within the larger structure of the Ten Commandments. He acknowledged our human frailties and offered the grace and mercy of God.

This was the kind of church I had been hoping to find for our family—a church where fun and laughter were mixed with sermons that applied to real life, and stories were filled with love and justice.

In the Broad Church tradition of the Episcopal Church, I was not told what to believe but invited to think for myself and work out my relationship with the Divine in the company of others who wanted to mature in faith. I hadn't known such a church existed.

Attending worship at St. Luke's, I received the Eucharist every Sunday. I really didn't have an informed appreciation for what taking the Eucharist regularly meant to others raised in the Episcopal Church. What I knew was that I was, in some mysterious way, participating in the death and resurrection of Jesus. Preparing to receive the bread and the wine, I prayerfully acknowledged my shortcomings, which involved a kind of death and a new beginning each time. I set my intention to receive God's grace to begin to let go of the past, learn from my experience, and start anew, forgiven and free.

Holy Communion was not just remembering Jesus' death and resurrection as Presbyterians and Baptists believed, nor did it literally become the body and blood of Christ upon being consecrated by the priest as the Catholic Church taught at that time, but I was beginning to experience that in some mysterious way, it was a vehicle of grace that released old, blocked energy and opened a road to repentance, the unconditional love of God, and hope for new life.

Re-membering the body of Christ, bringing the parts of the body back together, and kneeling at the altar rail as we individual members became one body through sharing the bread and wine fed my mind, body, and soul. It was an experience that held both mystery and hope for healing the broken places in me and in all of humanity.

When I was growing up, Presbyterian sermons in the suburban homogeneous congregation often focused on the letters of Paul, which dealt with living a moral life, individual salvation, and evangelizing the unchurched. The outreach of the church largely took the form of supporting missionaries who worked to convert people in other countries but did not focus on issues of racial justice, generational poverty, or oppression in our mostly white middle-class neighborhood.

In the diverse community of Lower East Side Manhattan, I experienced oppression closer to home. I couldn't see or hear the oppression and injustice until I lived among and came to know and care for many who had endured oppressions I hadn't known. If our intention is to love everyone, we have to pay attention to whoever is saying, "I cannot breathe: you have your knee on my neck, and I cannot speak my truth or get up," which was the experience of George Floyd, among others who died from similar police brutality—not a member of the dominant group in our country. He died in the street in 2020 with the knee of a policeman on his neck.

Although I was not raised in poverty, nor am I a person of color, when I entered seminary, I felt as though I could no longer breathe in church. I had to do something to stand against institutional racism, the exclusion of women in leadership, male-only gendered language to describe God, and the poverty I saw among my brothers and sisters in Christ.

Why was the church so important to me? I somehow had a sense that the church, synagogue, and temple were essential to support the shared values of truth, moral behavior, justice, and sacrificial love that enabled us to be united as Americans. We needed to find purpose, meaning, and faith in one God and belong to an intergenerational community that valued the wisdom of the elders and the care for children and those in need.

Living in Lower East Side Manhattan, I had come to embrace a perspective that enabled me to transcend race and culture to meet human to human. I did not want to be destructive or vengeful but rather to allow my growing awareness to propel me to act constructively to bring about change in the Christian Church. I wanted to develop the inner openness to allow the Spirit of Love to move through me to love "my enemy." It didn't come easily because I was used to thinking of "us" versus "them." I had a lot of maturing to do.

I could bring my mind, emotions, and experience to bear as I studied scripture in context and sought to apply it to my current situations. And, as I learned about the traditions of the Episcopal Church, in particular, I could decide what was true for me and my limited experience and what seemed to be true for humanity in general. I could participate in therapy, pray to have my emotions freed to trust and love, and focus my energy on a vision for the good rather than on what was not good.

When I began graduate school in 1973, my family and I became regular attendees of St. Luke's, and I enrolled as a special student in seminary. I had not experienced a "call" to ordination. I began as a part-time student to find a safe place to study scripture and church tradition and be free to ask the questions that had been burning a hole in my soul for years: Why can't women preach the gospel and interpret the scripture in light of the female experience?

If humankind is created male and female in the image and likeness of God, and the Hebrew word for "image" is gendered female and "likeness" is treated in Hebrew as having the male gender, wouldn't men and women working together hold equal authority to express God's full humanity? Wouldn't people attending religious services benefit from both men and women preaching and interpreting scripture in today's cultural context?

Our move to Atlanta gave me a safe place to open the shuttered windows and doors of my mind and heart to seek truth. At seminary and in Episcopal worship, I found encouragement and guidance that helped me pursue an honest and loving relationship with God. I remember clearly how I felt when I learned in a class called "The Religious Affections" that feelings were neither good nor bad; they simply emerged as a result of a triggering event. All feelings are a part of the human experience; none should be ignored or denied but rather felt and expressed in prayer and to a trusted friend, wise clergyperson, spiritual director, or therapist who could provide guidance in discerning a need for any action to be taken.

Anger and love, for example, were both legitimate feelings and did not carry a moral judgment of being right or wrong as I had been taught to believe. Through prayer, scripture study, and other spiritual practices to develop the religious affections of love, joy, peace, patience, generosity, kindness, faithfulness, gentleness, and self-control, I could ask the Holy

Spirit to guide me on whether and how to express my feelings. I hoped these qualities would mark my character as I matured in love, forgiveness, and grace. This was my deepest desire. But could I live that way?

Acknowledging that I am human and will never be perfect, and thus will make decisions based on ego needs or unresolved emotional issues from the past rather than the good of others, I nevertheless wanted to be whole and healthy and become my best self. I had so much negative baggage—fear, distrust, and jealousy—to let go of. It seemed daunting to keep growing and shedding my old skin as I faced letting go of old beliefs and embracing new ones.

Would the Episcopal Church be where I would find belonging and acceptance? I didn't feel as though I was Protestant or Roman Catholic, Methodist, Lutheran, or any longer a Presbyterian, but instead I could find truth in each one.

I remember a conversation I had as a teenager about these questions. It went something like this: "Mom, I have been wondering what my ethnic heritage is. When I asked Grandma why her potato salad was so different from the potato salad in the store and why hers included bacon and vinegar and not mayonnaise like we eat at picnics, she said she learned how to make it from her German grandmother. So, I know I have some German in me. Grandma also told me she had a Bishop from the Church of England in her background, so I guess I have some English, too. Are there any others that you know about?"

"Well, in fact, Jeannie, there is Swiss and French from my father, Ralph's, side. Your father, Clyde, was Irish, so that comes from him. I would say you are a mongrel, a mix of many different genetic and cultural strains. It's good to be a mongrel," she said. "Pure breeds can sometimes be high-strung and difficult," she added. The corners of her mouth lifted into a playful smile.

"Well, that's all well and good," I said to myself. It means I can claim to belong to many different cultures, just as I have blended into many different families throughout my childhood. But the question remains in the back of my mind, always present and mostly unconscious: *Where do I belong? Where are the roots that will hold me firm and nurture my faith in a healthy way as I explore who I am, who I am becoming, and what I believe?*

It felt disloyal, and to some degree blasphemous, to question some of the stories I was told that were basic to a certain way of knowing God. Although not feeling I belonged in any one family caused me much confusion, it also offered me some freedom to explore and wrestle with God. I was in the process of forming a faith practice that made sense to me, rather than accepting the "party line" of my male and female ancestors.

My struggle for my father's blessing continued with my clinical pastoral counseling supervisor at Georgia Baptist Hospital. Even though we had arguments and didn't always agree, he surprised me by staying present and engaged, which had not been my experience with many of the men in my life. I trusted his authenticity, and he didn't abandon me. I still received his blessing, which contributed to my healing journey. Now, it seemed, I was wrestling with God to receive "the ultimate blessing." Would God love me for me even if I expressed my doubts?

Two parachurch organizations, Young Life and Faith at Work, also significantly influenced my faith during adolescence and young adulthood. In retrospect, they each gave me a push toward seminary. Young Life, an interdenominational Christian youth organization, exposed me to a gospel message that communicated to me the love of God incarnated in the life and teachings of Jesus Christ in a teenage language I could understand. We met in a family's living room among high school peers. Our conversations focused on a personal message that included God's love and Jesus' sacrifice for our sins, inviting an emotional response.

In the leadership of Young Life, I saw adults who were fun-loving and living their faith. What they had was attractive to me. One night, lying in bed during my junior year of high school, I prayed a prayer of the heart that went something like this: "God, if you are there and can hear me, and if your Son loved me enough to sacrifice his life to show me how to live with purpose, then please take my life and use it for good."

That night, I decided to follow the way of Jesus. I didn't experience any particular voice from above or sign in response, but making that commitment was life-changing. It set me on a course that had direction and purpose. Although I often failed to live up to it, my intention from then on was to love God with all my heart, my soul, my strength, and my mind, and my neighbor as myself.

I had no idea where that commitment would lead me or even what it meant. Over the next few years, I felt an oppressive patriarchal strain in the church and Young Life. Everything in me rebelled against a hierarchy with men at the head and women following. I was hoping that the love of God incarnated in Christ and the new life offered through his death and resurrection were not bound by the patriarchal tradition or tied to a theology and practice that devalued women, made us dependent, and limited our choices regarding our bodies and our work. I hoped that wasn't the truth of what it meant to follow Jesus's Way. I went to seminary to find out.

My commitment as a high school junior to follow Jesus, the Christ, started me on a faith journey I never could have imagined. I didn't understand then how much my commitment was culture and gender-bound. Although Young Life gave me a "family" in which to belong that was nondenominational, fun, and relevant to my immature understanding of faith, once I left the homogeneity of my middle-class hometown and moved to NYC, it didn't hold up to the reality of racism and poverty I was exposed to on the Lower East Side of Manhattan.

Faith at Work gave me a different model. When Bill and I married and I moved to the Lower East Side of Manhattan, I had completed my teaching degree but did not feel prepared to teach in a multi-racial, economically diverse public school system. Straight out of college and needing some seasoning before entering this new community as an elementary school teacher, I looked elsewhere for work.

Faith at Work was looking for a receptionist. I applied and was hired even though I typed 20 words a minute with 10 errors in the first interview. I was intrigued when we were invited to give each other animal names during a get-acquainted exercise at a staff retreat. The President, Bruce Larson, smiling, turned to me and said to the group, "When I first met Jean, I would have given her the name Dove, but as I have come to know her better, I would name her Tiger." I celebrated that Bruce saw both sides of my personality and blessed them.

Working at Faith at Work, I learned why the ministry was referred to as every man's (sic) AA. Small group sharing, following the guidelines of the AA groups, made one's faith journey personal, relational, honest, and practical.

Later, serving on the Faith at Work board of directors, I received encouragement and support from older men and women to share my story at board meetings and in the FAW magazine. They became my mothers and fathers of faith. When Marjory Bankson became president of Faith at Work in 1985, the women of the board created a robust women's ministry. I was glad to support that ministry. Through women's retreats, many women found their voices and a deeper relationship with the Holy One who created them in the image of the Divine.

My internal struggle and questions of faith had become difficult to ignore by the time we moved to Atlanta in 1971. I no longer believed what I had been taught about my role as a woman, wife, and mother in my Presbyterian Church and the evangelical tradition of Young Life. And I was vocal about it. It was time to clarify what I believed to be true. Seminary seemed like a good place to begin my exploration. I needed to find a place and people to help me put the pieces of my life together coherently.

As I mentioned, enrolling as a special student allowed me to take a few courses at a time. I was not consciously preparing for work in the church; I just needed to find a solid ground to continue making choices about my family and my work in the world. Most of the students were Methodist since it was a Methodist seminary, but there were a few students from other Christian denominations and religious traditions.

I was pleased to find a small group of Episcopal women who had begun seminary study even though women were not yet being ordained in the Episcopal Church. It was an open-minded, cosmopolitan environment, and since I had enrolled not planning to be ordained but simply to sort out what I believed, I was free to explore and learn, taking in what made sense to me and discarding what didn't. I felt as if my soul was thriving, and I could breathe.

Although our financial resources were limited, Bill supported my taking a few classes. We were living, as I've said, in an economically poor, predominantly African American neighborhood in a communal household with another family of six and several single men and women who wanted to participate in this experiment in sharing our resources with each other and our neighbors.

By our standards, we were living very simply; however, some neighborhood children perceived us as wealthy white people. We were robbed several times by the children who had been in the house to play with our children and knew their way around. We didn't have much of value to steal, but it was still more than most of the neighboring children had.

The last time we were robbed, although our family was still a part of the intentional community, our nuclear family had moved into a single-family home across Grant Park, which housed the Atlanta Zoo complex. The thieves took the front door off with a crowbar this time, entered, and went through all our drawers, looking for money and valuables.

Bill was out of town when this happened, so when he arrived home and walked in the door, I exploded in tears, repeating the issues I had discussed with the Bishop. "I am done living in a place where I rarely feel safe. I find dead rats in my kitchen drawer. You are traveling a lot of the time. Our children aren't safe in this neighborhood; the public schools are terrible. My volunteering in the classroom does little to change the quality of education the children are receiving. I am ready to move."

Bill had been traveling to Washington, D.C., regularly. His board advised him to move there because it was the headquarters of many companies and would help him connect with people who could help build and sustain the work of Communities in Schools. We made plans to move as soon as I finished my seminary degree and my training to be certified as a pastoral counselor.

When did I first start to become a priest? Was it on the day I entered seminary or when my advisor and the Dean suggested I was suited for ordination? Or was it the day I received my Master's of Divinity degree, my ordination to the diaconate in 1978, or the priesthood on December 6, 1980? These events had particular dates I can point to that involved a public affirmation of my being formed as a priest, as when the Bishop and priest colleagues laid hands on me to affirm my becoming a part of the ancient line of apostolic succession from the time of Peter, Jesus' disciple and head of the one holy catholic and apostolic church.

These days were landmarks similar to November 6, 1965, the day I committed to a lifetime covenant of marriage. My commitment to follow Jesus had taken on institutional expectations and responsibilities, such as the choice to marry had. Could I honor both and be a mother and homemaker, too? I wasn't sure.

Camille, Claiborne, and I were a cohort of three Episcopal women approved by the Bishop to study at the Methodist Candler School of Theology in 1973. The Episcopal Church was not yet open to the ordination of women. In 1974, the door was burst open by a small group of 11 women and several retired male bishops, supported by many members of local churches. Before that time, many women who had grown up in the Episcopal Church had experienced a call to the priesthood, were theologically trained, and were prepared via long service to the church as lay ministers, but were excluded from ordination to the priesthood. Camille and Claiborne grew up in the Episcopal Church and had a clear calling to ordination. I was new to the Episcopal Church and had not received a call to the priesthood.

The first women were regularly ordained to the priesthood in the Episcopal Church in 1976. The group of 11 women who were irregularly ordained in 1974 before it was certified by the General Convention, the ruling body of the church, paved the way for change to happen. The vote of the General Convention, which includes two houses like our federal government—the House of Bishops and the House of Lay representatives, sent from each diocese around the country, finally agreed that year that women could be ordained to the priesthood. The vote wasn't unanimous by any means. Many of the all-male House of Bishops and the clergy, who were all men, vehemently objected.

Perhaps my formation as a priest started much earlier. As a child, I learned from my mother's example to be a caretaker of others. After my high school conversion to follow Jesus, I may have considered consulting with my senior pastor about ordained ministry in the Presbyterian Church, but since that wasn't an option for women, I chose one of the two most approved professions open to women in 1961, teaching and nursing. Since I fainted at the sight of blood and had no idea what I wanted to do besides marry and have a family, becoming a teacher seemed like the better option of the two. Becoming an elementary school teacher fulfilled my mother's unfulfilled dream to be a teacher and provided me with a career that could be integrated into having a family and receiving family approval.

My decision to marry and move to New York in the fall following my college graduation meant I had to cancel my teaching contract in an elementary school in Delaware. It required that I make a sharp turn to shift my focus from learning how to teach elementary school children to learning how to live in a racially and culturally diverse community. I had no models for a marriage of equal partners who respectfully communicate with each other about the hopes and dreams of each person in the family, so I set my mind and heart on figuring it out. I was living in a different time and place.

I had to embrace a new vision for myself as a woman, but how? The pattern of taking care of others, depending on Bill to care for me financially, and practicing a faith based on following moral rules and believing the right doctrine gave me a structure to live by.

That system worked for a while, but in time, it began to constrict like too-tight jeans. The desire to know and respect myself as a woman and to engage in a living faith that embraced mystery and doubt pushed me out of my comfortable religious box and into unfamiliar territory.

A path to find myself and a road to an authentic faith was provided to me by the feminist female theologians who began to reinterpret scripture in a way that included women who were created in the image of God and were equal to men. In seminary, I learned about two creation stories, one that told the story of women being partners and equal to men and the other commonly interpreted to mean that women are secondary to men in the hierarchy of creation, which has been the scripture most referred to in sermons. The Hebrew word "ha-adam," or "'adam," has been translated by most translators as "man"; however, the literal translation is "the adam." It is the root word for both man and humankind.

Genesis 1:27 says, "God created ha-adam in [God's] image. In the image of God, [God] created them, male and female [God] created them" (NRSV with Apocrypha.) A better translation of "adam" or "ha-adam" in this passage is "humankind" or "humanity," which includes both genders. Rather than translating it as a proper noun, Adam, it can be understood as a generic term for human beings. This illustrates why it is important to have women, as well as men, working together to translate and interpret scripture.

The complexity of interpreting scripture came home to me most profoundly at a 60th birthday party for Bill's high school classmate and our friend, Joe Bellanti. Sitting at a table along the wall in the smoke-filled room of the VFW with two other friends, Bob, another of Bill and Joe's high school classmates, sat down. He greeted Bill, "Hey Bill, I don't know if you remember me, but I am Bob from Wilkinsburg High School." He proceeded to tell us a story about Joe. Joe had been a part of the mob in Pittsburgh. One of his fellow mobsters thought Joe had sold out to the FBI and shot him three times.

On his deathbed, Joe turned his life over to God and ultimately survived. When he recovered, he began to visit some of his former associates in prison and told them to read the Bible, beginning with the book of Genesis. The next time Joe visited, one of the men said, "Hey, Joe, this is amazing stuff; they are killing and maiming people; they are doing just like we used to do in the mob." Hardly missing a beat, Joe replied, "Stop reading the Old Testament. Begin reading the New Testament."

For new followers of Jesus, starting in the New Testament to read about the life and teachings of Jesus makes sense. However, as one of my teachers cautioned, bypassing an informed reading of Genesis would be a big mistake because there is so much truth regarding human nature if understood in the cultural context in which it was written.

He emphasized the importance of readers considering the whole message of the Hebrew and Christian scriptures and which passages carry the whole truth of who God is. Is God a God of love or a God of judgment and vengeance? And does the New Testament show us a path to becoming our best human selves in a community modeled by the life and teachings of Jesus and guided by the Wisdom of the Holy Spirit? Jesus' faithfulness to fulfill his life purpose showed us the way of love, forgiveness, and courage.

The second significant influence on my being formed as a caretaker of people was the overuse and abuse of alcohol by the men in my family and the women who took care of them and adapted to their behavior. By the luck of the draw, or by grace, I didn't inherit the genetic predisposition to alcoholism. Like my mother and Grandmother Vogel, I could manage one alcoholic drink before I got dizzy or sleepy.

Years of therapy, training as a psychotherapist, and learning spiritual practices kept me from long-term overuse of alcohol or marijuana to escape the anxiety and fear I felt deep inside. These resources helped me deal with my confusing emotions, thoughts, and lack of self-worth, rather than following the way of some in my family to use alcohol and divorce to survive. I didn't, however, avoid the compulsion to try and control circumstances, to minimize angry outbursts, or to care for the needs of others while denying my own.

The challenge for me was to identify destructive adaptations to an alcoholic system and first discern and then acknowledge my needs as I learned to care for myself as I cared for those I loved. My personality was formed by watching my mother take care of everyone in the family while denying her own need for care, expressions of appreciation, and emotional connection.

Growing up, I wanted to have a relationship with my stepfather, but alcohol kept me from having a meaningful relationship with him. He would arrive home from work, pour himself a tall glass of whiskey, sit in his reclining chair, and watch the evening news until dinner was on the table, when he expected it at 5:30. Dinner conversation was often stilted since the smallest thing could trigger his anger.

After dinner, he would again retreat to his chair facing the TV and take a nap before heading back to work. Several hours later, he would again arrive home, pour himself another drink, and usually fall asleep in his chair, waking up to go to bed for the night. I don't remember any of us, my mother, younger sister, brother, or myself, trying to engage him in conversation in the evening about anything that mattered to us. Upon reflection now, it seems that he, like many other men of his generation, suffered emotional pain and spiritual disconnection in silence, using tobacco and alcohol to provide temporary relief.

My mother modeled a way of being a wife and mother that asked very little of the rest of us to invest in the emotional or physical maintenance of our family life. Although she never said as much, I can imagine the hardship she experienced caring for the two of us after my birth father left. I also imagine those years of hardship contributed to her being submissive and grateful to have a second husband who provided financially for our family. He was a man who accepted me, a sassy nine-year-old stepchild, as his own and did his best to be a good father to me and my two younger siblings, his biological children. I saw glimpses of his kind, compassionate heart, which he had no tools to express.

For example, one Christmas after our mother died, Linda, Kurt, and I decided we would give him a puppy to keep him company and provide companionship. He couldn't stand to leave the puppy alone in the kitchen. The puppy would cry, and it would make him so sad he would cry. Finally, he gave the puppy away. I learned an important lesson: Don't give someone a puppy for Christmas that they haven't asked for and are not prepared to train, even if you think it is a great idea.

Dad was proud of us children as we grew into adults, was faithful in marriage, and worked hard to provide for us financially. Like many men of his generation who had served in the Marines, he didn't talk about the horrors of war that he had experienced, and he believed his role as a father was to mete out discipline. Therapy at that time was seen as a weakness and only for those who were mentally ill, so most men suffered the trauma of war in silence and did their best to wall it off.

Any time I expressed an emotion my mother deemed "bad," like anger, jealousy, hate, envy, sadness, or competitiveness, her response would be, "Oh, Jeannie, you don't really feel that way."

Like Dad, she, too, repressed her painful feelings; there was no way to work them through, so she passed on the only way she knew how to deal with them. Soon, I didn't acknowledge that I felt any of those feelings or wasn't conscious that I felt them, and in time, my feelings went underground and became stuck in my body.

I knew I had feelings; however, I was taught to hide and be ashamed of certain ones, and I didn't want others to know I had them. I became head-centered and a people pleaser, unable to feel the whole range of emotions, trust them, and decide how to act on them. My survival strategy was, "Figure out what the people around you need or want and give it to them. What you want and need is not important. Be good. Be perfect. If you work hard enough, you can please everyone, and then you will be safe, and they will be happy."

This way of being seemed to work well throughout high school and college. In seminary, I began to realize that I could be myself and speak my truth and that there was a solid theological position grounded in a feminist view of the world rooted in love and justice for all.

Reading Janet Kalven's 1989 article, "Women Breaking the Boundaries," helped me define what it meant to be a feminist.[9] The word "feminist" can be like raising a red flag in front of a bull. For some people, it can trigger negative, fearful emotions and associations.

As I began to listen to, understand, and embrace the vision laid out by feminists, I realized I was a part of a larger community of men and women who believed as I did in the importance of men and women co-creating a healthy future together.

I felt empowered to claim my role in the family and society as a responsible adult, joining with my husband and male colleagues to define the values of the culture in which I lived. I could trust myself and my perception of truth rather than handing it over to men to create cultural and religious institutions they controlled, which primarily served their needs.

Feminism was no longer just about women's issues but a perspective on reality that would create healthy partnerships at home and in society. I could speak my fierce belief that a woman's body should be protected

---

[9] Janet Kalven, "Women Breaking the Boundaries," *Journal of Feminist Studies in Religion* 5, no. 1 (1989): 119–42, https://doi.org/10.2979/fsr.2009.25.1.180.

from violation by anyone and could express both romantic love and be a vehicle of spiritual love to pass through her to others.

A feminist point of view rejects a hierarchical system of domination of "power over" to embrace "power with and among," with the possibility of creating wholeness, connectedness, and mutuality in relationships.

A choice to live life from a feminist point of view can still cause some tension for Christian women. From a feminist perspective, women begin to trust their own experience rather than following rules set down by the church or the dictates of their fathers and husbands. Sexuality is not to be feared or controlled by another but is a source of power to be responsibly exercised.

In time, guided by these principles, I did find my voice and began to speak up, but my voice was fueled by anger and self-righteous judgment, not by love. As a result, some men in our extended community did their best to avoid me.

Enrolling in seminary required me to commit to classes that fed my mind and heart and enabled me to say "No" at times to requests from family. Writing papers, attending classes, and dialoguing with fellow students and professors were the saving grace that pulled me out of a dark, paralyzing depression and into a life-giving community where I could begin to name my needs as well as care for the needs of others.

Being grounded in a theology of a loving God and a community that respects women gave me hope for my future and the future of the church. If our faith communities are the bodies that help us explore life's meaning and our particular "call," we can sustain a healthy society if we are undergirded by a theology of a loving, just, and merciful God.

A belief in an angry, judgmental, punitive God yields violence, revenge, and injustice and promotes fear. That is not the God I choose to follow; God is love, plain and simple. As scripture says, "Love casts out fear." Clarence Jordan, founder of Koinonia Farms, captured this truth when he said, "Fear is the paralysis of the Soul that keeps one from walking in faith."[10]

---

[10] Clarence Jordan, *The Substance of Things Hoped For: A Theological Memoir* (New York: Harper & Row, 1977), 45.

Power in Priesthood

When I decided to leave the Presbyterian denomination of my mother and grandmother and become an Episcopalian, I was again moving into uncharted territory. My reasons for moving to a different denomination involved more than doctrine, however.

The notion that God causes suffering as well as blessings no longer seemed true to me. God is the creator of everything and sees the future, but does not control my free will nor my responses to my suffering or the suffering of others. Looking for life-giving possibilities in suffering makes more sense to me than being angry or blaming God.

Each decision I made provoked fear that I would be criticized, misunderstood, or abandoned. I left the teaching profession I had prepared for in college to seek my truth, which ultimately led to ordination. Rather than seeking a position as full-time clergy, like the others in my graduating seminary class, I chose part-time work as a pastoral counselor and priest. These choices energized me to live a balanced and purposeful life.

I am so grateful perceptions have changed regarding how women's psychological and spiritual maturity are assessed. A study of spiritual maturity done in 1970, for instance, revealed that for men, psychological and spiritual maturity were the same, but for women, psychological and spiritual maturity seemed to be gauged in terms of how competently they nurtured children and supported husbands or clergy with whom they worked. In other words, how well they fulfilled a popular ideal of "good wife" and "good mother." According to this study, many women were psychologically "immature."[11]

Traditionally, up to this point, spiritual and psychological maturity had been defined in terms that largely reflected male characteristics. The way maturity is measured is now more balanced and is the same for women. Churches' decisions to open their doors to women in leadership have changed the definition of spiritual maturity for both genders.

---

[11] I.K. Broverman, D.M. Broverman, et al. (1970). "Sex role stereotypes: A current application to social and clinical judgments." *Journal of Social Issues,* 26(2), 77-91.

Women have grown into institutional authority as well, partly due to integrating skills generally taught only to men: learning how to engage in conflict, being assertive, and developing financial literacy and management skills. In the same way, it has become more acceptable and expected that men take on and integrate traditional nurturing roles like pastoral care and teaching children.

In the early years of women being ordained, female assistants were often assigned the pastoral care role in lieu of shared preaching and teaching adults. Power in churches has changed now that women have become rectors and biblical scholars who join their male colleagues in translating and interpreting sacred scripture to inform the preaching of both men and women.

I remember how agonizing it was to choose the thesis topic for my Doctor of Ministry degree at Wesley Theological Seminary. By 1992, having been ordained to the priesthood in 1980, I had served part-time in a number of large and small congregations and was working for the Diocese of Virginia as a part-time deployment officer while serving in a congregation and maintaining my pastoral counseling practice. I saw men and women clergy in that role and listened as a pastoral therapist to the stories of others serving the church as assistants.

For a long time, I struggled with what power and authority looked like when exercised by women in leadership. Was it different from our male colleagues? I was curious about how women moved on from being assistants to being the head of staff of congregations, and if it was different from male assistants.

I sought a vision for spiritual maturity and creative leadership in male and female rectors whose congregations were thriving. This became the focus of my doctoral work. The title of my doctoral thesis was *"Power, Authority, and Spiritual Maturity: Women Clergy Serving Congregations as Rectors or Vicars in the Episcopal Diocese of Virginia."* I began to notice the similarities and differences in clergy leadership and where the differences were gender-related.

Power is a strong word that carries a great deal of ambiguity. Power encompasses both the ability to act and an internal state of being. The word often carries a hint of intimidation; it demands respect and some-times engenders fear.

To me, power is simply the ability to accomplish something that needs to be done. Defined in this way, power is neutral. Its purpose is neither to dominate nor to intimidate but to free creative energy to act and to get the job done. Feminist thinkers have been working for many years to re-create our understanding of power, ascribing dominating, intimidating power to a misguided, outdated patriarchy and seeking to empower those who are powerless to become equal to the powerful.

In the course of my journey to find my voice and understand my deep well of resentment of men and their power over women and chil-dren, it became clear that the level of rage that was sometimes trig-gered in me was a response to present injustices that had roots in my childhood.

In the New Revised Standard Version of the Gospel of Matthew, God is referred to as Power. In Matthew 26:64, Jesus said, "... you will see the Son of man seated at the right hand of Power ..." Just as power, when it is ascribed to a human being, carries many nuances, it is also true that the power of God is multifaceted. Is God the One who uses power to create fear, punishment, and intimidation, or the One who empowers us to use our free will to act justly in love to do our part in healing the world's and our own broken places?

To summarize briefly what I've learned about power: personal power comes from self-esteem and self-worth, which have developed and grown based on how one has been loved, nurtured, and educated in childhood, developing a secure attachment. Spiritual power comes from a relationship with the Divine One, which results in finding one's call through various stages of life and gaining wisdom and compassion for oneself and others. Both are relevant to institutional power.

Having power in one's professional life, marriage, and family means you can initiate change and get a job done. Having spiritual authority is when role and personhood come together, and others trust what you say and look to you to use your power to lead. True authority is present when one speaks and acts with integrity, guided by the wisdom of the Holy Spirit to be a compassionate truth-teller who uses power to act justly.

My colleague at Faith at Work, the Reverend Bruce Larson, once told me that preachers advertise their weaknesses. If someone preaches about the same subject, like love or forgiveness, over and over, there is a good chance that is what they are working on to understand themselves.

I have been interested in power and authority for a long time: what it is, how men exercise it, and how women exercise it. And I have been curious about why power and authority have been such a persistent theme for me. I've rejected power as "power over." I've embraced power as "power to." I've joined like-minded men and women to push for equality at home and work with some success; that has felt powerful. I served apprenticeships with good mentors and gained power by association. I secured the symbols of power through education, title, and position—becoming The Reverend Dr. Jean.

And this has become clear: if a person has done the internal work to gain individual power through increased self-esteem and self-knowledge, has been graced with Divine power by opening her heart to listen to the Spirit, and has become wise, skilled, and compassionate but is not given institutional authority to exercise her gifts, then her creativity is lost to the church and institutional life is stifled. Life energy is stuck, and everyone loses. I have seen this happen in corporations, churches, and schools when historically marginalized individuals have been prevented from exercising their gifts and offering their insights.

Jesus shared power with his disciples; he empowered them to do what he did. He had the authority to discern what was right and wrong. None of us carries that level of personal and spiritual authority; we are not God. Yet, we must make choices and be accountable for them. The leaders on whom we bestow authority often betray our trust. Maintaining integrity requires a commitment to be in a community where we are held accountable in love to live out what we say we believe, and admit it when we are wrong. Without a community that holds its members

107

accountable in love, the exercise of power is a fearful thing because we are so easily misguided and so often self-serving on our own.

Janet Hagberg's book, *Real Power: Stages of Personal Power in Organizations*, served as an important guide in my exploration of the use of power in churches.[12] She had studied power in secular settings, and I adapted her stages for women gaining personal and institutional power in a church context. I also learned from listening to the stories of many female clergy as they were growing personally and professionally while I was working as one of the deployment officers for the Diocese of Virginia. I integrated what I learned from them into my doctoral research.

Stage One of Hagberg's book, defined as powerlessness, applies to seminarians. At this stage, neither men nor women have any power or authority within the institutional church. A candidate in the process of preparing for ordination is dependent on the approval of others and is under constant evaluation. I remember the nervous anticipation of waiting to meet with various committees and a psychiatrist who was to determine whether I was psychologically healthy. I then moved on to be judged again by various groups tasked with discerning a valid "call" to serve the Episcopal Church in Atlanta.

This process precedes ordination to the priesthood. Once approved for holy orders, the candidate is first ordained as a transitional deacon, committed to serving those in need in the community. After that comes ordination to priesthood. Even though I felt personally powerful, had reasonable self-esteem, and a clear vision of a call to ministry coupled with a strong sense of being guided by the Spirit, I still depended on those in authority for institutional validation.

This was a long and challenging process for me. Because I hadn't grown up an Episcopalian, I had to learn the liturgy of worship and the symbolic vocabulary—what the colors of the season meant, for instance, and what the words spoken at the altar meant.

---

[12] Janet O. Hagberg, *Real Power: Stages of Personal Power in Organizations* (Long Grove: Waveland Press, 2024).

I was first called to be a deacon and serve the needs of our neighbors. I was serving as a hospital chaplain as part of my seminary studies when a call to priesthood surfaced. While my two female classmates in seminary were clear about their call to priesthood, mine came more gradually. I could only follow the pull forward, discerning each step as I listened to the wise counsel of those accompanying, encouraging, and praying with me for clarity.

I learned about Stage Two, or "power by association," working with a rector who was a skilled mentor. He was vital to my professional growth. This was when I learned the ropes and the culture and was protected by the buck stopping with the rector. I gained new self-awareness and competency.

Given the fact that I served with a number of male rectors (at this time, there were only male rectors), it was important to my growth as a clergyperson to serve with a man who had a healthy relationship with his marriage partner, respect for female friends, and clear relational boundaries. Rectors who had developed their feminine side could effectively nurture and mentor new clergy.

A commitment to serve the needs of those in the wider community and provide opportunities for a clergy assistant to develop new avenues of outreach was another way to share power. When I served with a colleague who respected me and saw me as an equal, affirmed my gifts, and wasn't threatened by my suggestions for change or my assertiveness in a given area, the congregation thrived, and so did I.

Generally, the men I knew in seminary who had become assistants in churches were motivated, as Hagberg suggests, to move to Stage Three to seek their own congregations and assume power and authority. Generally, we women were not, and many congregations were not even ready to accept us as priests. I wasn't, at that point, planning to seek a rector position due to family obligations.

Stage Two was the most difficult stage for me to move beyond, possibly related to my resistance to assuming external symbols of power. I had much still to learn about the Episcopal Church. Some of that resistance was practical: like many women who considered seeking a rector position, I was married, had children, had limited financial resources, and knew I would be taking on a double load of responsibility to nurture two "families." In my case, not only were these things true, but Bill's frequent travel added to the complexity of my role as wife, mother, and priest.

A significant challenge at this stage was to develop the confidence to be assertive at work and available for pastoral duties while at the same time caring for myself and asking for help in appropriate ways from family, friends, and the church community. Often, the women of my generation served congregations that were small and unable to pay salaries that would support the kind of help a female rector would need to ensure that her home and children were cared for without a significant second income.

Sometimes, marriage partners could not sustain the major role changes required for the wife to attend to two "families" and for the husband to do more home and childcare. This was certainly true for us during my early years in seminary and after ordination. Living communally enabled us both to pursue our "call to serve" and helped us raise our children with housemates who served as surrogate aunts and uncles. That community was its own kind of wealth, which many women didn't and still don't have.

However, even with this support, I decided I could not be a full-time rector. I concluded my marriage wouldn't survive, and our children would pay a high price. At times during seminary and the early years of serving congregations, I thought our marriage would tear apart at the seams.

Stage Three posed a new challenge. It's the most masculine of all the stages, according to Hagberg. It demands that a woman exercise what Jung would call her masculine side. If I chose to seek a rector position, I had to be willing to take on symbols of power like managing a large endowment. I had to learn to be assertive (rather than aggressive or defensive), decisive, expert, savvy, ambitious, willing to take risks, confront conflict straight on, show individual achievement, and compete with others. And I had to learn to enjoy all this and be task-, fact-, and detail-oriented. I also had to learn not to show my emotions so readily.

The emotional toll of these demands showed up when, as I recounted earlier, I met with my bishop, overwhelmed with competing duties, and he told me not to cry in front of the vestry. It was a confusing moment. I remember thinking at the time that it should be safe to cry when in the presence of my Bishop. I needed pastoral care—I thought the bishop was supposed to be a pastor to the clergy, someone with whom it is safe to be vulnerable.

But this was not the case for me then or for many other women. Women's tears, or any display of emotion, often take men out of their comfort zone, but the awkwardness is too often construed as the woman's problem.

I kept questioning whether I was called to be the rector of a church. Though I felt I had moved into Stage Three in my personal development, I never felt as though I could make that leap in the institutional church. I began to consider other options that would allow me to both serve the church and honor the covenant I had made in marriage and continue to grow. The men in my family had all started their own businesses. Maybe I could, too. Thus, the seeds of my future company, Pastoral Counseling Network Inc., were planted.

At this stage, I was challenged in a new way to be "in the world but not of it." How could I be in the church and not lose my sense of who I was—a mother and wife as well as a priest? I needed to develop a vision that went beyond others' definitions of professional success and learn a more intentional way to be a leader as a woman. The women I interviewed for my doctoral research, who were rectors and vicars, were doing just that. They gave me hope.

In the early years of women's ordination in the Episcopal Church, the desire to fit in and be accepted by our male colleagues and male bishops was a powerful force. It was a challenge not to become male-identified. Too many men we worked with modeled an authoritarian way of being. Some of them even enjoyed telling jokes that demeaned women right in front of us. We were supposed to laugh.

As women, we needed each other to stay grounded as we navigated encounters like these and trusted the wisdom of the Holy Spirit to enable us to respond with both grace and self-respect and stay present in conflict to hold the space for dialogue. This was part of the motivation for a number of us to go to the beach together each year for a week to clarify our call to ministry and get some distance from the daily pressure to seek approval from men and renew our vision for the future.

I noted how each of us chose to dress, the tone of our voice, and the language we used to communicate power and authority. At the same time, I knew our self-esteem had to come from inside, from knowing we were created worthy in the image of the Divine.

We were also fighting cultural and scriptural stereotypes, like, for example, the notion that a Christian woman should be under the authority of a man. We were aware that the men in our lives—the rectors, bishops, and husbands—were acculturated to expect that, even if they would deny it.

Bill Gothard, a popular evangelical leader in the 1960s, preached complementarianism—a notion that held a lot of authority among evangelical Christians. It was an interpretation of scripture that taught that although men and women were equal in the sight of God, in family life, and in the life of religious institutions, men and women were to have different roles. And men were the ones in charge.

In his New Testament writings, Paul presents the matter of gender with two very different emphases. "I permit no woman to teach or to have authority over a man; she is to keep silent" (I Timothy 2:12). As I mentioned previously, in Galatians 3:28-29, Paul states an egalitarian view: "There is no longer Jew nor Greek, there is no longer slave or free, there is no longer male or female; for all of you are one in Christ Jesus. And if you belong to Christ, then you are Abraham's offspring, heirs according to the promise."

As with so many other passages of scripture, I had to decide how to contextualize these statements and which passages held authority for me. Did I believe the scriptures taught complementarianism or egalitarianism? And, more importantly, which interpretation could I live by? It seemed to me that interpretations by men who thought women should have no voice in the church kept women from speaking their truth and gave implicit permission for the emotional, physical, and sexual abuse of women in the church and in society to continue. As David Von Drehle wrote in the *Washington Post* on June 13, 2021, "Bad theology begets bad policy, and bad policy begets moral decay."[13]

My questions continued as I wrestled with what I believed to be true for me. If the man is the "head" of the household and the woman is the "heart," and most decisions and actions are actually driven by the heart or emotions, why wouldn't a woman's point of view carry at least equal weight? It seems that one needs both head and heart to make wise decisions at home and in the church.

Complementarianism still defines practices even in denominations where women can be ordained. Often, the male senior pastor acts as though the woman clergy assistant is to serve his needs rather than to be a colleague and a collaborator. Our leadership practices need to be grounded in sound theology and informed by the Spirit—flexible, sensitive to the moment, and hospitable to each leader's gifts. When they aren't, when shared leadership and mutual respect are not practiced among the staff, those attitudes influence family life and congregational culture.

I have worked with many rectors over the years, and only a very few believed that my choice to work part-time to care for my marriage and my children could also allow me to make a significant contribution to caring for the church congregation. At a number of the churches where I served, only full-time clergy were invited to attend staff meetings, which limited my effectiveness in doing my job since my voice was not part of the full conversation regarding care for the congregation and staff. I felt as equally committed to serving the congregation as the full-time staff, but I was excluded from many meetings where decisions were made that affected my ability to do my job because they did not believe that part of my time was as important and impactful as all of my time.

Sometimes, it felt like the institution of the church wanted my whole soul. We women were also struggling, as our male colleagues in seminary

---

[13] David Von Drehle, "Bad theology begets bad policy, and bad policy begets moral decay," The Washington Post, June 13, 2021, https://www.washingtonpost.com.

were, with the tensions of bearing worldly symbols of power and, at the same time, responding to Christ's call to identify with the powerless. How might we use our power and privilege for the sake of those who were not born white, who were excluded from a good education, and who lacked financial resources? How could we avoid being seduced by power ourselves?

A valuable source of personal power came from learning alternative translations of Hebrew words. This led me to a deeper understanding of the third person of the Trinity, Sophia/Wisdom/Holy Spirit, who is one with God, the Creator, Redeemer, and Sustainer of all life. Reading scripture in this light was like taking film into the dark room and watching a clear picture emerge. I felt awe every time I revisited familiar texts with this new lens, which prepared me for Stage Four.

Moving from Stage Three to Stage Four (looking inward, moving off center stage, and mentoring others) was a less difficult transition than moving into Stage Three. In my observation, men seemed to have a harder time with this one, being more comfortable functioning in Stage Three, relying on external symbols of success as measurements of achievement: a growing congregation, increased lay leadership, larger budget, increase in salary and discretionary fund, competence in preaching and management of staff and serving in leadership positions in the larger church. I came to believe, as Hagberg suggests, that to define success in other terms, I—and they—had to look inward.

For men, the transition to Stage Four could be understood as taking on the task of integrating the feminine side—affirming and developing gentleness, intuitive awareness, relational skills, and handing over power and authority to the next generation of leaders. If they hadn't done so already, they would have to learn to look inward, discover, and become comfortable with their own tears, occasionally feel out of control, and maybe even shed a few tears at a vestry meeting.

The men in this stage were going to have to develop qualities they might have undervalued, like the capacity for intimate friendships with people of the same gender, the capacity to nurture others, including one's own children, the capacity to move from a focused awareness to a diffused awareness, to move from tunnel vision to seeing long-range patterns of interconnectedness and how parts come together to make up the whole.

Male clergy may differ a bit in this regard from men in general because they may already have developed or at least come to value these qualities, traditionally considered feminine, because they are essential to good pastoral care and nurturing community life. But in our militarized culture, one that places a high value on masculine-focused consciousness and power by domination, it seemed to me especially important that people of faith come to value the feminine aspect of God. Of course, even to say the Holy Spirit manifests a "feminine" dimension of the Triune God might seem heretical to some, but this may be a problem of translation and interpretation rather than a truth about the nature of The Holy One.

For me, the process of moving to Stage Four, Power by Reflection, involved balancing masculine and feminine qualities that were actually modeled by Jesus. It meant creating my own personal style by integrating the skills I had developed in Stage Three to incorporate a pastoral counseling practice that allowed me to decide how much I worked, where I worked, and what I would charge for appointments.

I have observed that men are often teachers of women at Stage Three. And women are often teachers of men at Stage Four, encouraging them to nurture friendship, pay attention to needs for self-care, and care for others while continuing to do competent work.

As I matured, I found that my beliefs have been repeatedly challenged in serving on mixed-gender boards like Faith at Work, participating in Bible studies and a Covenant Group with whom Bill and I have worshiped for over 30 years, and listening to sermons and praying for clarity and wisdom. I have been challenged to love those with whom I may have differences of belief or perspective and challenged to grow in faith as a result.

Both men and women who have responded to a call and committed themselves to a life purpose that extends beyond themselves and have developed healthy ego strength but are not ego-driven have entered

Stage Five, according to Hagberg and Joseph Campbell, an author and writer integrating spirituality and psychology describing the "Hero/Heroine's journey."

I found this example in Jane Goodall, a woman who has given her life to studying chimpanzees, conservation, environmental sustainability, and animal welfare. Women and men who recognize and claim their purpose cannot be co-opted. Their time and energy go to mentoring others, sharing power, and letting others lead. Others seek them out for wise counsel. Some have embraced the feminine nature of God and draw on Her wisdom in decision-making. They are committed to just action and living interdependently with nature while staying in community with others committed to loving everyone, including one's enemies.

Stage Five people may look like Stage Two people in that they are unassuming. However, the difference is that Stage Five people are comfortable sharing power; Stage Two people have never fully understood their power or claimed it. Stage Five people are conscious of their strengths and weaknesses and are willing to change a behavior pattern if it is called for.

Few people enter Stage Six, the last stage in Hagberg's stages of power. It comes in one's final growing season—the stage at which one does not get meaning from attachment to things or people. They seek Wisdom from above to know what is good and just in a particular situation. They don't fear death but accept it as part of the cycle of life. They spend periods in silence and solitude, inviting the Holy Spirit of Wisdom to heal their body, mind, and spirit in preparation for the end of this mortal life. They are oriented to serving others, and their wisdom and energy clearly come from a source beyond themselves.

Head Meets Heart

Many male clergy who have come to embrace what might be referred to as their feminine side have increased their effectiveness in ministry by integrating the wisdom of the Spirit from their heart with years of academic study and reflection on their life experiences. This integration has helped them be better listeners, nurture spiritual growth in members of the congregation, and trust their intuition.

Some have matured by giving up an authoritarian style of leadership to share ministry with the laity and have embraced a partnership model of leadership. They still carry the authority of their role as senior pastors, and their male identity is not at stake, but their power and authority are more effectively used for good when role and personhood are aligned and power is shared.

If Carl Jung was right that men reach maturity by integrating their feminine side and women by integrating their masculine side, emotional androgyny would be a mature model for both male and female clergy. Spiritual maturity and competent ministry call for an integration of the masculine and the feminine in both men and women. I think of the widely admired British actor Maggie Smith, for instance, as a woman who gave us all a sense of what that integration looks like in the way she interpreted so many roles with edginess, humor, sensitivity, and authority.

When an understanding of what it meant to integrate masculine and feminine qualities came together for me in my seminary studies in 1974, it felt like the ground underneath my feet was finally solid. I, like men, was formed out of "The Ground of Being," Paul Tillich's name for God.[14] I now had language and a vision of myself that was life-affirming. I was created out of the same essence from which men were created. Out of that exhilarating sense of emergence, I wrote the following poem to articulate the life-changing learning I was doing:

Father, God, Full of power and might,
Is that all you are?
Can it be that you are the "Ground of Being" as well,
that expresses the knowledge of the unity of all that is?
My ecstatic spirit–mind struggles to express

---

[14] "God as 'Ground of Being'—Paul Tillich," Religious Naturalism, accessed November 12, 2024, https://religiousnaturalism.org/god-as-ground-of-being-paul-tillich/.

to my rational mind–spirit
how you can be both masculine and feminine in essence,
It seems beyond reason yet not irrational.
How shall I contain the tension?
I want to give up and polarize!
I am Eve, I am a woman,
I am Adam, I am a woman.
You are Adam and Eve, you are a man,
The weight of the guilt of separation from God,
a heavy load for womankind to carry alone for all these years.
The pride of blame, self-deception, and irresponsibility
a heavy load for mankind.
We are one in essence—a theonomous moment.
Adam and Eve are me, Adam and Eve are me.
Yet you, man, are different from me.
You respond naturally to separation, focus, and change,
While I listen, watch, respond, know, and participate
in relationship.
Will you teach and enable me to develop the rational
potential that is present in my essence?
I will lead you to the wealth of collective unconsciousness
inside of you
so that you may know the unity of all growing things …
If you will not be afraid to discover the potential of your essence.
Who will mediate between us, male and female?
Or between the masculine and feminine
Inside of you and me?
Or between our warring human spirit and God's spirit?
Christ mediates.

In the years since I wrote this, I have learned that in ancient Hebrew, head and heart were equal signifiers and symbols. There was no hierarchy between them as there is in Western culture. Much of what is gendered in European languages is gender-neutral in Middle Eastern languages and cultures.

In a study of Proverbs, the translation into Greek imposes some of the differences we are used to seeing in our current translations of the New Testament, but in Hebrew and Aramaic, those differences aren't there. We need Biblical scholars and church leaders to keep offering us a wider, more inclusive, more egalitarian understanding of gendered language to correct so much preaching and teaching in our churches that has been based on problematic translations.

As I keep reflecting on gender and leadership in the church, I find myself raising again the questions I posed early on: "What is spiritual maturity?" Is it different for men and women?

Over the years, I have become increasingly conscious of the choices and triggers that pulled me backward to a time when I was dependent on others to make choices for me and to tell me what a woman's attitude and role should be in relation to church leadership.

Once I realized women were excluded in so many ways from leadership in the church, limiting their spiritual maturity and the growth of those in their congregations, addressing that exclusion became a driving motivation for me. It was a dimension of my call. My challenge was to listen to my feelings and desires even when others told me I shouldn't feel restless, discontent, or longing, or told me what I hoped for wasn't possible. Following my deepest promptings gave me the courage to enter the seminary, though the path to ordination wasn't really open to me at the time.

I began to understand this journey invites constant revision and change. "Jesus is not the answer," as my husband is fond of saying to those who would put the Christian faith in a box. "He is the question."

This isn't a question any of us answers once and for all. It keeps coming up, often in small, daily, unglamorous ways—from greeting a stranger on the street to enduring the tedium of HOA board meetings. It requires that I keep being present in my life every day, not in a way defined by schedule or role fulfillment, but with an awareness of where the Spirit of God might be leading me.

One of my assignments as a pastoral counseling resident and chaplain at Georgia Baptist Hospital was to visit patients in the cardiac unit who were preparing for surgery. Frequently, I would find myself sitting at the bedside, listening to a patient's life review. I listened to confessions about mistakes, sorrows, joys, and gratitude for loved ones. Some patients were afraid they wouldn't survive surgery; some were calm, ready for it, and hoping for a successfully repaired heart.

Having your chest bone sawed down the middle and cracked open to expose your heart is no small thing. The question was always present, spoken or unspoken, "Will I survive this surgery? Are there things I have done well and people and events I am grateful for that need to be expressed to them and things I have not done in this life and need to ask forgiveness for?"

As a hospital chaplain, I listened intently to understand the patient's language rooted in their religious traditions as they spoke and sought hope, comfort, trust, and confidence that all would be well. Sometimes, their language was not my language of the Christian faith. Sometimes, it wasn't religious at all but an angry tirade against God or someone or something done to them by a person whom they trusted that was unfair, that released old blocks being held in their hearts. My intention was to attune myself to where the patient was and do my best to speak their language and be a loving presence.

For me, no matter how clear my thinking is or what is in my heart, provoking conscious or unconscious triggers from the past can allow for deeper engagement with others if I can bring it to consciousness and clear it with the Spirit's help and or the help of a listening ear of a trusted friend. A familiar prayer from the Episcopal *Book of Common Prayer* that I pray regularly to begin my meditation is, "Cleanse the thoughts of my heart by the inspiration of your Holy Spirit." Learning to mindfully listen to the Holy Spirit of Wisdom to reveal what is in my heart has taught me how to be fully present in my life and my relationships.

At the Beach

What was the pull that drew nine of us clergywomen back together each year for many years, leaving our church leadership responsibilities and our families to spend time together for a week at the beach? It didn't matter which beach, as long as it was far enough south to be warm enough to walk on the beach in our bare feet and keep the windows open at night to hear the ocean waves beating against the shore, lulling us to sleep.

We have a few requirements for the house. It has to sit right at the oceanfront, have enough bedrooms so each woman has enough space, and a living room with comfortable chairs to invite long, into-the-night conversations.

The time of year is important, too. We gather after Easter, when many of us are exhausted from the intensity of pre-Easter week worship preparations and before the rental rates go up, making the cost too much for our collective budget to bear.

Those close enough to drive bring sheets and towels to provide for those who fly. I have to fly, and I choose to fill the valuable space in my suitcase with murder mysteries and the latest books on theology to invite dialogue rather than linens and towels.

We enter the house full of anticipation, curiosity, and questions. If the house is new to us, we explore the bedrooms: "Which will be my room?" "Is it my turn to have an oceanfront room?" If we all come, "Who is willing to share a room?"

Sometimes, gifts are brought to share. "I have brought each of you a bar of organic handmade lavender soap," Nancy announced to the group one year as she laid them out for each of us to choose.

In more recent years, we have arrived to receive a mug for our coffee made by Eloise, who is a potter/priest/social worker. "I have etched your names on the side of your cup and baked them into the clay and glaze. Each year, the size, shape, and color will be unique as I experiment with different processes I am learning."

In the early years, we came together to help each other survive the challenges of being female priests in a church trying to get used to the idea and reality of our presence. Parishioners who had come from the Catholic tradition were comfortable calling male priests "Father" but somewhat sheepishly would say, "Do I call you 'Father' or perhaps, 'Mother'?"

I remember the first time this question came up during my time at St. Luke's Church in Atlanta. A kind, white-haired Southern gentleman tentatively approached me and said, "I hope I don't offend you, but I don't know what to call you. It doesn't feel respectful of your role among us to call you Jean, and our tradition doesn't refer to clergy as Pastor, so since I am used to calling our clergy "Father," is it okay if I call you Father Milliken?" I smiled and thought that at least being called father would help minimize the positive or negative transference of being referred to as mother. But Father Milliken also invited transference, either positive or negative—I wasn't so sure the title fit. "Father" did call forth an authority of office that I found intriguing.

His question evokes a memory of a moment when I publicly "put on" a masculine role in a ceremonial and psychologically meaningful ritual.

For several days, the television covered the coronation of the new King of England. As I watched the procession, the red velvet robe draped over the prince's shoulders, and the crown being placed on the head of Charles III, my mind reverted to St. Luke's Church on Epiphany Sunday in the early 1980s when I became one of the three kings from the Orient.

Living in the role of a king who traveled from the East to bring gifts to the baby Jesus, I began my long, slow walk down the center aisle. St. Luke's was a familiar place to me. I was welcomed into the Episcopal Church and ordained a priest there as the sun shone through multicolored stained glass windows, sparkling and dancing across the pews and the people.

I don't remember how the decision was made that the three clergy would proceed down the center aisle dressed in cope and miter, the cape and hat, i.e., vestments worn by bishops. Preparing for Epiphany Sunday, we looked through the vestments that might look kingly and borrowed what we still needed from the Bishop's office. Regaled in tall miters and floor-length copes clasped together at the neck, we lined up at the back of the church.

The organ began playing, and the first clergy/king began his slow procession down the polished stone aisle, singing, "We Three Kings Of Orient are, bearing gifts we traverse afar …" By the time the first king got midway down the aisle, it was my turn to move forward. My knees began to shake. I had never sung a solo before, and I was scared I would open my mouth to sing the second verse and nothing would come out.

When I took the first step, a voice emerged that was strong and on key. I didn't recognize my "king" voice. Holding my head up high so that the miter, which was too big for my head, didn't slip over my eyes, and grasping the too-long cope in one hand and holding my hymnal in the other, I walked forward with confidence.

I learned something new about myself that day: the masculine was alive and well in me. It showed up as a strong, confident voice as I played the part of a powerful man with authority. I just had to internalize the strength and power I was experiencing and balance it with my feminine voice, which was softer and gentler yet so powerful in its own way. Not only that, but I now believed both were an equal part of the nature of the One True God, and claiming both was a good thing to do.

Just recently, I viewed the documentary *The Philadelphia Eleven*, chronicling the years of lobbying for and waiting for laywomen to first be admitted to the House of Deputies in 1970, which worked alongside the House of Bishops and was all male.

The documentary went on to show the courageous journey of the eleven women who were irregularly ordained in 1974 and the men who supported them. The male brotherhood of priests and bishops at the time argued that a woman could be President of the United States or a judge, for example, since her gender didn't matter, but she could not be a "father," so there was no way she could be ordained a priest since God was our Father.

Until I viewed the documentary, I was unaware of the way "God the Father" was used as a weapon to exclude women from the priesthood. I had never liked the Father/Mother title for clergy because of the positive and negative transference it invited parishioners into.

Something in me had always reacted negatively to Jesus praying The Lord's Prayer to "Our Father, who art in heaven." I somehow knew that understanding God as Father was limiting and exclusive of the feminine nature of God and wasn't the whole picture. Since it is the prayer all Christians learn to memorize and repeat, God, the Father, has become deeply ingrained in our collective psyches.

I hadn't been a part of the early struggle and the painful, sometimes violent, conversations in which gender was cited as the primary reason not to ordain women, so my friend's question from St. Luke's regarding my title didn't trigger me. I saw it as a legitimate struggle on his part to find a respectful way to address me that carried the authority and the responsibility of my role as priest of the church.

Of the nine of us, all ordained priests for many years, our family situations varied over the years. Some were married, some were divorced, and some remained single. Some have born and raised children, and some have not; some have been rectors, senior clergy in charge of churches, counselors, social workers, artists, and writers, in addition to serving the church as priests.

Now, we can acknowledge and appreciate our differences. We no longer have to deny them to fight for legitimacy as priests in a church that, for most of its history, was unsure if we were created equal or called to priesthood. But some of us still carry the trauma and scars of abuse and exclusion that were inflicted on the women who bravely stood up to the male hierarchy of the Episcopal Church.

Gathering in the living room at night at the agreed-upon time for our yearly check-ins, the couches and chairs available for moving are drawn into a circle, our wine, whisky, or water glasses in hand, our hearts and minds ready to hear each other's stories. Someone takes the initiative to ask, "Who would like to talk tonight?"

Sometimes, I looked forward to my turn to share the events of the past year and volunteered to talk early in the week. The years I served the church at the Washington National Cathedral were filled with wonder and growth challenges as I learned to respect the faith of those who practiced religions other than Christianity. I had lots of questions about New Testament scripture that said a belief in Jesus as the only son of God was the only way to know God.

Although I had made a commitment to follow Jesus, which was my way to a relationship with God, I learned that judging the way others found God was not my role. Many followed "the way, the truth, and the life" of Jesus without knowing his name or were oppressed by those who used his name to do harm or serve their purposes, so rejected his name but not His Way.

They practiced sacrificial love, kindness, patience, goodness, self-control, and humility that could only come from believing in and being empowered by something or someone greater than self who loves all of humanity and works for truth, justice, and peace for all. Being together at the beach allowed me to explore some of my questions with my sister clergy colleagues.

Other times, I felt unsure about how open I wanted to be about what I was facing at home or the church, so I would be among the last. More often than I like to remember, I worked as an associate with a clergyman who didn't have good boundaries, took pride in his role as rector, and gave me the work that he didn't want to do rather than the work of ministry I was best suited for. Sometimes, the congregations we served fought over small matters that had nothing to do with building the Beloved Community here on earth by loving and serving each other and the needs of our neighbors. So we vented our frustration with our colleagues who could listen with understanding.

In the early years, I felt competitive with the women who had become rectors of churches. A part of me wanted to embrace that role in the church, to be in charge and preach often on Sunday mornings, but I had chosen marriage to a man who was constantly on the move. This meant I had to fill in the gaps and serve the role of mother and father, and I didn't see how I could provide for my family and lead a congregation.

I was also drawn to train as a pastoral psychotherapist, which provided time to attend to my own inner healing as well as to companion others on their healing path. When I preached, I wanted to preach good news rather than pass on my unresolved personal and theological issues, which were not yet life-giving.

Competition was a common theme in some movies I was drawn to during those years. The movie *Turning Point* featured two ballerinas: one who remained single and chose a professional career as a dancer, the other who married and had children and opened a dance studio as a way to continue her love for ballet. Jealousy and competitiveness became the focus of their relationship when they met years later, after they had been young ballerinas working together. The movie *Julie and Julia,* about the competitive nature of cooking, captured the same dynamic. And, of course, the Biblical story of Sarah and Hagar's competition regarding who would be the number one wife to Abraham is a classic story of jealousy and competition.

As a teenager, when I decided to follow the way of Jesus, a foundation was built for all the decisions I made going forward. It was the first covenant I made in my life.

Sometime later, I made three more. I chose to make a lifelong covenant with Bill in marriage and one to be a mother before the call to serve the church as priest came. In my attempt to honor all of these commitments, I often felt as though I wasn't doing any of them well. I had difficulty focusing on one relationship or task and felt diffused much of the time. My masculine-focused awareness wasn't operating very well.

During those early years, I only knew the traditional roles in the church to be prophet and priest. Those two roles fit to a degree as I was discerning my call. There were times when, as deacon, I served as a prophet, interpreting the church to the world and the world to the church by working for a city council person to explore part-time employment for those who were also caring for children at home and needed to be gainfully employed.

While serving as a hospital chaplain during my required quarter course at seminary, I listened to the confessions of patients and was moved to offer them absolution and assurance of God's unconditional love for them. I could and did offer assurance of God's unconditional love as a chaplain and sister Christian, but I could not as a priest of the church, which was important to many patients facing serious illness or surgery. Thus, I began to seek discernment about whether I was called to ordination to the priesthood.

Years later, now sitting with my colleagues at the beach, after becoming ordained as a deacon, priest, and now certified as a pastoral therapist, I felt like my identities as a prophet (deacon), priest, and wisdom teacher (pastoral counselor), had coalesced, and I was able to exercise all three on behalf of the church. I no longer felt like a stepdaughter in the church, having never served a church full-time as a priest or rector. I had found belonging by integrating all three.

Discovering the writings of Episcopal priest Cynthia Bourgeault gave me solid theological and historical grounding in another spiritual tradition in addition to the prophetic and priestly traditions, the wisdom tradition.[15]

As I have said before, I have always been attracted to the character of Wisdom in Holy Scripture. When scholars began to name it as a legitimate part of the Judeo-Christian tradition exemplified by the life of Jesus, The Christ, the self-criticism I had felt that something was missing from how the scripture and tradition were being understood and preached was transformed into affirmation of what I had come to know to be true. The nature of the One True God included the feminine, but it wasn't being spoken or respected in the church. The feminine nature of God was missing in our understanding and in our language to communicate it.

In the Hebrew tradition, Wisdom was the embodiment of the divine presence of God dwelling on earth, and Wisdom/Sophia present in the apocrypha and Christian Scriptures helped people become friends with God. When I learned of the character of Wisdom in the sacred scriptures during seminary, the scriptures took on a whole new

---

[15] Cynthia Bourgeault, *The Wisdom Jesus: Transforming Heart and Mind—A New Perspective on Christ and His Message* (Boulder, CO: Shambhala, 2008).

authority for me as a woman. It was no longer just a book about male spiritual leadership interpreted by males; the feminine was alive in the character of Wisdom/ Sophia, making available God's wisdom to men and women alike.

Human beings, male and female, were both created in the image and likeness of God. The feminine was present from the beginning with God and was a part of God. Names for God the Father and God the Mother were both of value in relating to God, especially if you had had a difficult relationship with either parent. God was Mother, Father, Sophia, Holy Spirit of Wisdom, the Source of all goodness and light, Creator of all that is, and much more.

I didn't fully trust my own discovered truth about the feminine nature of the Holy Spirit until I read Bourgeault on the Wisdom Tradition. Even though Jesus was a man, he fully embodied the nature of God as masculine and feminine, transmitting the Wisdom of God through his teaching and the guidance of the Holy Spirit. Adding Wisdom Teacher to the traditional roles of Prophet and Priest, all three being incarnated in Jesus, The Christ, is what drew me to pastoral counseling and gave me the spiritual grounding to integrate all three into the call to ordination to the priesthood.

After many years of often feeling like I was an impostor priest, I felt legitimate. The path I had chosen as a wisdom teacher/priest was based in scripture, lived out in the life of Jesus, and Sophia/Wisdom expressed in the third person of the Trinity, the Holy Spirit, was feminine in nature.

As the years have passed, some of us clergy women who met at the beach each year have retired. We have paved the way for the next generation who have taken our places presiding at the altar, running the business of the church, and providing pastoral care to the sick and dying and those in need of support.

They will now invite those who come to share in the Eucharistic meal to find solace and courage and offer gratitude there. They will choose colleagues/friends and serve congregations who will shape them over time and encourage them to be what they invite others to be: inclusive of all, beloved of God, and growing in faith and kindness by God's grace to serve the common good.

Maybe they will take our place at the beach, too, making it a priority to set aside a week to meet friends and colleagues who will speak the truth to them in love and be renewed by the sound and motion of the waves, the soft brush of the breeze, the delight of seeing the dolphins surfacing and diving in the water as they swim by, and walks on the sand at the water's edge in bare feet.

Sitting in a sacred circle long into the night, they will listen and speak about the joys and sorrows of their lives and work over the past year. Maybe they, too, will learn from each other creative ways to balance their roles of priest, wife, mother, friend, and caregiver to the elderly, children, animals, and nature. Their shoulders will be the next generation of men and women to stand on to create an inclusive spiritual community. It will be their responsibility to translate the good news of the Christian tradition to respond to the needs of their generation to find belonging, purpose, and a value system that supports life, conveys truth, and builds trust in the unconditional love of God for them and everyone everywhere.

A NEW CALL

Vision Quest, 1992

Diane had been leading women's wilderness expeditions into the mountains of California for many years. During the year we lived together in the communal household in New York City, she often mentioned how much she would like me to join the women's expedition she led each summer.

Diane and I had gone through a lot of ups and downs during that year while sharing the brownstone's third-floor apartment. She was a California girl through and through—a free spirit who loved the ocean and the outdoors, hiking, and camping, and I was a proper East Coast dweller who spent my summers at my grandparents' cottage during my teenage years on a lake in Pennsylvania baking in the sun, reading novels, and thinking about boys.

We often saw the world differently. She disliked the institutional church and learned to distrust ministers due to her family's experience with a clergyman who violated her family's trust. On the other hand, I was looking to the church for answers to my questions and to find meaning and purpose. When she decided to knock down the plaster wall in the living room of the apartment (serving as their bedroom) to expose the brick and refinish the floors, our kitchen/bedroom filled with plaster dust and toxic odors.

I sat on my resentment for a while until the dust got the better of me, and I confronted her. "The bathroom and our bedroom are covered with a layer of dust. No matter how often I clean, the dust comes back; I am really frustrated."

"I did my best to block the dust by putting rags under the doors and taping what I could," she replied.

I knew Diane wasn't thoughtless, but from my perspective, it felt like she was. I wasn't used to expressing anger directly, but my relationship with Diane invited honesty and trust since I knew she was generally considerate of others and cared about me.

Another area of conflict emerged when I found myself feeling jealous about how our children loved to be with her. She enjoyed them, played with them, and took them to fun places. Unconsciously, I wanted to have the courage to venture out to explore the city with my children and be able to play and have fun with them, but I didn't know how to play and was afraid to risk the unknown parts of the city.

Several days a week, Diane rode home on her bike from her half-day work at IBM in midtown Manhattan, folded up the bike, put it in the closet, and showed up to care for our children. This allowed me some free time and supported me in finding what I wanted to do with my life. In the beginning, my jealousy contaminated my deep gratitude for her sacrificial commitment to me and our children.

Jealousy, competition, and fear of loss have plagued me in a number of relationships throughout my life, including my marriage. I have disliked these qualities but couldn't find their source back then or find a way to remove them from my heart.

As fiercely as Diane and I disagreed sometimes, we fiercely loved each other more. When Diane and John returned to their home in Berkeley, California, we kept in touch.

She knew my 50th birthday was approaching in February. To celebrate, she proposed that I join her and a group of women on a two-week expedition into the California mountains. Our children were grown by this time, and I was enjoying my work as a pastoral counselor. I had just completed a Doctor of Ministry degree and felt poised to make a major internal shift, which I anticipated might provoke a need to make changes in my work and my marriage.

During my doctoral research on women clergy and their exercise of power and authority, I began reading creation theology and exploring new life-sustaining images of the Divine in nature. It took me four years to integrate what I was learning from my research and reach the point where I could write about it.

At this point, having been in urban or suburban settings my whole life, I felt somewhat disoriented by a newfound awareness of my inter-dependence with nature. I was naive, scared, and insecure about how to relate to nature, but at the same time, I felt ready to risk opening myself to both the wonder and the harsh realities of it as God's first creation.

Trusting Diane's assurances that she would see that I was safe and intrigued by the physical, emotional, mental, and spiritual challenges of this rite of passage as I approached my 50th birthday, I agreed to go with her and a group of women the following summer.

Several months before we were to embark on our journey into the wilderness, Diane was diagnosed with kidney cancer. She was so healthy; she exercised, ate well, and had a positive spirit. She did every-thing right to be healthy. It was devastating news that seemed to come out of nowhere. We grieved that she could not lead the Summit Expedi-tion trip we were so looking forward to doing together.

After overcoming the shock of the diagnosis, Diane focused all her energy on getting well and being with her husband and children. She was happily married, the mother of three children, and a college pro-fessor. She had a lot to live for. She began to explore various healing modalities in Eastern and Western medicine and focused on recovery.

Her friends and family were wrestling emotionally and spiritu-ally with the possibility that the cancer had come from being held in a warehouse that had previously stored nuclear waste while protesting the Vietnam War. She and a group of protesters were rounded up and put there by the police. It wasn't fair; the injustice of it gave focus to our anger and fear of losing her.

Diane's death was earth-shattering for me. She was a bright light for me and many others. I knew I still wanted to enter the wilderness to honor my commitment to her and to myself to face this major challenge during my 50th year. Hebrew scripture normalizes the wilderness experience as a time when we are tested and called to trust God.

After some weeks of prayer and meditation, it became clear that I did not want to go with the group of women in California without Diane, so I sought out another way to keep my promise. I was introduced to Animus Valley Institute and connected with Janet, whose husband, George, had made a vision quest with this group several years before. Vision quests were often practiced by indigenous cultures as a rite of passage, surviving physical and spiritual challenges in the hopes of returning with a vision for the next phase of one's life.

Janet also wanted to challenge herself to go into the wilds of Montana. We were prepared to receive guidance through dreams and other signs, alert to receive a vision and strength from the spirit world to discern our purpose for going forward. We began to plan our trip.

Janet's husband George's stories were part of our preparation. He took lurid pleasure in telling us scary stories about scorpions, snakes, and bears that almost made us change our minds about going. "Just make a lot of noise or curl up into a ball if you see a brown/black bear. If the bear isn't hungry, it will likely leave you alone," he quipped. Lowering his voice, signaling danger and foreboding, he continued, "If you come face to face with a grizzly, however," pausing to make sure he had created the proper level of curiosity, anticipation, and fear, he said with a smile, "just know your time has come."

Despite being told scary stories of brown and grizzly bears inhabiting the region, I still wanted to go, so I began to prepare by walking miles with a heavy backpack loaded with books and rocks.

By the time I left for Montana, I was physically much stronger but still apprehensive about my ability to complete the 14-day journey. I knew what I would face in the wilderness was totally unpredictable, and I had never spent even four days camping in a protected campground with showers and bathrooms available, let alone going on a four-day solo without food.

I was most concerned about my physical stamina hiking into the wilderness, climbing steep terrain with equipment for 14 days strapped to my back. Even though I had been walking several miles each day in all kinds of weather conditions, carrying a heavy backpack, I still wasn't sure I could do it.

As Janet and I entered the airport terminal in Great Falls, Montana, we were stunned into silence as we were greeted by a huge brown grizzly bear standing on hind legs, claws outstretched, and sharp white teeth bared. My adrenals went on alert, and my cortisol level shot up. The memory of George's stories fueled my fear and anxiety. I was paralyzed and glued in place until my fight-or-flight reaction calmed down. My mind reengaged with my body, and as I returned to reality, I remembered that we were in an airport and the life-like grizzly was stuffed. But it looked so real!

Turning to the sound of a friendly "Hello," we were greeted by the smiling face of a driver who was to take us to Blacktail Ranch, about an hour's drive away.

Peering out the window of the van after leaving the vicinity of the airport, I found myself in awe of the world we had just entered. The beauty of the rugged terrain, fields of colorful wildflowers, and snow-capped mountains surrounded us. The horse ranch where we would begin and end our quest was located on 3,000 acres in the heart of the Rocky Mountains at the base of the Continental Divide, where the Rocky Mountains meet the prairie.

Driving into the ranch property and up the winding road to the main lodge, a tall canvas teepee stood to our right with symbols painted on the sides in black and red. We were taken to sleeping accommodations in the rustic cabins, which slept six to a room with three bunk beds. Janet and I both chose a bottom bunk; our younger roommates didn't mind climbing the ladders to the top bunks.

After taking a short time to settle in, we joined 30 fellow participants and, with the guidance of four leaders, began our internal preparation to enter the wilderness a few days later. I didn't know any of our leaders except that they were experienced in leading vision quests, and George had returned safely the year before, alive and able to recommend it.

A biblical understanding of wilderness is a place where we can hear the voice of God. It is often a place of testing that shows us what is in our heart and is ultimately intended for our good. Something that often happens is that we come to see the ways we have resolved the unconscious trauma of childhood by transferring our relationship with our parents onto our relationship with God.

I knew one of my challenges was that I could never fully trust God, "the Father," to be present and love me unconditionally, given my father's early abandonment and the lack of adult support to express my grief and sadness when he left. Would I ever get over my two-and-a-half-year-old child's need for my father's blessing? The love and security I had experienced came from women, and I am deeply grateful for their faithfulness. I desperately needed to draw on the feminine nature of God to keep me safe.

Sitting in a circle in a massive canvas-walled yurt, I looked into the faces of those with whom I would make this journey over the next 14 days. We were young and old, skinny and overweight. These would be "my people" for the next 14 days. I might need to depend on them for my survival.

Using the Native American ritual of passing the talking stick, we each took the stick, expressed our hopes and fears, and began to get acquainted. For five days, we did various exercises designed to prepare us to enter our inner wilderness and engage with the challenges of nature we might confront along the way.

We learned how to listen to ourselves at a deep level and how to listen to each other as we passed the talking stick. Our religious affiliation didn't matter. We were Jews and Gentiles and nonreligious males and females. Our leaders guided us to open our hearts and minds and use our imaginations to seek and connect with the Power Animals found in the energy centers (chakras) of our bodies. Like angels, they became our guardians and guides. Sometimes, the animals we met were injured and needed healing. Sometimes, they were called into council to work on particular issues that needed resolution. Our imaginations were set free to help heal our hearts, minds, and souls.

Out on the lawn on the third day, each of us opened our backpacks. We laid out all the items we had brought with us from the list we were given to be evaluated for their usefulness in the mountainous wilderness come rain, shine, or snow. It was suggested to us while we were still at home that packing our things was a "self-generated" severance ceremony, selecting from our past the things that would make it possible to walk into our future and discover a delicate balance between security and freedom.

This choice of self-severance was generated again many years later as I went through the experience of downsizing and letting go of our family home, including rugs and furniture that had been passed on to me from previous generations in my family.

The guides reviewed the items in our backpacks. Even though it was summer and the weather was warm, we were strongly advised to bring warm clothing in case the weather turned cold. It was suggested, too, that we include a first aid kit, two one-gallon plastic water containers, a metal cup and spoon, toilet paper, two large plastic garbage bags, a small day pack, a knife, a sleeping bag and tarp, matches and a candle to light a fire, water purifier, a journal, and pen and pencil.

After being made ready inwardly and outwardly as best we could, it was time to go. We were bussed to the entrance of the trail; I left the security of the bus and slung my heavy backpack over my shoulders. Folding myself into the middle of the group, we began the treacherous, single-file trek up the mountain, over rocks, and through streams and foliage to our base camp and temporary Rocky Mountain home in the wilderness.

After several days in base camp, my body adjusted to eating less food and learning about engaging with the environment. The day finally arrived to go out and find my place, my special spot, which would allow me to delve deeply into my soul's center and seek a vision for myself and my people.

I wandered for several hours alone, looking for the right spot, and finally found it. It was bordered on one side by an Aspen grove and on the other by a steep gorge with a waterfall tumbling down its rocky center, landing in the swirling water of a riverbed below. A five-minute walk took me to a small stream that fed into the river, where I could collect and purify my water for the day. It was perfect.

Having identified my place, I returned to base camp and was paired with another person whose spot the leaders had determined was within walking distance of mine. We were instructed to go to a central location between us and change a rock formation each day to let the other know we were mobile and safe. One more night in base camp, and then the four days of solitude would begin.

I took nothing with me to eat but a bag of dried fruit in case my blood sugar dropped too low to provide energy to get me back to base camp at the end of my four solo days. I took no books to escape into but a pen and journal to record my thoughts and visions. I discovered pretty quickly in the changeable weather the importance of taking a warm sleeping bag, a tarp to hang over a tree branch covering my sleeping spot to keep me dry, a water filter, containers to hold the two gallons of water I needed to drink each day, and layered clothing for hot days and cold nights.

With my bag of dried fruit tied to a branch high up in a tree to discourage animals from eating what I might need to give me energy and my tarp hanging over a sturdy tree branch, I climbed under my shelter and onto my sleeping bag to get acclimated to my temporary wilderness home. I stayed there for a long time, just breathing in the warm, fresh air filled with the scent of pine and listening to the rustling of the aspen leaves on the trees that surrounded me.

Each day, I walked to the stream to filter water for drinking. At night, I could hear someone drumming and singing on the mountain above me, far in the distance. The sound of another human being provided a welcome distraction from wondering if this night I might become bear food.

I didn't sleep much the first night but lay listening to the drumming and sounds of nature around me. The steady sound of the water rushing down the side of the mountain and the wind moving through the

Aspen trees offered comfort as it blew over the plateau where I had set up camp. I felt a deep satisfaction; I had chosen a good place to be and was learning to be brave.

During the day, I walked, journaled, and slept. As I became weaker from only water to drink, even the ants who crawled over me while I lay on my sleeping bag became companions on my quest.

By the second day of the fast, I felt really hungry and a little nauseated. I kept drinking water, hoping the nausea would subside. By the third day, I was no longer hungry and fell into an altered state of awareness.

The quiet isolation and intention of my mind and heart led me to wrestle with the Spirit of Wisdom and the angels to obtain a blessing—my father's blessing, which I had sought to receive my whole life but which seemed unattainable—a blessing I continued to long for even though my stepfather had blessed me in his own way. I listened to the wind of the Spirit and felt the solid ground of Grandmother Earth beneath me, surrounded by her children, the animals and plants.

Slowly, a vision began to form, and a medicine name and a song emerged from my heart. Like Jacob in Genesis 25, I wrestled with an angel and was given a new name. I heard the new name and was given a song to sing when darkness threatens to overcome the light, and when I forget to remember to hope and trust. The medicine name that was given to me was "Dances in Light." The song, sung in a minor key, follows.

> *Dances in the light; dances in the light,*
> *full of joy and wonder.*
> *Singing in the light; singing in the light*
> *Full of strength and power.*
> *Praying in the light; praying in the light;*
> *Full of God's own Spirit.*

I discovered that a key to hearing the voice of God is often found in the past. As a vision for the next phase of my life began to form, I concluded I would focus my pastoral counseling practice on working with couples who wanted to heal and grow. That call had emerged out of the pain of the divorces of my parents and my maternal and paternal grandparents. "My people" were couples who wanted to find a way through conflict, misunderstanding, and disconnection to safely communicate to each other their hopes and dreams for the future.

I was called to be a companion to couples who put their time and energy into experiencing emotional and physical intimacy with each other again and recommitting to their marriage. For couples with children, I wanted to hold the space for couples to create a home that provided emotional and physical safety for the whole family.

I knew some couples might conclude that their relationship was no longer life-giving and would choose not to continue in the marriage. But hopefully, they would learn tools to communicate and gain clarity about what they wanted for the next phase of their lives, respecting themselves and each other as they parted and planned for the health and safety of their children. If they chose, I would walk with them through a process of saying "goodbye."

I returned from the vision quest with a new sense of calling, a new, clarified sense not only of my physical stamina but of a power I had found and claimed in myself. Maybe this was the blessing I had longed for. Although I had been trained before then in family systems to work with couples and had begun using my training in Imago Relationship Therapy, I now wanted to focus on working primarily with couples.

Calling

Living into a personal "call" is transformative, a truth that is strongly affirmed in both Hagberg's *Stages of Power* and Marjory Bankson's *The Call to the Soul: Six Stages of Spiritual Development*.[16] Their books suggested to me a way to put into words what a call is and how it continues to unfold. For many, an understanding of receiving a "call" means a call to ordained ministry. According to Bankson, anyone can be called to

---

[16] Marjory Zoet Bankson, *The Call to the Soul: Six Stages of Spiritual Development* (Minneapolis, MN: Augsburg Books, 2005).

fulfill a need and find purpose in life by responding to a call. In Bankson's system of the call process, a new call begins with resistance and continues as an inward experience of reclaiming parts of ourselves, leading to a revelation of a specific call to service.

Initially, when Diane invited me into the wilderness, I resisted. It felt completely out of my comfort zone. She held the dream for me that in the quietness of nature, I would have an opportunity to listen to my inner voice, interact with the earth around me, and come more fully to realize what form the next chapter of my life might take.

Bankson's second stage is reclaiming forgotten or rejected parts of our story in light of a new call, even as we deny or resist it. In my case, I identified the desire for my birth father's blessing and the childhood pain of loss and abandonment as still holding me back. I realized these childhood experiences were still alive at the core of my unconscious past and needed to be called to consciousness and released. I needed to reclaim and transform a part of my past that had been frozen in childhood.

The middle or neutral phase starts with a clear *revelation* of what we might do and how we might do it. That vision creates tension between what we have been doing and a call to a new way of being. None of this is automatic. We do have the power to refuse a "call." We can stay on the side of dreaming and possibility without moving to act. We can hesitate and turn back, repeating the first three stages, in Marjory's words, in an "endless waltz of agitation."

Doubt and fear loomed large as I considered taking action. There were so many ways I could talk myself out of taking the next steps. Self-critical thoughts kept coming: "I am not smart enough, I don't have the skill, I don't have a business partner, I don't have the financial resources, I might get hurt or fail." All along, my deepest fear was that I might step out to take a risk and fail. After all, my husband was the risk-taker, not me.

I was learning how to "let go" and what I needed to let go of in the context of my inner spiritual journey toward healing. Wholeness meant I would begin to see the denied, repressed, and rejected parts of myself that I didn't want to acknowledge. I didn't want to recognize their power to control me.

Rather than turning against myself in self-criticism or self-hatred, or hiding my gifts and talents out of false humility, I wanted to claim my belovedness to the One who created me and knew my broken places. I wanted to take full possession of my gifts to be used for the good of others. I felt a new freedom as I embraced all the self I had come to know up to this point, including the blind spots.

The movement from death to resurrection, while central to the Christian story and uniquely understood in the life of Jesus, can be found in other traditions and psychological models embodying transformation. The theme of death and resurrection is an archetype, as is Erik Erikson's eight-stage psycho-social model, for example, which sees us all as capable of moving from despair to generativity.[17]

It is a lifetime process of transformation, of letting go of who people say I am and who I thought I was to come to know more of my core self or true self, the self God created me to be. It's a process of growing into ways I can offer my gifts in service to the community, reaching up for guidance, and reaching back to invite others to fulfill their potential.

I was mulling over what I had learned from these writers as I sat alone in the wilderness that week of vision quest. Weak from four days of no food but empowered by newfound insight, I slowly folded up my sleeping bag and tarp, packed my journal, pen, and other belongings, and dragged myself back to base camp.

Food that our stomachs could handle was waiting for us by the fire. We had all survived the time alone. With renewed vision and purpose for ourselves and our people, we shared our experiences as we prepared to return home, ready to convey our new vision to "our people," whoever we had identified them to be.

On the bumpy bus ride back to the ranch, I reflected on the leadership qualities displayed by our guide, Bill, who was sitting next to me. Hesitantly, I said, "I hope you don't mind my asking, but are you a priest?

---

[17] Erik H. Erikson, *Childhood and Society* (New York: W. W. Norton & Company, 1950).

Your ease at performing and leading rituals for our group facilitated a profound experience for me and, from what people have said, for the rest of the group, too, so I was just wondering."

His answer took me by surprise at first. "No, in fact, I am Jewish and a transformational therapist."

His answer intrigued me, and I tucked it away to revisit it later. I thought that is what all religion is supposed to offer people: transformation that opens the way to new life, meaning, purpose, and connection to the natural world, God's first creation. A provocative question arose: Is this what I have been doing as a priest and pastoral counselor? Have I been helping people face the death of a committed relationship that needed to end or finding a new way to begin or a way to redefine the faith tradition they have outgrown to find hope in the possibility of new life emerging from the ashes? My eyes had been opened to the essence of true spiritual guidance: transformation and connection to a deeper purpose discerned and empowered by the Divine Spirit.

Now, 30 years later, I understand better what I was experiencing in his leadership: a quality of mind and heart that opened the way for transformation. He was a "Moshel Meshalim," a teacher of wisdom who saw in the ancient traditions a way to transform human beings.

The "Kingdom of Heaven" is a metaphor for life lived out of a transformed mind and unitive consciousness. We are one with the Source of life and love, other humans, and the natural world if we choose to see it and live that way. The Christian tradition in which I was born and raised and which I claim for myself as an adult offered me a way to understand this life path in the suffering, death, and resurrection of Jesus, the Christ.

The depth and breadth of the profound transformational lessons we learned from the Hebrew scriptures are combined and summarized by Jesus in the Great Commandment, found in three of the Gospels in the Christian scriptures, "Love the Lord your God with all of your heart, mind, and strength (will), and your neighbor as yourself" (paraphrased).

This scripture has been interpreted by many to mean that loving yourself means practicing self-care first, and only when you have achieved a new level of self-love can you love your neighbor.

I have come to think about it differently. "Your neighbor *is* yourself." We are all interrelated. When, for example, black lives matter, all life matters, including mine. When one among us suffers unjust treatment, we are all imprisoned. My neighbor is my window into the areas in my life calling for healing and transformation to experience the fullness of life.

If I stand in judgment of another or hate another, that quality I hate also unconsciously lives in me. The judgment or hatred I feel is an invitation to become conscious of how it lives in me and to seek release from it. That doesn't mean that I don't take a stand against the wrong done to me or another; it simply means that the judgment is not the ground on which my stand is built, but rather is grounded in stopping the harm and caring for all involved.

At the same time, what I admire in another that causes me to put them on a pedestal sets me up for disappointment when I see they are not all I had imagined them to be. Also, it denies that the quality I admire also lives in me. As long as I project it onto another, I postpone taking the risk to develop it in myself through trial and error.

For example, my admiration for our leader Bill's ability to lead meaningful rituals during our vision quest is an invitation to me to develop meaningful rituals for "my people." I just need to be willing to put in the work and take a risk.

If I become envious of a colleague's gifts, I can use that awareness to focus on developing my gifts and free myself to appreciate theirs. If another person's gift or calling is not mine, I can celebrate their gifts and rejoice in the reality that each is a part of the whole.

The last three stages of the call cycle also involve fear and doubt. As I made plans to risk making my vision public and to share it so others could relate to it, I was worried about how my clients and clergy colleagues would react.

I decided to finish with my clients who were in a committed partnership but with whom I had been working individually, and either invite their partner to join us or refer them to a colleague to give them an equal start with someone new. I no longer felt it was ethical to continue seeing individuals who were growing and changing when their partners were not a part of the process. I knew I was now called to work primarily with couples.

Never Stop Learning and Check Your Sources

Entering the second half of life, I am less preoccupied with collecting more goods and strongly desire to give back to the world a bit of what I have received. I am very aware of how much I have been given from my family and friends, from society, and from guidance from the One God, Creator, Redeemer, and Sustainer.

Erik Erikson's concept of a generative person captures my imagination as a vision for a life well lived, which he describes as a stage where emotional independence grows, ego diminishes, and one is drawn to reflect on universal spiritual truth.

Erikson's eight-stage theory of development contrasts ending one's life with integrity rather than despair. At this stage, a "generative" person lives as part of a family, has found meaningful work, and is eager to share what she has learned from her life experience to benefit younger people. Thinking in black-and-white terms is not appealing. A generative person is curious and eager to keep learning from others.

Any lasting wisdom I have gained from reflecting on my experience comes from the Holy Spirit. Therefore, I cannot claim it as my own. There are things I wish I had known when I was younger, mistakes and poor choices I have made, and yet I am not left with despair or bitterness but rather freedom, knowing I have learned from my mistakes, am forgiven, and bathed in the Spirit of love.

Each Thursday morning, I join an ecumenical Bible study on Zoom, expecting to be challenged in my understanding of faith. Without fail, that happens. As 9:45 a.m. approaches, familiar faces appear on the screen. Some I know well, and others only from sharing this time on Zoom. Some of us teach, some do administration, and all of us are thirsty to grow in our experience of faith in community. This, we have come to know, is a safe place to share our doubts, questions, explorations, and wisdom.

Our first teacher, Jonathan, an Episcopal priest friend who is now retired, had been teaching this ecumenical Bible study for years. When I tentatively stuck my foot in the water, I hoped this would be a place to share my whole self and my experience as a priest. I had served congregations in Atlanta and Virginia as part-time interim clergy, worked with a multi-religious staff at the Washington National Cathedral, served as Chaplain at Georgia Baptist Hospital, and as a pastoral therapist, caring for people across religious traditions. I hoped I would be free to express my doubts and confusion and my growing, evolving experience of God's expansive love.

I didn't know the language then, but I was in the process of deconstructing and reconstructing my faith based on current scholarship to integrate it with my life experience. A friend quoted a line I've come to love attributed to Bill Moyers: "Religion was where I got my questions answered. And life is where I got my answers questioned."[18]

Following the first meeting, I knew this was a community of people who could receive me as a sister seeker of truth who wanted to grow in faith as they did. Jonathan's approach was one of "both/and" rather than "either/or": "This is what this passage of scripture says. However, this other passage says this: they seem to be in conflict." He suggested that we look at the whole arc of scripture. Although there are passages where God is pictured as a judgmental God, and although there are consequences that result from our choices that are sometimes painful, forgiveness and grace are the operating principles of God, who loves humankind and all of creation.

As humans, we make judgments regarding what is right and wrong, which guide our actions, however, God is a God of a continual wellspring of love, no matter what we do or think. God's Holy Spirit will guide us when we open our hearts and minds to hear.

Some months after I joined the Bible study, Jonathan, recalling his many years of teaching and now approaching 90 years old, said, "I think I have given you all that I have to give right now, and I would like to pass on the teaching to Larry. I will now become a participant." What

---

[18] Bill Moyers, *The Language of Life: A Festival of Poets* (New York: Doubleday, 1995).

an amazing model of leadership transfer—discerning a call to hand over the reins of teaching and become a fellow learner!

Larry had been participating in the Bible study group for some time. He knew scripture and had enriched our understanding of Hebrew scripture with his knowledge of the Hebrew language and the historical and cultural context of when various passages were written. He welcomed questions and contributions and offered alternative translations of the Hebrew scripture. Larry had grown up in an evangelical church community, become an attorney, gone to seminary, learned Hebrew, and studied with several Rabbis. He and his wife, Vivian, though she was mostly quiet during the Bible study, were partners in life and ministry. Together, they held the space for us to talk, listen, and learn.

Because I didn't study Hebrew in seminary and found much of the Hebrew scripture confusing, I was looking forward to learning what Larry had to offer. The way the creation story, for instance, had been interpreted to me as a woman was damaging to my faith in God. I was open and ready to learn a new way to make sense of passages in Hebrew scripture that had made no sense to me in the past. I was intrigued by the way the Hebrew words could have a variety of meanings and were largely dependent on those who translated them in a particular historical context.

Currently, a critical mass of male and female clergy in the church have studied Hebrew, Aramaic, and Greek. They can present important corrections to English translations where a gendered term that would have been ungendered in the past can now offer richly ambiguous and more inclusive translations of scripture.

We pondered the possibility that the Garden of Eden story was a coming-of-age story rather than a story that cast the woman as the one to disobey God's orders as a temptress to get her husband to follow her lead to disobey God. My mind and heart were totally engaged: I saw an alternative truth in these stories as I considered alternative translations from the Hebrew. Perhaps the Garden of Eden story, like the creation stories in other ancient cultures, was a metaphor rather than literal history.

No one was there at the beginning of time before language was created or written down. Perhaps those who did ultimately write the Hebrew/Christian creation story were guided by the Spirit of God, but the interpretation is culture-bound.

So, should this story be the literal truth or a metaphor that carries with it a universal truth regarding our relationship with our Creator? The point of the story could be that it was not wrong for Eve to be curious, to want to become conscious; it was the natural evolution of humankind, but rather, it was not the right time. She wasn't ready to accept the responsibility of knowing, so she took control rather than waiting for guidance and seeking the wisdom of God. Adam, rather than taking responsibility for his choice, chose to blame her and follow her lead.

The consequence of their actions was to be separated from God and hide once their eyes were opened, and they saw the result of their decisions. Together, they abandoned a way of life that gave them a constant connection with eternal love and made them responsible for choosing between what was good and not good. Ego, pride, power, money, and self-interest would now affect the life choices they made in the future with the guidance of the Spirit of God walking along with them.

Perhaps it was inevitable that, in order for humankind to mature, we were given free will to choose and learn how to distinguish between what was good and what was not good. Eve's lack of obedience and ignoring Wisdom's instruction were the problems. She didn't listen to God, nor was Adam, her partner, listening. She thought she knew what was best.

Neither Adam nor Eve was mature enough to assume the responsibility that eating the apple would require. God was saying to wait and seek Wisdom from above when the time comes for you to make a decision. It is how I feel when I see a young person engaging in behavior they are not ready to be responsible for and refusing to listen to the wise counsel of their elders.

Larry encouraged us to read scripture considering its historical context from four perspectives: the literal; the implications of the literal understanding; the metaphorical, since much of scripture is parables, story, and poetry; and mystery, which is beyond our human understanding. But all scripture is written in the context of relationship with the creative energy of the universe we call by many names: God, the Eternal One, the Source, or The Divine, who is good, loving, merciful, and just, rather than not good, judgmental, or punishing.

Over the succeeding months, as the study guides have arrived each week, I have resisted reading them before we meet on Zoom, even though I know it would be helpful to be more prepared. I want questions to emerge spontaneously in the context of the interdenominational church gathered on Zoom so that we can wrestle with what we are hearing and arrive at our own insights in the process.

I come away from these conversations feeling as though I want to cry, grieving the many years I believed I was not sufficiently orthodox in my understanding and thus didn't belong in any faith community. I jump for joy and shed tears of gladness at the same time at the freedom I now feel. The closed doors of my heart, sealed shut by a fear of and inclination to reject people who didn't follow my path to faith, open as I come to know The Creator of the Universe at a deeper level.

My doubt and inability to trust are being transformed into a new understanding of Scripture and God, the life-giving Energy of the universe, rather than a punitive father and moralistic judge. Those fear-based images continue to recede as I bring my imagination and creativity to reading these texts. Eve's choice taught me that my knowledge, curiosity, and desire are not enough when making a decision; the guidance to act comes from seeking discernment from the source of all knowledge and wisdom. I was being propelled to a new place of trust in the One God, responsible for seeking the Wisdom of God and following the way of Jesus, who is the exact embodiment of God's nature.

I increasingly see the Hebrew and Christian scriptures as living human documents containing divine revelations, which mysteriously make them relevant to every generation and culture. The more inclusive translation of the Hebrew in the first three chapters of Genesis, and seeking to understand the culture-bound perspectives of those who have interpreted them in the past, can provide a strong foundation for living in the Light and continuing to grow in faith.

Misunderstood or mistranslated, those scriptures can serve the purpose of tribalism rooted in fear and judgment. They can be twisted to suggest that only men are created in the image of God. They can put God in a box called Christian orthodoxy or Christian Nationalism, the latter a distortion that has afflicted the church in some form since Constantine made Christianity a state religion. The concept of "sin" and judgment that emerges from both nationalistic and literalistic readings of scripture both distorts and, for many, extinguishes faith.

The current push among Christian Nationalists to post the Ten Commandments in classrooms indicates how their understanding of God is rooted in scriptural images and stories of following the rules and judging others who break them, which leads to division and contempt for those who falter.

Rather, the life of Jesus teaches us that we will do wrong either by making a mistake or violating the spirit of God's law on purpose because we are human. However, we can become conscious of the wrong we have done, admit it, and reconnect with God's grace-filled love. It's telling that the Christian Nationalist movement's followers have not suggested posting The Beatitudes, which speak of the habits of the heart and caring for those in any kind of need, rather than standards of behavior given in the Ten Commandments that call forth judgment and seek to control.

The church, in some cases, has done us a disservice by teaching that sin as a pathway to hell, based on "bad" behavior, encourages its members to be a community of judgmental people. Jesus' victory over sin on the cross has served as a "get out of jail free" for some, without repenting from the wrong that has been done and taking responsibility for it to make restitution. What is taught in some faith communities is, "I have accepted Jesus as my personal savior. He died for my sins, so I am saved no matter what my attitude is toward others or what I do to stoke the fires of fear, hate, revenge, discrimination, and violence."

In my experience, there is often little or no curiosity about what is unconsciously driving behaviors or attitudes that violate everything

150

Jesus stood for or taught among some who claim to be Christian, nor is there a desire to rid one's soul of the need for control and dominance to be free of the bondage of those emotions.

One could understand the concept of sin as a mistake made or missing the mark of what is good and loving, take the responsibility to learn from it, and make it right if possible, intending to do better next time. I believe Jesus' words on the cross, "... forgive them for they know not what they do." We are human and will make mistakes. Sometimes, we think we know what we are doing when we align ourselves with those who hate, lie, and want to control. Or we make personal decisions that satisfy our desires that do harm to others seeking revenge. Ultimately, we don't know what we are doing; we are short-sighted. But hopefully, we will wake up, see the truth, and repent.

Nevertheless, the grace of Eternal Love is always present, but not the "cheap grace" that lets one off the hook of doing the inner work of uncovering what drove the action in the first place. Of course, there are those who justify whatever wrong they have done and consciously do wrong without regret or repentance, but those are not the ways of Jesus, The Christ, either.

In childhood and even adolescence, I was taught that to be a faithful Christian, one must take the scriptures literally. Yet interpreting scripture that way often didn't make sense. I fell into the habit of ignoring my feelings and not trusting my intuition. After all, the male preachers had the authority and training to know what the scriptures taught, didn't they?

Their preaching limited my sense of "call" to go where my passion and gifts were leading me because there was much my church and culture said I could not do as a girl. I am grateful that many faith communities have changed as the culture has changed to embrace the gifts of women in leadership. We are all the better for it.

What we make of our contemporary experience of God and our reading of scripture with new eyes to update the "faith of our fathers" and "quiet, often hidden faith of our mothers" is what matters now. The quiet discernment of the Holy Spirit of Wisdom is needed now more than ever before. It is our work to do. It is our choice to decide what kind of human beings we want to be and how we want to live out Jesus's message of love and justice in our contemporary situation.

To summarize what I have said before, following the Way of Jesus is not confined to a particular political party or sociological, racial, or cultural group. We all fail in our efforts to live a moral and ethical life. If we try to follow rules and judge who belongs as part of the kingdom of God and who doesn't, based on right doctrine and good behavior, national identity, or according to our religious and cultural standards, it will make us brittle and judgmental and exclude those who don't look like us or talk like us.

It takes courage to explore the childhood beliefs embedded in our unconscious selves that violate following the Way of Jesus, the way of love. If we do our inner work, we can be free to let the Spirit do the work of conviction and judgment of the other if and/or when they are ready to listen. We can be brave to stand in protest when harm is being done.

The Feminine Nature of the Divine

In *The Power Code,* Katty Kay and Claire Shipman write that 80% of women in leadership focus on the needs of the whole, as opposed to men, who tend to focus on the task at hand—a tendency the authors describe as "ego-driven." Their data confirms that, in general, women have a stronger diffuse awareness and a capacity to hold all the pieces together, making them better at multitasking.[19]

This aligns with my findings from pastoral ministry and theological studies on the significance of feminine qualities within the divine character. A woman's nurturing role in society mirrors attributes of the divine feminine, including the ability to see what is of value and true regarding how we live. One might say it is the capacity to see the forest while the masculine-focused consciousness sees the individual trees.

---

[19] Katty Kay and Claire Shipman, *The Power Code: More Joy, Less Ego, Maximum Impact for Women* (New York, USA: HarperCollins, 2023).

But these are generalizations. Some men can multitask and are not ego-driven, and some women are thinking types, sidelining their emotions and getting jobs done faster because they can focus. These qualities are not inborn; there are gender tendencies, but they are developed and grown in the context of family and community. A healthy family or community fosters a range of skills and strengths in both men and women as they join together to support life and the health of all.

What is most interesting to me in reading Kay and Shipman's book now is that the authors are asking the same questions I was struggling with in 1992 as I wrote my doctoral thesis on women clergy's exercise of power and authority and also on the question of whether spiritual maturity looked different in men and women.[20]

As a part-time deployment officer in the Diocese of Virginia, I had opportunities to listen to the stories of women clergy who hoped to be considered for rector positions after years of serving the church as assistants. I became curious about how women clergy's leadership in the church was undercut and limited by the image of God as male.

This male-gendered language shapes our understanding of women's value to God, the church, and society today. As women, we are now present in the leadership of the church, but the language still undercuts our authority and creates a psychological dissonance. While doing my doctoral research on women's exercise of power and authority in the church, I concluded that deep, systemic changes were needed.

The question is now more frequently and urgently raised: how can Christian communities offer any vision of partnership and respect for the integration of masculine and feminine qualities in both men and women without acknowledging that the feminine is a dimension of both creation and the Creator? If we need to speak of the Creator in

---

[20] Jean Milliken, "Power, Authority and Spiritual Maturity: Women Clergy Serving Congregations as Rectors or Vicars in the Episcopal Diocese of Virginia," A Project Thesis in Partial Fulfillment of Requirements for the Degree Doctor of Ministry, Wesley Theological Seminary, Washington, DC, May 1992.

gendered terms, then the Source of Life and Love and the Creator of all that is is not only our "father" but also our "mother."

Despite the centuries of patriarchal language, Julian of Norwich, a 14th-century mystic widely respected in the church, wrote in *Revelations* 60, "This beautiful word, mother, is so sweet and kind in itself that it cannot be attributed to anyone but God."[21]

Father Richard Rohr points out in one of his daily meditations (August 12, 2024) that Julian's words were "courageous, original, and yet fully orthodox." I fully agree. There is something primal about our connection to our mothers, whether or not they have fulfilled the social expectations assigned to their role. Many who have had conflicted or painful relationships with their mothers continue to depend on that relationship despite the challenges. It is not easily relinquished; the need for what mothers teach us and the nurture and discipline they provide runs deep in our bones.

The Bishop of York, addressing the General Synod of the Church of England in 2023, suggested that praying to God, Our Father, in the Lord's prayer is problematic because of its patriarchal associations. Referring to God as Father and imaging God as male can be destructive for those whose earthly fathers were abusive or those who have suffered the worst cultural oppressions of patriarchy. Though the prayer has been prayed for 2000 years, he pointed out that its focus on fatherhood reads very differently in the context of Western rationalism than it may have in the context of the ancient Middle East.

One of the female clergy attending the synod meeting asked, "Do we really believe that God believes that male human beings bear his [sic] image more fully and accurately than women?"

The Bishop's answer, and mine as well, is absolutely not. I believe that when Jesus prayed to "Our Father," he was praying to Abba, not to

---

[21] Julian of Norwich, *Revelations of Divine Love,* ed. and trans. Edmund Colledge and James Walsh (Mahwah, NJ: Paulist Press, 1978), 192.

God as a masculine person, but as the Creator, which in Aramaic and Hebrew understanding included the feminine as well.[22]

In 1973, when I entered the seminary at Candler, not many people in Christian circles were interested in Sophia/Wisdom. Some of my professors would have said it was heresy to equate what was called Sophia/Wisdom in the Hebrew Bible with the wisdom figure mentioned in Psalms, Proverbs, and Ecclesiastes and in the Apocrypha.

Some still hold the position that the Holy Spirit could be nothing but male if gender were to be assigned. At first, I was confused because it made so much sense that Sophia-Wisdom was a feminine dimension of the Holy Trinity. Why didn't they see it? I saw with considerable irritation that their logic was deeply flawed and self-serving. We all have been taught that by praying the Lord's Prayer, we are to pray as Jesus prayed to God the Father, not the Mother, though some scholars of Aramaic insist the language he spoke was more nuanced than we can replicate with our two-gendered language.

According to Aramaic scholar Neil Douglas-Klotz, though the Lord's Prayer begins with "Our Father," a translation of the word "abba," the actual Aramaic transliteration is *"abwoon,"* which is a blending of "abba" (father) and "woon" (womb), Jesus's recognition of the masculine and feminine source of creation.

Douglas-Klotz explains that *abwoon* is the first word usually translated as "our Father," and *D'Bashmaya* is multiple words [together] translated as "Which art in heaven." The translation of *abwoon*, as "Our Father," is, if not wrong, very misleading in that *abwoon* is inclusive of both the masculine and feminine. And *D'Bashmaya*, translated as "Who art in heaven," is an activity of creation, always being created and recreating, pointing to the eternal connection between the creation and the divine.[23]

---

[22] The Bishop of York, "Address to the General Synod of the Church of England," General Synod of the Church of England, February 2023, https://www.churchofengland.org/synod/speech-address-bishop-york.

[23] Douglas Klotz, *Prayers of the Cosmos: Meditations on the Aramaic Words of Jesus* (1994), pp. 10-14.

As I understand the point, the nature of the Divine Being is best expressed as a verb, beyond male and female, but inclusive of both in God's dynamic of ongoing creation.

So, for some people, especially those who hold a doctrine of belief in God as Father, there is no room for the feminine in the Trinity if Father, Son, and Holy Spirit are all believed to be, or at least imagined to be, male.

There is no question that ancient Hebrew culture was male-dominated in ways that have left a long lineage of patriarchy. Women could not own property, for example. When Jesus fed the five thousand, that number didn't count women and children.[24] The women simply didn't count and were accustomed to not being counted. And after all, since Jesus prayed to God, the Father, how could God be anything but male?

When I learned that in the seven books of the "Deuterocanon," those still found in Roman Catholic translations like the Jerusalem Bible and a few others, parts of Daniel, Esther, The Gospel of Mary, and other books included references to Wisdom/Sophia, it opened a new and exciting dimension in my relationship with God; I had a lot to rethink. The books of the Deuterocanon, or Apocrypha, were written by early Christians and included in the original canon of scripture until the Protestant Reformation, when they were removed. I was then and still am curious about why these books were removed, and what was in them that caused the early church fathers to decide they were not divinely inspired and therefore held no authority as Holy Scripture.

The seven books of the Apocrypha are Baruch, Judith, First and Second Maccabees, Sirach or Ben Sira, which is also called Ecclesiasticus, 1 Esdras, Tobit, and Wisdom, also called The Wisdom of Solomon. Wisdom/Sophia appears repeatedly in these books and the ones mentioned above, some of which are still included in the Protestant canon, i.e., approved books of the Bible.

Sophia is a voice of wisdom. As the scriptures say, she helps "men," i.e., human beings, know God. She is a kind friend and teacher. She

---

[24] "And those who ate were about five thousand men, besides women and children," Matthew 14:21 (NRSV with Apocrypha).

embraces what supports life. As I understand her, she is a member of the Trinity, as Jesus is—an expression of the one God who is not only our father but also our mother and the face of the Holy Spirit.

I believe the Holy Spirit can be understood much more broadly than most churches teach. *Chokhama*, the feminine word meaning Wisdom in Hebrew, and *ruach*, also a feminine Hebrew word meaning Spirit, can refer simply to breath, wind, or the invisible moving force that hovers over the surface of the waters in the process of creation, like the Holy Spirit, who blew through the crowd on Pentecost. This rich understanding of Spirit came well before Christian tradition funneled it into a male identity. It moves me deeply to hear Sophia's voice in passages such as these that have survived into the translations most Protestant Churches still use (from the New Jerusalem Bible):

> *Wisdom calls aloud in the streets, She raises her voice in the public squares; She calls out at the street corners, She delivers her message at the city gates.*
>
> *—Proverbs 1:20-21*

> *Yahweh created me when his purpose first unfolded … before the oldest of his works, From everlasting I was firmly set, from the beginning, before earth came into being.*
>
> *—Proverbs 8:22-23*

> *I was beside the master craftsman, delighting him day after day, ever at play in his presence, at play everywhere on this earth, delighting to be with the children of men.*
>
> *—Proverbs 8:30-31*

> *Teach us to count up the days that are ours, and we shall come to the heart of wisdom.*
>
> *—Psalm 90:12*

When I admitted to myself and a few others that Sophia's femininity had become an important part of what I had come to believe about God's nature, I felt both great relief and fear that I would be judged as a heretic or someone who had "gone off the deep end" and was no longer orthodox by clergy colleagues and/or brothers and sisters in the church. My desire to belong and be accepted in a church that had never fully accepted women's authority competed with my need to honor and speak my truth.

Although not many would see it as an expression of my love for the church, this admission was exactly that for me. Many modern women have looked elsewhere to find spiritual truth and belonging. Many of the educated women in my circles have left the church, or they remain for community, social involvement, and outreach, but not because they find the language used to talk about God meaningful. Many screen out the judgmental doctrines of sin and hell. They find an encounter with the living God in the terms they've been offered elusive. Often, it is difficult to state one's doubts and explore spiritual truth in a religious community where one's questions can be received without judgment and be both challenged and affirmed in respectful dialogue, thus deepening one's experience of the Divine.

Why would God, they wonder and I wonder, have made humankind, plants, and animals gendered and, in some cases, mixed-gendered if they weren't intended to be a full expression of the many-sided nature of One who is their Creator? Yes, Christian tradition is rooted in Hebrew tradition and scripture, which were rooted in a culture that recognized males as more valuable: anytime a man was present, the language used was male. However, a mature faith calls us to work through oversimplified representations of God as male that are culture-bound.

Some preachers now acknowledge that God has no gender, but as soon as the sermon ends, we all join in a prayer that begins, "Our Father." We import those words into our personal relationships with God, making no room for the Psalmist's image of God in Psalm 91:1-4 as a mother hen protecting her young under her wings—an image Jesus invoked in Luke 13:34.

We need to imagine The Divine as One who will help us, both men and women, as we pursue the question of purpose which Mary Oliver poses in "The Summer Day," "Tell me, what is it you plan to do with your one wild and precious life?"[25]

I sometimes wonder if perhaps insisting on the feminine as an aspect of God is prophetic rather than heretical. Perhaps Sophia herself is appearing among us with a warning that if our religious institutions do not respect and embrace the feminine as a true dimension of God's nature and teach respect for grandmother/mother earth and care for the environment, they will continue to dwindle toward impotence and will no longer offer a place to grow in wholeness, freedom, and trust in a loving Creator. And grandmother/mother earth will continue to be abused and misused, no longer being able to nurture and feed us.

Amid an unprecedented decline in the Southern Baptist Church, the nation's largest Protestant denomination, the news on June 23, 2023, carried the story of Rick Warren, founder along with his wife, Kay, of the 57,000-member Saddleback Church and author of *The Purpose Driven Life*. Warren was making a plea to be reinstated into the Southern Baptist Convention and to authorize the Convention to call women pastors. He warned that the church would continue to lose members if it did not embrace the pastoral ministries of women. The members of the Southern Baptist Convention (SBC) did not agree with him and voted to keep the policy to exclude women pastors in place on the grounds that their exclusion was scriptural.

The significant decline began in 2000 when the prohibition of women as pastors was added to the SBC constitution, which for 400 years has been anti-creed. In 2015, the removal of churches from the convention began to be enforced.

In his plea to the SBC, Warren said, "I should note that men treat this as a theological issue. Women, however, see it as an existential issue because it denies the gifts, talents, and skills they were sovereignly given by God. It thwarts their identity ... We need everyone in the church to

---

[25] Mary Oliver, *New and Selected Poems, Volume One* (Boston: Beacon Press, 1992), 91.

use all of their gifts. We cannot finish the task with 50 percent of the team forced to sit on the bench. We need everybody on the field."[26]

I find it difficult to understand the decision unless the church sees it as the continuation of a hierarchical system where men are the head of the household. For example, Paul writes in Ephesians 5:22-23, "Wives, be subject to your husbands as to the Lord; for the man is the head of the woman, just as Christ also is the head of the church … but just as the church is subject to Christ, so must women be to their husbands in everything" (New English Bible with Apocrypha).

It is true that men with more testosterone tend to be more aggressive and thus perceived as strong leaders. Still, I choose to follow leaders who are assertive and confident, who have studied the facts, are emotionally clear, and can listen to other wise voices and varied opinions, male or female, before they make a decision. This is my image of what it means to be a man.

The church, synagogue, mosque, and temple are sacred spaces where people gather who are dedicated to passing on faith traditions and interpreting the Holy Scriptures in light of their contemporary context. These Holy Places are among the very few where people of different ages can gather and grow into the stories of the faith of ancestors and mature their understanding of what it means to be a human being created in the image and likeness of God in the present time.

Women know deep in their bones the experience of being bearers, nurturers, and caregivers of new life. Many women who have not birthed children also know their bodies as nurturing places to greater or lesser degrees. We know what it means to care for living things, whether humans, animals, or plants, that depend on us for survival.

Historically, we have been largely confined to the roles, in themselves generous and noble vocations, of teachers caring for children and nurses caring for people who are dependent and ill. Even though these roles of caregiving are essential to the health and well-being of society, women are still paid less for the work they do in these fields and other

---

[26] "Evangelical star takes on Southern Baptists," Washington Post, June 11, 2022.

professions. Jesus himself affirmed the particular value of that work. Many Christians don't.

The other day, I was at dinner with my husband and several friends when a child of two or three years began to cry at the next table. The mother and the other woman at the table looked at the child, ignored her, and ordered another martini. The father picked her up and tried to distract her by giving her a french fried potato, teaching her to soothe herself with food. The child was pulling at her ear and rubbing her eyes. It was about 8:30 p.m. It seemed to me that the parents were not attuned to her needs. The baby was obviously tired, perhaps had an earache, or was teething.

Caring for the needs of a young child was long considered to be the mother's role, and now is becoming recognized as part of the father's role as well. But I wonder how those qualities that have so long been identified as the woman's work, like carrying healthy snacks for a child to dinner in a restaurant or providing a teething ring, can be taught and fully valued in a culture where parents are both working outside the home, and are exhausted at the end of the day.

We are living in a time in history in which patriarchy remains so deeply inscribed and where making money while overlooking attunement to the needs of children, the elderly, and the community at large is justified as "My work is providing for the family. I am tired, so I should be taken care of when I get home from a long day of work."

A view held in the past, in which the traditional role of the male as provider still matters more than the work of nurturing and caretaking of children and the elderly, is shifting. Changing this imbalance may require both partners to sacrifice making more money for the greater health of families and communities. Our son made this decision when our grandson was a teenager. He and his friends needed parental guidance, so our son put his career and well-paying job on hold to provide that care.

Not long ago, I heard an evangelical Christian leader speak about a curriculum he helped create for small groups in churches to foster dialogue among people with different points of view regarding their faith.

161

After the presentation, I approached him to ask in private if the curriculum included any reference to the feminine nature of God, referring to biblical passages in the Hebrew and Christian scriptures. He took a deep breath and responded by mentioning that it would cause people to leave the group immediately and dismiss the study.

At first, I was surprised and then came to realize that to see the Holy Spirit as feminine and value the role of women was still a minority point of view. To affirm the feminine as part of the nature of God was still considered heretical by many Christians.

As I walked away, I was overcome by sadness. I understood that the purpose of this curriculum was to explore the way the Christian Church has been torn apart by politics and to rediscover the core of the faith—certainly a worthy goal. At the same time, so is recognizing womankind as having been created in the image and likeness of God alongside mankind.

The doctrine of the Trinity developed over several centuries. It is a man-made doctrine that was formalized at the Council of Constantinople in 385 CE. Until then, Christians experienced God in three ways as father, son, and holy spirit, and over time, the councils of the church concluded that each was fully divine, sharing the same essence but distinct in personhood, resulting in the doctrine of the Trinity.

As the doctrines of the church continue to grow, we could grow too, and the Holy Spirit could be reimagined in light of our current understanding of the feminine voice of Sophia/Wisdom captured in little-known passages of the Bible. The teachings and Spirit of Wisdom chronicled in the book of Proverbs, Psalms, and the Apocrypha make legitimate what women's voices can contribute to transform faith traditions to be more relevant to members of the church as well as to enrich public dialogue about issues of faith.

The trust in and authority of the church have been undermined by clergy whose actions have done significant harm to their families and congregations. I can only speculate that traumas and unmet early emotional needs have led some church leaders to justify romantic involvement with married members of their congregation while married themselves or to make destructive choices like stealing money, lying to preserve their jobs, or molesting children. Clergy abuse of trust has made it nearly impossible for many children and adults to feel the church is a safe place any longer.

Homophobic speech, abuse of children, and/or racist behaviors have similarly hurt and excluded people from faith communities, where lying is acceptable and injustices are overlooked. As I became more exposed to those outside my white, evangelical Republican "tribe," who followed the way of love and truth, and as I embraced more and more fully the feminine nature of God, I rejected that value system and withdrew from the religious institutions that perpetuated it.

Finding a language of faith that speaks of love, kindness, and justice, and is relevant to our current culture, can attract people to become a part of a community where the language of faith is meaningful and relevant. A spiritual life is not meant to be lived in isolation, excluding those different from us. We cannot bridge the gap with those who have a different worldview without a value system and community to ground us in truth-telling, hope, and forgiveness; a community that nurtures in us the desire to develop love, joy, peace, patience, kindness, goodness, faithfulness, gentleness, and self-control (Galatians 5:22-23, paraphrased).

How do we find meaningful language for The One who created all things and whose energy is eternal love? The character of Wisdom as a feminine expression of God in the Apocrypha and the Hebrew canon offers possibilities for enriching our relationship with the Divine. Ruach, the feminine name for the Divine Spirit moving in the hearts of the Hebrew people, translated as pneuma in the Greek New Testament, can guide us wisely. Just as the goddesses of the ancient Greek myths offered women models of divine feminine power, the divine character of Wisdom offers an image of God as both masculine and feminine, modeling nurture, moral teaching, playfulness, friendship, eroticism, and discipline.

It is impossible to stress too much that Christianity cannot claim universality without an understanding of the nature of the Divine as both male and female. Could the Spirit of "Lady Wisdom" be what is missing in our public dialogue today? The following passages from the NRSV with Apocrypha illustrate more fully the feminine expression of the nature of God, the Spirit of Jesus, and the Holy Spirit, all an expression of the one God who created everyone and everything.

> *Although she is but one, she can do all things, and while remaining in herself, she renews all things; in every generation she passes into holy souls and makes them friends of God, and prophets; for God loves nothing so much as the person who lives with wisdom.*
>
> –Wisdom of Solomon 7:27-28

> *Wisdom is radiant and unfading, And she is easily discerned by those who love her, and is found by those who seek her.*
>
> –Wisdom of Solomon 6:12

> *There is in her a spirit that is intelligent, holy, unique, manifold, subtle, mobile, clear, unpolluted, distinct, invulnerable, loving the good, keen, irresistible, beneficent, humane, steadfast, sure, free from anxiety, all-powerful, overseeing all, and penetrating through all spirits that are intelligent, pure, and altogether subtle … For she is a breath of the power of God, and a pure emanation of the glory of the Almighty. For she is a reflection of eternal light, a spotless mirror of the working of God, and an image of his goodness …*
>
> –Wisdom of Solomon 7:22b, 23, 25-26

> *Search out and seek, and she will become known to you; and when you get hold of her, do not let her go. For at last, you will find the rest she gives, and she will be changed into joy for you.*
>
> –Ecclesiasticus/Ben Sirach 6:27-28

She gave to holy people the reward of their labours; she guided them along a marvellous way, and became a shelter to them by day, and a starry flame through the night.

–Wisdom of Solomon 10:17

Therefore I prayed, and understanding was given me; I called on God, and the spirit of wisdom came to me ... All good things came to me along with her, and in her hands uncounted wealth. I rejoiced in them all, because wisdom leads them; but I did not know that she was their mother.

–Wisdom of Solomon 7:7, 11-12

And if anyone longs for wide experience, she knows the things of old and infers the things to come ...

–Wisdom of Solomon 8:8

Whoever loves her loves life, and those who seek her from early morning are filled with joy.

–Ecclesiasticus/Ben Sirach 4:12

Whoever fears the Lord will do this, and whoever holds to the law will obtain wisdom, She will come to meet him like a mother ... he will lean on her and not fall and he will rely on her and not be put to shame.

–Ecclesiasticus/Ben Sirach 15:1-2, 4

According to research done by Susan Cady, Marian Ronan, and Hal Taussig and published in *Sophia, the Future of Feminist Spirituality,* there are more passages about Wisdom/Sophia in the Hebrew Scriptures/Old Testament than about all other biblical figures except God, David, Moses, and Job.[27]

---

[27] Susan Cady, Marian Ronan, and Hal Taussig, *Sophia: The Future of Feminist Spirituality* (San Francisco: Harper & Row, 1986).

Western Christianity has, for the most part, chosen to ignore Sophia. She has been either repressed or invoked only superficially. According to scripture, she is clearly Divine and not human, so biblical scholars have not known what to do with her. There has been a surge of literature on the subject of Sophia as she is found in the Bible. Two notable voices in this conversation, in addition to Cynthia Bourgeault (*The Wisdom Jesus*), are Sally Douglas (*Jesus Sophia*) and Jann Aldredge-Clanton (*In Search of the Christ-Sophia*).

The character of Sophia challenges Jewish and Christian believers in two significant ways. First, she encourages and demands reflection on the meaning of a wide variety of happenings in the world—suffering in war zones, the plight of refugees, changes in the political process, and evolving understanding of gender identity. She runs counter to those in the priestly class who want to revert to earlier, holier times. She calls humans to think about what is happening in their world and promises that this kind of reflection will be rewarded.

According to Cady, Ronan, and Taussig, Sophia's gender was a challenge. She calls people to herself like God does, presenting herself as a saving figure in history. Is that opening the door to more than one God? The Christian belief in the Trinity—Father, Son, and Holy Spirit—is seen by the Hebrew mind as creating three Gods in the place of one, rather than an attempt to name the three functions of the One God: Creator, Redeemer, and Sustainer.

Although Sophia challenges the Hebrew faith in this way, writers of Hebrew scripture carefully protected monotheism and the covenant between God and Israel while including Sophia in the Biblical story. Ecclesiasticus, also known as "Wisdom of Jesus Ben Sirach," states that Sophia is within God's agreement with Israel.

More recent studies of Sophia by women Biblical scholars shed light on why stories about Sophia would be included in the Bible. As I have mentioned previously, Jesus, though called "Rabbi" by his followers, was from the Middle Eastern Wisdom tradition. Jesus draws much of his teaching from Wisdom/Sophia, but translators of Christian Scripture and many contemporary scholars still do not acknowledge his reliance on that source. In his humanity, Jesus sought wisdom from God, the Source, and was guided by the Holy Spirit of Wisdom as he taught his disciples. Every dimension of the divine emerged in those teachings.

If it is true that the feminine character of Wisdom/Sophia is the source that enables humankind to become friends with God (Wisdom of Solomon 7:27-28), it is sad that she has been so feared, neglected, and repressed by our biblical tradition. Just as women are called to face their fear of physical violence perpetrated by aggressive men who sometimes dominate them in their homes, workplaces, and society at large, in the biblical tradition, men are called to overcome their fear of the engulfing, abandoning, annihilating female. The fear of men toward women and women toward men cripples our faith, our equal-partner relationships in marriage, our work, and the ability of our elected officials to lead in diverse cultural communities.

HOMECOMING

"What"?!?!? I was surprised and pleased when one of my college classmates, a male Presbyterian minister, invited me to preach at our 50th reunion. Two of my senior-year roommates, Cathy and Joy, would be going. The reunion offered me a rare opportunity to see these old friends I hadn't seen for many years.

Still, would it be worth all the effort and expense to get there, not to mention the hours of preparation it would take to prepare a sermon? I was also dealing with extreme hearing loss, which made conversing in groups very difficult. And why would a male Presbyterian minister ask a female Episcopal priest to preach when he could have chosen to preach himself?

Women weren't admitted to ordination in either the Presbyterian Church or the Episcopal Church when we were in college, and even now, it is somewhat rare in parts of the church. Although I was ordained long ago, I am not an experienced preacher, having served largely as a pastoral counselor and a part-time clergy assistant.

I felt unprepared and scared to say yes. Like too many young women, I worked so hard to be liked by everyone in college. I kept part of myself hidden to be popular. I believed I wouldn't have been elected May Queen, Homecoming Queen, or President of my sorority if I had shared my whole self. Could I now be honest and brave enough to speak my truth about what I believe about God and share my faith journey, knowing some might not like what I have to say?

Chapel had been central to our experience at this small college. The requirement to attend several times a week was often received with a good deal of grumbling and, in some cases, outright rebellion. Would anyone even attend this chapel service when it is not required?

Despite my anxieties, I agreed to preach. Then, the hard work of crafting the sermon began. Did I dare preach the hard truths I had arrived at over decades of growth? The sermon emerged from days of wrestling with myself and listening for the guidance of the Holy Spirit of wisdom. (I have added it in its entirety as an appendix at the back of the book. One of my favorite parts of the sermon was the story about a woman named Rose and a man named Larry.)

The return to Westminster College after 50 years was an important homecoming for me. It united my present with my past. In the introduction to an updated version of Richard Rohr's *Falling Upward*, Brene Brown wrote about another kind of homecoming: a spiritual homesickness not as a temporary going back to a place of temporary belonging but rather a longing for "a home that exists only inside me."[28] Longing for home, a place I really belonged, is one of my earliest memories and perhaps a longing we all share.

---

[28] Richard Rohr, *Falling Upward, Revised and Updated: A Spirituality for the Two Halves of Life* (Jossey-Bass, 2023).

A NEW SEASON

Moving & Downsizing

What a roller coaster of grief and joy I am feeling. I woke up yesterday holding back the river of tears that came on me suddenly at 6 a.m. Bill felt the bed shaking, so he turned over and wrapped his arms around me and held me until I was ready to talk.

I was so grateful he didn't ask, "What's wrong?" I didn't want to talk right then; I just wanted to empty the well of tears I had been holding back since we decided to move out of our family home, where we had lived for 38 years, and leave the neighborhood and community where I had put down roots. I loved our home, our backyard, and the gardens surrounding the house with camellia bushes, the red and white ones that bloomed at Christmastime, and the pink and white ones that blossomed in the spring, even though they had become too much work for me to maintain even with a gardener's help.

The purple irises and fragrant daffodils and lilac bushes I had planted over the years alerted me that spring was here and summer was not far behind. The numerous azaleas of many colors, which had begun as small cuttings from our neighbor across the street, were now mature and filled one side of the house next to the driveway.

Our son, Sean, was aware that I, in particular, would be interested in downsizing if we could find a smaller home with an elevator in which we could age in place, so he was looking for a place near him that we could move to. One day, he spotted a three-story town house six blocks from their new town house, which seemed like it might be just right for us. It wasn't far from our current home but in a different county, about a 20-minute drive away.

We had previously decided to stay where we were and add a chair mover to our wide entrance hall that could take us up and down the stairs when we could no longer navigate them. For now, Bill and I were healthy and could still manage to do much of the maintenance work in our home. We loved the peace and quiet of our private backyard in the suburbs. We planned to hire someone to help us do the things we could no longer do when that time came.

We were both avoiding the reality that Bill had already turned 84, and I had stepped over the 80 line. How much longer would we be mentally and physically healthy? And, too, I felt the burden of caring for a house that was too big for us now that our children were grown and gone. Although it was good to have extra space to welcome friends and family on holidays, it was a lot of house and landscaping to maintain.

Even though it had become increasingly clear that I no longer wanted to spend my time and energy in that way, I had resigned myself to staying since we didn't see any better option. It was comfortable and familiar. I had friends close by and knew where the cleaners, gas stations, and grocery stores were within a short driving distance.

Intending to stay put, I had the upstairs bedrooms painted a beautiful soft blue and light aqua, had window treatments installed to match the slatted blinds downstairs on the front of the house, and moved Bill's office upstairs into one of the newly decorated rooms. He loved looking out his windows to the front yard and street below while working at his desk.

My office overlooked the backyard, which was alive with butterflies, squirrels, and chipmunks scurrying around the flagstone patio and birds flitting from the ancient oak to the miniature maple and flowering bushes. The house and yard were just like we wanted them.

Then we went to see the town house. It had everything we were looking for but was so much smaller than our home, and most of our furnishings would no longer fit. It was in the middle of Covid, so no one was having open houses or moving sales. My beautiful blond oval dining room table with a border of inlaid darker wood around the edge, which could seat 14 for dinner, would have to go to auction or Goodwill. The eight comfortable black and beige striped upholstered parson dining room chairs, my grandmother's colorful oriental rug, and our new side tables in the sunroom would all have to be donated or sold. Oh my, how could I let these things go? All the memories held in three generations of furniture and rugs, all the time spent looking for just the right piece of furniture and art for the walls to create a place of beauty and peace.

I suffered in silence for a while and then spoke to Bill, "I don't know if I can do this; it is so much loss all at once. I have spent a lot of my energy renovating, creating, and maintaining our beautiful home." At the same time, it made sense to move closer to our son and downsize, and it was clear these town houses sold very quickly. We needed to make a decision right away.

We put in an offer on the town house, and it was accepted two days later. Immediately, we began the agonizing process of getting our home ready to sell, emptying the garage and attic, and seeing that everything was in tip-top shape. We celebrated that we had maintained our home so well over the years, so it didn't take long to get it ready to show. We grieved that our home was finally the way we wanted it to be, and now we would leave it. It went up for sale and three days later was sold.

Respecting the social distance required to be safe during the Covid pandemic, our son, granddaughter, daughter-in-law, and daughter all came to the house and looked at what we could not take with us. They didn't want many of the things that have been in our families for at least three generations. I learned what our children and grandchildren value and how their lifestyles differ from the one I knew as a young person and as an adult, having grown up with parents who had lived through the Depression and saved everything. Things like a well-made brown dresser and twin beds passed on first to my mother and then to me were of no interest to them. They wanted white furniture and modern rugs that could easily be replaced when they became worn or stained. My friend told me about a book she had read that captured the essence of what

I was experiencing. The message was, "Nobody wants your old brown furniture or your grandmother's china."

Even though I looked forward to the freedom I imagined would come with fewer choices of what to wear and less home and garden to maintain, I was surprised at how attached I was to books, china that I rarely used, furniture and art we no longer had walls to hang it on, or clothes that were well made and barely worn, one size too small, but that I imagined I would at some point get back into when I lost weight.

I had already retired from my last church position. I maintained a small counseling practice, preparing couples for marriage, and had already begun the process of letting go of a professional identity.

The other day, I pulled out a bag containing clerical stoles and women's clerical blouses. "I will keep a few of the black ones for occasions when I still need to wear a clerical collar," I said to myself, "but the rest I will pass on to young women preparing for ordination who need them."

The freedom from attachment to material things, however, has been and continues to be hard-won. I wanted to take back the blue striped clerical blouse and the gray one, which were two of my favorites, but I resisted. Washing and ironing the blouses allowed me to be grateful for the years I wore them and to pray for those who would wear them in the future.

The first time I downsized, I was getting ready to move into our current town house, which was half the size of our current home. The second time I downsized was when we got to our new home and I realized that we had little to no storage space. I stuffed everything I could into the space I had with no order to it. I am a pretty organized person, and for these first two years, I told myself, I would get to reorganizing my closets and drawers in time. But now, I have to get rid of even more things that have memories. Christmas tree ornaments made by our children and grandchildren, baby blankets that belonged to our children, and a second set of china will be discarded.

Now, I am downsizing for the third time. This time, I have help from a professional with a home organizing business. I engaged her to help me once I came to terms with the fact that I couldn't do it myself.

I had too many memories attached to things I didn't have space for. I needed help.

As we worked side by side, my helper, Allison, turned and looked at me as I tried to decide about the multiple sets of flatware and china I wanted to keep and gently asked, "When do you think you will be having 20 people for dinner again? Do you remember when you last used that platter?" Or, "How long have you been saving that bar of organic soap? Do you think you will use it?" The saved soap is like the half-burned candles I save to use until they are stubs, when I have a whole drawer full of new candles waiting to be used. The truth is that I have been saving that soap for a special occasion that hasn't presented itself for 15 years, and we mostly use liquid hand soap, so it would be good to do something with it now. It is so hard for me to throw something away if it might be usable, but if I don't plan to use it, would anyone else want to use a bar of soap wrapped in a yellowing cellophane wrapper clearly showing its age?

Slowly, I am beginning to realize that I am in a different phase of life. We won't be entertaining large groups, both because we don't have the space and because I don't have the energy to do all it takes to prepare for large group meals.

The conscious awareness to live in the present and detach from what was invites me to make space in my life and declutter. Earlier in my life, when Bill and I were newly married, making a home and preparing for children, I was nesting and accumulating things I would need to entertain guests and raise a family. At this stage of life, I don't want to withdraw. I want to stay creative and engaged in my community and serve where I can, but age requires adjusting my goals and being realistic about my energy to clear space to act on my new priorities.

I feel lighter, having gotten through the kitchen and bathrooms, keeping only two sets of sheets for the beds and two sets of towels for each bathroom, giving the rest away for someone else to use and to create space. And, it is okay to buy a few things to make our current home a place I love living in, like a matching set of towels for the bathrooms.

We added a Murphy bed in Bill's office to create more open space and make it primarily an office rather than having a queen-sized bed taking up a large portion of the room that is only used once in a while; then, it isn't either a guest bedroom or an office. Now, Bill can have an office and a comfortable chair to sit in and enjoy his space, with the bed tucked into the wall with a beautiful wood front and desk attached. Now that I am more settled, I ask myself, *Am I happy? Or is happiness the goal of my life right now?*

Neil Pasricha, a *New York Times* bestselling author, has written ten books on happiness, gratitude, habits, and resilience that share how to cultivate a positive mindset. There are practices one can do each day to help one's mood and feel happier—practices like doing what you love, being grateful for small things, exercising each day, outside if possible, getting away from technology, saving time, and wearing the same clothes over and over if you feel comfortable in them, nurturing meaningful relationships, making a to-do list the night before, and doing the hardest ones first in the morning. I like Pasricha's idea of creating daily disciplines in one's life to bring order out of what could be a chaotic day and, thus, feel happier. At the same time, I am not sure this gets to the deeper question of inner happiness the scripture points to.

As I read The Beatitudes in the Good News Bible, I was struck by the fact that words matter. In some translations, they begin with "Blessed are those …" In this translation, they were translated as "Happy are those who are humble," "Happy are those who are merciful to others," and "Happy are those who work for peace."

In our culture, happiness is primarily understood in external measures, such as "I am feeling good, and everything in my life is going well." However, I know that everyone experiences suffering, conflict, and loss. In our corporate life as a nation and among our work colleagues, sometimes things are not going well, and happiness is beyond reach, no matter what we do to create the conditions. I have come to see that living in a state of happiness is a false hope; happiness comes and goes and depends on external circumstances or whether my expectations of how things should go are met.

Perhaps the Beatitudes would be better translated as "Hopeful are the meek," "Hopeful are the merciful," and "Hopeful are the peacemakers." Embracing hope does not deny the reality of living in a painful situation. It isn't the same as having a positive attitude or seeing the glass as half full; it can exist when it is nearly empty.

Hope is grounded in possibility. As humans, we will fail in our attempts to love ourselves and others unconditionally because we have free will to choose. Sometimes, we make poor choices, and sometimes, we believe negative things we have been told about ourselves that aren't true but are buried in our unconscious mind and cause us to feel unworthy. And terrible things happen … just because they do.

Focusing on the hope of the resurrection gives me eyes to see the seeds of new life emerging from personal and corporate suffering and pain. It frees me of guilt and shame and prompts me to set my intention to do better next time once I face the harm I have done if I have been the cause and make restitution if possible. I can question things I have been told about myself and ask, "Is this really true?" Then, I can get back into the flow of the energy of the created universe, which is love.

An image that has helped me understand this came from a boatman on the Snake River at the base of the Grand Teton Mountains one summer. He explained that it is the heat and the flames of the forest fire that split open the pine cones and release the seeds for new trees to grow.

Having a perception of the new life that is possible out of loss gives us a vision for the future. For me, that vision includes the hope that new life will come out of the suffering I experience as an individual but also as a nation and world.

And too, that image of new life growing following the fire in the forest sparked my hope that we will come to our senses about the destruction of our environment. We must reform our thinking from dominating the earth to being partners with our natural world and stop using and abusing our resources so that we can have more and more and more. Hope doesn't mean that the wrongs of this world will be made right now or even in our lifetime, but it is often the energy behind the just action that begins things to move in a positive direction.

Rebecca Solnit wrote in an article for *The Guardian* in 2016, "Your opponents would love you to believe that it's hopeless, that you have no power, that there's no reason to act, that you can't win. No matter who or what your opponents are in life, hope isn't something you have to give up, ever."[29]

My hopelessness was pervasive when Bill and I had reached a point when there seemed to be no way forward in our marriage. But then, I began to see small steps I could take, propelled by a value system grounded in love and hope. Being engaged with people who supported our vision for our family and community kept us from giving up the hope that, with help, we could sustain the lifelong marriage covenant we had made. And I sought training to help us learn how to communicate respectfully.

Having crossed the threshold of 80 years, I am shedding old skin and growing a new layer to sustain my life and relationships for the future, based more on "being" than on doing and possessing. I am finding a newfound freedom to be myself and care less about how others see me. That doesn't mean I take my relationships for granted; I care when there seems to be a disruption or misunderstanding and move to clear the air.

I came into the world dependent and powerless. I will leave it, having let go of the symbols of power accumulated over time, contained in material things, titles, education, etc., to discover the power of just being myself. In the end, I will be dependent and powerless again, dependent on family and friends and perhaps paid nursing care.

Do I have a new call emerging now? If so, what will it be besides being faithful to my marriage to Bill and caring for family and friends? Who will be my partner to share in, encourage my vision, and support me in finding a new purpose? As I engage this time of discernment, I ask myself, "What am I good at? What helps others? What gives me joy? What do I have the energy to do?"

---

[29] Rebecca Solnit, "The Case for Hope," The Guardian, January 23, 2016. https://www.the-guardian.com/commentisfree/2016/jan/23/the-case-for-hope.

Whatever it is, now that I can hear again, I wonder who needs to be listened to. Perhaps I can offer a listening ear to facilitate folks seeking to let go of beliefs and patterns that no longer serve them in their relationship with the Divine to develop a faith that sustains them now. Although that seems spontaneous and ordinary, the trajectory of my life has moved from being special and structured to being an ordinary human being living consciously and spontaneously in the present.

Letting Go of the Roles That Define Us

Having retired from my position as adjunct clergy at the last church where I served and having moved into a new community, I thought, *Where is my institutional religious belonging rooted now, and is that even a relevant question to be asking? How do I make friends in a new faith community without a role to define me?*

The Reverend Samuel Shoemaker, Episcopal priest and advisor to Bill W., one of the founders of AA, wrote *I Stand By the Door*. I found myself drawn to the same position Sam took in the church. I wanted to stand by the door and welcome seekers wanting to explore faith in community and find someone who would care to listen to their story and care for them.

Although he was the rector (i.e., senior pastor), having served a number of large churches over the years, Sam saw himself as someone who stood by the door, not going too far in like a monastic nor too far out, which is the position of many "nons" who have left the institutional church and who describe themselves as spiritual but not religious. Sam chose to welcome everyone and invite them in no matter where they were in their faith journey or the circumstances of their lives.

So today, I ask myself, "How do I stand by the door?" I don't feel called to go too far in so that I become insensitive to those who cry for justice or too far out, detaching from the many things the church offers that could deepen my faith and provide opportunities for service.

When I walk into church now that I am retired and have moved, I know almost no one. There are good things about being anonymous as

179

a clergyperson entering a church, including the freedom to truly focus on my relationship with God and worship apart from greeting people.

At the same time, I am looking for friendship and belonging in my new community, and my sense of loss regarding what I have left behind and feelings of isolation increase when I know no one at church. I feel stuck and conflicted.

I want to belong to a church community, but I no longer have the energy to invest in the many worthy service projects of my local church. My now more limited energy to serve is being invested largely in being Bill's traveling companion. He is invited to give the history of the movement to new staff and volunteers around the country at Communities in Schools sites and celebrate their steady growth and success in support of children and young people to stay in school and graduate on time. And I am drawn to be at home in silence more and more, thinking, reflecting, and writing.

One place I felt that belonging and community was in the group of people who responded to a blurb in the Arlington County newsletter for retired people. The group met just up the street from our house. After the first meeting, it just felt right. I knew I would commit to this group, which was being guided through a book by Julia Cameron called *The Artist's Way*.

I decided to leave the group when I no longer lived in Arlington. It was at the beginning of Covid, and we were isolated in our new home. I was sad and lonely, but decided it was important to let go of past community involvement, a 30-minute drive away, to invest in the present.

I pondered how I would make new friends when I'm now in my 80s. I have many friends, but they are scattered around the country, in DC or out in another part of Virginia, in my old neighborhood, and in several worship communities I have served as a clergy person. I am living side by side and just across the courtyard from neighbors, but how do I go about meeting them and developing friendships at this age, especially when everyone, for the first two years we've lived in our new home, was hiding behind closed doors, fearing they would get the Covid virus?

Reflecting on starting again in a new church community, some of my earlier questions surfaced. I wonder if I have internalized the need to receive the bread and wine in community as a part of my regular spiritual practice. It seems that I do because, again, it feels like something is missing when I don't receive the consecrated bread and wine in a gathered church community. What do I believe happens when the bread and wine are consecrated by the priest? Have I truly internalized an understanding of the Eucharist as in some way a real presence, yet mysterious at the same time?

Although many have tried to explain it, the Eucharist is a mystery at its core, and each person experiences it differently. It is one thing to believe that the physical elements somehow offer me life-giving energy that can comfort me when I am sad, open my heart to feel gratitude and joy, receive forgiveness for myself and others, and give compassion to serve those in need. It is another thing to experience the mystery of the Holy Spirit entering my heart and providing peace and love while kneeling at the altar rail.

Or, outside the context of liturgical worship, do I enter into the resurrectional life of Jesus and become "his hands, feet, and heart" in my relationships and daily life by acting in love in simple ways that seek nothing in return but serve the needs of my neighbor?

Of course, my hearing loss and cochlear implant surgery kept me close to home when my hearing was limited and during the time of healing from surgery. I have to remind myself of my age and to listen to my body and heart to do what I am called to do and say "no" to those things I am not drawn to do.

Looking from another angle, my feeling of detachment in the church now, without a role to define my place and my belonging, may be rooted in my childhood sense of not belonging and the loneliness of being an only child. Now that that thought has surfaced, it is worth exploring. It offers me another opportunity to let go of old "baggage" I no longer want to carry, although it will take time and energy and is not something I look forward to delving into.

CELEBRATION OF LIFE

Completions

In my work as a priest, I have been called now and then to be present to those who are sick and near death, usually older people who are reaching the end of a long life's journey. Most were church members who had come to a place of peace, believing they were going home to God.

I have also talked with people who have left their bodies and come back. Such stories are more widely known now than some years ago, as people have written accounts of their experience. The people who tell them are full of assurance, having seen loved ones and felt the pull toward indescribable light and love. Each encounter has helped make me willing and hopeful to think about the end of my life.

Some months ago, I received a phone call and was asked if I could visit a young woman who was dying. I hadn't had much opportunity to walk someone through the long process of letting go of life. But this time, the invitation was to stay with her—to come frequently during those hard weeks, sit with her, and grieve with her friends and family as she continued to decline physically and fought to stay alive.

The homily I was asked to preach at her Celebration of Life was challenging for me. Though her family shared my Christian faith, neither the woman nor her close friends talked about their faith. They seemed to share a general belief in Divine Presence and practiced a sacrificial love for their friend daily by caring for her physical and emotional needs. I wanted to honor her wishes and those of her family and friends, and speak of my faith that might offer hope. I include the sermon here because it reflects some of my unfolding thoughts about death as I increasingly think about my own.

Celebration of Life Sermon: Rachel

May 13, 2024

It has been a privilege to have visited with, listened to, and prayed with Rachel over the last six weeks. I didn't know Rachel before she became very ill. Her friend, Rebecca, who is also my friend, asked me to visit her since she didn't connect with the hospital chaplains who dropped in.

Sometimes, when you least expect it, a person or situation calls you or "Has your name on it," so to speak. It became clear to me that the relationship Rachel and I developed very quickly was mine to midwife through to the end, and it was my task to find common language to speak about the Source of Life and Goodness that offered us *both* a way to speak our truth to each other in love.

Although Rachel did everything she could to reverse the cancer in her body, it continued to grow. On my last visit with her, as I sat by her bedside, holding her hand, praying silently and aloud, while she could still hear but conversation was very limited, her tears came, and she asked, "Why?" Soon after that, she went into a coma.

In the moment she asked, the answer that welled up inside of me was, "It's not fair." Even as I said that, my thoughts turned to the great mysteries of death and life. How does one engage with the mystery of death? I imagine one of the purposes of our religious rituals is to help us confront that question in a meaningful way and enter the mystery of life and death to seek, and hopefully find, comfort and hope, if not an answer to the question of WHY.

We are all born into the belief system of our families, be it one of the three Abrahamic faiths: Christian, Jewish, or Muslim, or no institutional religious practice. No matter what was passed on to us from our families, part of the challenge of maturing and growing to become a more loving human being is to find our own path to the God of our understanding, as they say in AA.

Rachel did just that. Baptized as a Christian in the Roman Catholic Church, she began her journey toward finding the truth that made sense to her and connected her with a loving energy she found in meditation called *The Source*.

During one of my early visits, after Rachel had left the hospital and gone home to hospice care, I asked her, "How is your heart today?"

She responded, "I have been having a recurring dream of a flowing river, and in the river are these little things floating by that look like fortune cookies. When I pick one out of the river and open it, I read the message, and sometimes I say to myself, 'This isn't true'—messages like, 'It's your fault' or 'You are being punished,' and I put those messages back, knowing it isn't true. Then there are others. When I open them, they say things like, 'Gratitude,' or 'You are loved,' and I keep those."

Rachel continued to do her inner spiritual work, releasing the past and getting ready to enter the next dimension, letting go of all that troubled her or didn't serve her highest good. It was such a privilege to be a part of Rachel's Care Circle. Her fiancé, friends, and family surrounded her and faithfully responded to her requests and needs with amazing respect and tenderness. Day after day, week after week, they embraced her suffering and pain and loved her through it. It was an amazing community of love and grace to behold and be a part of.

I suppose that when we are called into another's moment of dying or loss, it may be for our healing and growth, as well as for the person for whom we are caring. Being with Rachel brought back memories of sitting with my mother, who was in hospice care when she, too, a young 63, wanted to beat the cancer that had invaded all parts of her body. She, too, had a lot to live for, dreams yet unfulfilled; she didn't want to die.

Saying "goodbye" to a loved one is so hard. It is hard for the person who is dying, too. They need to be kept safe and use their energy to deal with physical pain and the grief of passing from this world to the next, especially when you are young and letting go of unfulfilled dreams.

I learned a lot from Rachel. Her sense of the unfairness of dying so young when she had tried so hard to care for her health makes sense to me. Her willingness to speak her truth about her connection to The Source of Life, which she accessed through meditation, also makes sense. I respect the courage it took for her to be so clear and honest with an Episcopal priest, whom she barely knew, who represented the institutional church, about her personal understanding of the source of life, love, and truth.

Our conversations prompted me to ask myself again: what is *The Source of my faith?* Is my language for God, the Creator of the world of nature—the trees, the mountains, the oceans, and humankind, created male and female in God's image, different from Rachel's understanding of The Source?

And what about Jesus? Rachel and I didn't have time to explore who Jesus was to her. I am twice Rachel's age and so have had a lot longer to live with Jesus, the human expression of the Divine, as my teacher on the path to forgiveness and to develop the sight to look for new life to emerge out of death and loss.

Because Jesus was human, he knew it is human to make mistakes as we live our lives and use our free will to choose between the good and the not good. His message was to keep your eyes open, learn from your mistakes, know you are forgiven and forgive others for the wrong they have done to you, act out of love, and look for new life that will come out of the mistakes, losses, and pain to experience the joy of being alive.

And finally, the third part of my faith, "Was the Holy Spirit of Wisdom, whose discernment I sought through prayer and meditation to reveal truth and offer healing of the past and peace in the present, the same as The Source which Rachel accessed in a dream of a flowing river with fortune cookie messages floating by, revealing truth, healing, and wisdom or by focusing on the breath and opening one's heart to love in contemplation? Was it the same experience, called by a different name?"

Having seen many faces of God while serving as a priest at the National Cathedral, a House of Prayer for All People, I no longer look for one way or the right way to talk about or talk to God, The Source of Life, Beauty, and Love. I do think we have a choice as to whether we say "Yes" to a loving presence in the universe and decide if we want to be a part of that flow, seeking understanding and moving beyond judgment to do what we can to restore connection with those who have done us wrong. That is the spiritual work each of us is invited to do—to engage mystery and find love, community, and hope.

May each of us have eyes to behold new life emerging out of our sadness. See the light and beauty Rachel saw through her photographer's lens. And may we find moments of joy in the midst of our grief, which can light our path going forward.

—Amen

Living in the fourth quarter of life, I think more often about coming to the end of my journey. I have begun to read David Gibson's *Living Life Backwards*, a reflection on the Book of Ecclesiastes. He suggests that "Left to our own devices, we tend to live life forward. One day follows another, and weeks turn into months and months into years. We do not know the future, but we plan and hope and dream of where we will be, what we would like to be doing, and whom we might be with. We live forward."[30]

Gibson suggests that we use our imaginations to consider what it would be like to live life backwards, beginning with the fact that our life on this earth will surely end. "Ecclesiastes invites us to let the end sculpt our priorities and goals, our greatest ambitions, and our strongest desires," he writes.

I know that time is coming, though I don't know when or how. But there is still more life to live, so I am pondering his invitation to let the end sculpt my priorities for today and for the future.

Finally, I am grounded in the promise that the Spirit of Love is in me and with me as my Companion each day going forward. In the

---

[30] David Gibson, *Living Life Backward: How Ecclesiastes Teaches Us to Live in Light of the End* (Wheaton, IL: Crossway, 2017).

end, there is nothing to fear. Jesus has shown me how to live in freedom and to know that through his resurrection, new life will emerge from my death.

At the end of my life on earth, life hasn't ended, it has merely changed, and my spirit has become one with the Spirit of Eternal Love. I give thanks for a long life, allowing time to let go of my fear of abandonment as well as the need to belong and embrace the knowledge that the Spirit of a loving God that lives in me now will go with me into the next life.

Celebrating Rosalynn Carter

When the invitation to Rosalynn Carter's Celebration of Life arrived, I struggled with whether to go. Bill was sure he would go; it was because of President and Rosalynn Carter that Communities in Schools gained a national presence. Plus, Chip Carter, President Carter and Rosalynn's son, worked for Bill. Years ago, the Carters had invited us to come down to the Carter Center to meet with them about coming back to Atlanta to apply the principles of Communities in Schools to a wider context in the community, not just in the schools. But we chose to stay where we were.

I continued to ponder whether to spend the money and time to go to celebrate Rosalynn's life. I often wonder how important it is for me to be at various occasions when Bill is the primary contact person with a closer relationship. What came to me as I meditated on going was, "Who are your heroes?"

I could never think of what to say when asked that question, but on this occasion, I suddenly thought, *Rosalynn is my hero(heroine)*. I don't usually think of people that way. Acknowledging her as one of my heroes made it important to go and honor her and myself, in a sense.

We flew down the day before the service. The family was hosting an event at the Botanical Gardens with a small group of people, mostly trustees of the Carter Center and out-of-town guests. We got there in time to attend the evening reception.

The Botanical Gardens were decorated for Christmas. It was so beautiful—like a fairyland—with so many colors and different constellations of waterfalls and lights. It was an unexpected gift that we got a taste of the beautifully lit gardens as we entered and left the reception.

We arrived early the next day at the Glenn Memorial Church on the Emory campus, where Lani had gone to preschool while I was a student at Candler School of Theology, to celebrate Rosalynn's life.

Months later, during a gathering to celebrate President Carter's life, one of his sons told the story of the President and First Lady driving back to Plains, Georgia, following his losing the election. Rosalynn would not speak to him. After they had arrived in Plains, he asked her why she wasn't talking to him. She replied that he had promised her that they would see the world, and now they were going back to their hometown of Plains, Georgia, to live.

His promise was providential in that, in time, she did see the world, but not on a cruise ship or touring from country to country, but by traveling around the world building Habitat Houses. What an amazing example of how a kind of death in losing the election and a promise made for a vision of the future could be fulfilled in a way that I am guessing President Carter did not anticipate or know how it would be actualized. It was a great example of how new life can emerge from a difficult ending if one has eyes to see.

Returning to the celebration of the life of the First Lady, the Atlanta Symphony Orchestra chamber chorus, string quartet, and brass quartet performed a variety of musical selections as we waited for the service to begin and family and dignitaries to be seated. Arriving at about 9:30 a.m., we sat in the church until 1:00, when the service started. The music played, and the chorus sang for much of that time.

The hymns included one of my favorites, "Morning Has Broken." The procession of the family, First Ladies, and Presidents Carter, Clinton, and Biden entered to the singing of "America the Beautiful." Then, there were opening remarks and the Lord's prayer. The orchestra played, and the chorus sang "Blessed Assurance."

Tributes were given by Judy Woodruff, Chip Carter, and Amy Carter, who read a letter her father had written to her mother when they were newly married and he was away doing military service. The grandchildren did readings from scripture. Their grandson, the Honorable Jason James Carter, who ran for governor of Georgia, also spoke.

Garth Brooks and Trisha Yearwood sang "Imagine." Then we all sang "Let there be Peace on Earth." I, along with many others, was really moved. We sang it through twice. They brought President Carter in on a wheelchair stretcher. He could sit up but had his legs stretched out in front of him. I was in awe of his commitment and love and hoped he would make it through the service. He was supposed to have only a week to live when he left hospice care, but months had passed since then. He was very frail, but he came, nevertheless. He wanted to be with her when she died, when the community celebrated her life, and when her body was laid to rest.

As I reflected on her life, I was struck by who Rosalynn was. She embodied a lot of my values. She was the first First Lady to go to a cabinet meeting. She would ask Jimmy what happened at the meetings—they were such close partners. He finally said, "It's hard for me to remember all that happened. Why don't you just come to the meeting?"

The same thing happens to me when Bill goes to a board meeting of organizations I'm also involved with and I'm not there—I want to know. I went to the last one of his LeaderComm Board meetings, and he said, "I'm so glad you were here. It would have been hard to tell it all to you."

I admired the way the Carters lived out their partnership in marriage. I know life wasn't always smooth at home with four children finding who they were while living in the public eye, but Rosalynn was always engaged with them and loved them. That was part of her character.

I was reminded again of Proverbs 31: "An excellent wife who can find? She is far more precious than jewels. The heart of her husband trusts in her." She was that kind of wife—the woman who went into the marketplace to add her energy and influence to help those who were suffering from mental illness, for example, but she also saw to the needs of her household. That's always been a model for me—to be involved in the world, offer my gifts to the wider community, and be a good wife and mother invested in making a home for us.

At the end of the service, when we sang "Let There Be Peace on Earth," I thought that is really all we can do: "Let there be peace on earth and let it begin with me." Otherwise, I get into judging women and men elected to serve in public life, their decisions, and what seems to be their failures of public trust. So, "Let it begin with me" seemed like something any of us could do to be peacemakers.

The words of the hymn were such a good way to honor Rosalynn, who, of course, was not perfect and made mistakes, but lived her life with such grace. As their minister from Plains, Georgia, said of her, "Rosalynn didn't worship the elephant or the donkey; she worshiped the Lamb."

On the way to the service, our Uber driver was a young man from Ethiopia. I could tell he had a good heart. I asked what he was interested in, excited about, and looking forward to, and he said, "It's hard for me to say because I feel as though all I do is drive for Uber 12 hours a day to support my wife and two children. When I was young, I had ambitions, but now all I can do is drive to make enough to pay the bills."

I said, "What's your dream for the future?"

He said, "I had a couple of small businesses, but they lost money. Now, I don't really have a vision for the future."

I said, "Would you want to go back to school?"

He said, "I'm not smart. I don't remember things."

Bill said, "I think you would be good at sales."

Bill told the young man his story about dropping out of school, getting work selling pots and pans, and making good money from new brides who were creating their hope chests. The pots and pans were of good quality, and Bill was a good salesman.

We all laughed. Then I remembered that our friend, Neil, had started Partners in Change, a nonprofit to help coach the parents of young people in Communities in Schools to help them get out of poverty while their children gain an education.

I have learned that coaching is different from mentoring. It's different, too, from the social work approach with which I am familiar, which is more directive. A coach sits with a person and asks the kinds of questions that help them envision their hopes for themselves; the answers emerge from inside of them.

I suggested we give Neil's number to the young man, and perhaps he could get a coach. Neil is training employees from various companies who want to do volunteer work to help adults move out of poverty. Rather than volunteering to paint a building, for example, they could volunteer and be trained to coach.

BlackRock, a global investment management company, for instance, has offices in Atlanta with many employees, some of whom want to volunteer their time to be trained to be coaches. Once the person receiving the coaching is trained, they "pay it forward" by committing to coaching another.

Bill gave our new young friend his card and put Neil's number on it. I felt as though, in addition to making the trip to honor Rosalynn, we were there to encourage this young man's hope for his future. He'd tried so many ways to get ahead, but none had worked. He was out of ideas and had lost hope. He said, "I need help; I have helped so many others, but now I have nothing left to give." He dropped us off. I don't even know his name, but it felt like the Spirit guided that conversation, offering hope for another chance.

Loyalty's Lessons

What does being a loyal American, friend, or marriage partner mean? And what does loyalty look like in the life of a Christian who embraces the values of truth-telling, kindness, love, justice, protection of the widow and orphan, and supporting life in all its forms?

Watching the news, I am confronted with these questions constantly. My community includes people with differing world views. There is a radical difference between identifying as a Christian Nationalist or a Christian Patriot. My definition of Christian Nationalism is "my country right or wrong." I am loyal to my country and a particular structure of governance, even if my country or its leadership erodes the values of truth-telling and justice and no longer supports the rule of law, moral behavior, or kindness and respect for all people.

That kind of blind loyalty is not life-giving, and it is not Christian. Also, we who have grown up in the Christian faith need to open our minds and hearts to the fact that people of different religions live in the U.S., love God, and live according to the way of love. To attempt to combine church and state and legislate our country to be exclusively Christian excludes whole groups of good, God-fearing people.

To me, Christian Patriotism means I am loyal to my country and will do all in my power to support life, just laws, and action, and care for the sick, widows, orphans, and children in need.

I love my country and, at the same time, can think critically about its laws, leadership, and the values it promotes. When power and money are the driving force and truth is no longer being respected, I can speak the truth about that betrayal and hold those in leadership accountable to realign the laws and actions of the country with who we say we are as Americans, encompassing many religious traditions.

We never fully know the consequences of our actions until we can look back, but we can know what our intentions are when we make the decisions we make. Will this decision be life-giving? Does it serve the greater good, not just my group's investment in its power and money or status? Is this decision in alignment with my value system?

We have just been through a very stressful national election to determine the future of our country. There seemed to be many single issues that drew people to vote a certain way based on their personal experience. There are multiple sides to every issue.

For example, people from Texas suffered from the influx of undocumented people who came with no resources and much need. However, many of those coming were running for their lives to escape danger at home. We are a country made up of immigrants. Some voted based on their view of abortion, for others, it was women's rights, for some, it was race or too much government regulation, for others, it was the environment, and for others, it was the price of groceries or the plight of Russia or Ukraine.

It reminds me of the various ways one can read the scripture, just like Bob, the man I mentioned earlier who began to read the scripture in prison following Joe's visits and was amazed at the maiming and killing that was taking place in the Old Testament that seemed to justify what they did in the mob. One experience can set a view of God that is difficult to change if one focuses on a single traumatic experience we or our family suffered in the past.

I hope we can read the scripture from the whole arc of who God is and what Jesus taught about living a faithful life, and do the same in our national politics. Who are we? Who do we aspire to be? What is good for the whole? How important is truth-telling? As we move back and forth between hopes and fears, we come up with our worldview, constantly confronting the old with the new, and are invited to face our fears and release them.

I have found this to be true for me as a follower of Jesus's Way of love, mercy, truth, and justice. I am one limited human who sees "through a glass darkly." To think otherwise leads to presumptuous self-deception. As we listen to each other's understanding of truth in the present time of scientific discovery and cultural change through prayer and meditation, we can ask the Holy Spirit of Wisdom to help us discern the most loving and best action to take for the good of all.

Forgiveness

Not long ago, I was taking my morning walk, gazing at the river, when I found myself pondering the question of forgiveness—what it is, how to do it, and why do it? I slowed my pace and sat down on a metal bench at the water's edge. I saw turtles swimming, bobbing up, then disappearing; seagulls swooping down, landing on the water with a practiced splash for a quick swim, then taking off; beautiful green-necked male mallard ducks and their female partners floating by.

I saw a female duck right in front of me, all alone. Every few minutes, she would dive for food. I have found that if I am silent and attentive to nature, I can get direction on something I am wondering about.

It felt as if she would be willing to engage in a conversation, so I asked her to speak to me about forgiveness.

I had come on this walk contemplating what it would take to fully forgive the men in my life who were unfaithful to their wives—my maternal and paternal grandfathers and my father. It felt as if the female duck was saying to me, "Dive deeper." When I did, I realized the spirit of unfaithfulness also lived in me. Rather than facing it, I have often projected it outward onto close relationships, feeding distrust and fear of being abandoned by my husband or betrayed by the women who worked with him while denying my capacity to be unfaithful.

It was hard to admit that the person I needed to forgive was myself for letting fear and jealousy distort my relationships. Fear has kept me focused on protecting myself from loss and from opening my heart fully. How would I survive the grief if something happened to my husband, children, or grandchildren? This fear, begun in childhood, has kept me shackled to the past, trying to control the future rather than living in the joy of the present.

I know it is human to want revenge when one has been wronged. We plot in our minds how we might make the other person suffer as we are suffering, or we act out in unpredictable ways. I also know that some offenses are much harder to forgive than others.

"I forgot to do something I said I would do, and I'm sorry. Please forgive me." This level of forgiveness is rather easy.

"I was cheated by a business partner and lost my business and life-time savings. I can't forgive myself for trusting my business partner. I am angry at him and blame myself for trusting him. I blame his betrayal on the loss of my marriage as well." Betrayal by a trusted partner you cared about and thought you knew is harder to forgive.

"I just learned that my marriage partner was unfaithful, and I can't forgive him/her." When a gap this wide is created, it is hard to imagine closing it and investing in the hard work to reestablish trust.

A fatal automobile accident caused by a drunk driver is a traumatic event that can cause a wound so deep that the path to forgiveness seems blocked forever. Seminary professor Jerry Sittser, author of *A Grace*

Disguised, How the Soul Grows Through Loss, tells the story of his own experience of catastrophic loss.[31]

His wife, mother, and daughter were killed by a drunk driver who hit their car head-on. The loss of three generations of one's family in a split second is almost more than a person can bear. He chronicles his faith journey as he wrestles with God, his despair, anger, desire for revenge, and his need for justice. As he wrestles with his faith, Sittser slowly discovers a pathway to forgiveness. Seeking justice, he acknowledges, reflects our belief in the moral nature of the universe. When wrong is done, we believe the wrongdoer should be punished.

I've come to accept that anger is a legitimate emotional response to suffering. When someone has done something hurtful to me, I want to strike back and hurt them. And I know grief is natural in the wake of loss. In the absence of someone or something we've lost, we express the pain in various ways. Passionate feeling responses indicate that we have begun the healthy but painful process of healing. But unforgiveness is different from anger, grief, or the desire for justice. It eats us up from the inside out.

Unconscious truth can surface in the course of seeing a good movie or hearing a good sermon. If we're listening, we can hear what we need. Watching *Oppenheimer* gave me a moment like that. Much of the movie spoke of how human beings live in community. You must have a strong ego to pursue a vision that could affect the global community forever. You have to deal with professional jealousy, the responsibilities of leadership, and much more.

I left the movie able to see more clearly how my jealousy had affected my relationships. For many years, I was jealous of Bill's time and attention and of anyone with whom he spent a great deal of time building Communities in Schools. I learned from my mother and grandmother that it was prudent to be suspicious and jealous of women who worked closely with him; after all, women assistants had seduced their husbands.

---

[31] Jerry L. Sittser, *A Grace Disguised Revised and Expanded: How the Soul Grows through Loss* (United States: Zondervan, 2021).

So, in a way, I could justify my jealousy as a desire to protect my marriage and family. I saw clearly how destructive one man's jealousy could be to those around him in the movie *Oppenheimer.*

I have also been on the receiving end of the jealousy of someone I loved. I didn't know it lay just beneath the surface, waiting to raise its destructive head. When she expressed it, I saw how it harmed our relationship and rippled out to our whole intimate circle. Although I know jealousy is often rooted in unmet and unconscious childhood needs and insecurity, I still found myself thinking on that occasion of things I could say to retaliate. I felt that wrong had been done. Although I believed it was just to feel indignant, I intended to let it go, but kept ruminating on the behavior and my hurt and made a need for an apology a condition for moving on—or at least some recognition that wrong had been done. My desire to forgive kept getting short-circuited. I knew it was unhealthy not to forgive, but I had trouble letting it go.

What does it mean to forgive another? I have found it helpful simply to suspend judgment. It is not that I am saying what was done is now okay, but an acknowledgment that I am not the judge.

Once I can acknowledge that truth, I can let it go and "Give it to God," so to speak, and let the other person deal with the harm they have done to the relationship. Then, I can be released from the judgment expressed by the tightness in my body and conflict in my mind and spirit.

As I reflected on this incident, I was reminded of the definition of sin as missing the mark. As in archery practice, you intend to hit the bullseye, but when you miss the mark, you keep trying. What was the mark I was trying to hit? Was it to find a way to communicate the harm that had been done to elicit an apology? Or was the bullseye to love unconditionally, let go of hurt and judgment, let life offer the lessons, and trust God to be the judge?

I have heard others comment in the face of deep hurt and loss that maybe it was partially their fault. For example, "If I had been driving more slowly, we would have avoided the drunk driver," or "If I hadn't been wearing a low-cut blouse, I might not have been raped."

Even as children, we can blame ourselves for our parents' divorce. "If I had been less trouble, maybe my parents would have stayed together." It did occur to me that my mother's life would have been very different if she hadn't been a single mother when she tried to re-enter college.

The self-critical voice is relentless. The first step on the road to letting go of the anger and hurt is to acknowledge that voice, bring it to consciousness, and speak it out loud to a trusted person who can hear it without judgment.

When I did that with my spiritual director, she helped me move toward letting go. She helped me see it wasn't my place to judge the other person; that was God's work. My work was to let it go so I could be free to love. It's certainly easier not to forgive, to withdraw, or cut off and let the offense sink into the unconscious where it festers. I know I have unconscious areas in my life that could hurt other people. When I don't suspend judgment of the other, it hurts me. I want to free up my heart space to love.

My experience working with ex-offenders newly released from jail was that those who could admit they had done wrong and ask for and accept forgiveness from those they had harmed could move on and find ways to make amends for what they had done. When their families or faith communities welcomed them home and provided support to begin again, they could embrace the truth that although they had done wrong, God loved them, and they could begin again. Others remained stuck in self-blame, anger, and victimhood.

It's not only hard to let go of the hurt and anger, it's also hard to accept forgiveness. I've wondered what keeps me and others from accepting forgiveness and moving on. We've all seen politicians who can't admit they have done wrong. I suspect it has to do with shame. They have not experienced unconditional love, which makes it safe to admit they made poor choices and did harm and to ask for forgiveness and make restitution. They deny the truth, attempt to hide from it, and hope it will go away. Maybe they have never experienced forgiveness, reconciliation, and acceptance, which can open new possibilities. They haven't been able to receive the truth that they aren't bad people—that, like the rest of us, they have made some poor choices. Or maybe they intentionally hide the truth to hold on to power, position, and money. There are, of course, consequences resulting from poor choices. Accepting the consequences is part of paying the price of being a responsible adult and valuing and submitting to the rule of law.

Suspending judgment of another is an action, an emotion, and a spiritual practice. If I've been harmed by someone, it doesn't mean I have to enter into a trusting relationship with that person again or vote for them, but when the chains of unforgiveness are broken, I'm free to invest my energy elsewhere. It certainly seems easier to justify not letting go.

Suspending judgment of others is costly. But the alternative is more costly. It drives resentment underground and poisons future relationships. To suspend judgment, I have to give up the right to get even, to require an apology, and to see myself as a victim.

Instead, I have to dig deep to consider if I might have contributed to the wrong that was done. To a follower of the Way of Love, that means accepting Jesus' prayer on the cross on our behalf, "Forgive them, for they know not what they do." We are forgiven, even if we don't believe it. In embracing God's unconditional love, we find freedom to go forward and open our hearts to love again.

Jerry Sittser wisely said that a desire for justice is not wrong: a person can both forgive and strive for justice. Wrong that is forgiven is still wrong done. "Mercy does not abrogate justice: it transcends it."[32] For a tragic loss like his, and a loss like the one we as a nation experienced on 9/11, for example, it might take a lifetime to be able to forgive and perhaps a daily intention to choose forgiveness rather than seek revenge.

Thoughts of revenge, the desire to see the offender punished, and the pull toward bitterness can be powerful, yet the Holy Scriptures challenge us repeatedly to seek life and freedom by embracing God's love. Release from the pain and suffering begins when victims realize that

---

[32] Jerry Sittser, *A Grace Disguised: How the Soul Grows through Loss* (Grand Rapids, MI: Zondervan, 2004), 141.

nothing—neither punishment nor revenge—can reverse the wrong done.

Some suggest that the road to moving forward is to "forgive and forget." I have tried that. It didn't work for me. In my experience, that slogan is a recipe for a spiritual bypass.

Sometimes, horrific pain gets stashed away in a corner of our hearts, sealed off in our unconscious minds where we suppose it can't hurt us. Forgetting does not automatically translate into forgiving. It can become lodged in our bodies and affect our relationships or cause illness until we bring it to consciousness and let it go. That moment of allowing it to become conscious can bring surprising liberation: the door swings open, the handcuffs are unlocked, and we walk free.

One day, my friend Blinky received a call from an acquaintance who visited inmates in prison. "Blinky, I was visiting the prison the other day, and I was approached by one of the inmates who asked me if I knew you. Nodding my assent, he asked if I would ask you to visit him. He is the man you and your wife forgave in the courtroom 30 years ago, the boy who killed your son."

Blinky, shocked, asked for time to process the request. He began to pray and fast to discern if it was something he should do. It was a hard decision to reopen the pain of loss and confront this man again, who had sneered at Blinky's words of forgiveness in the courtroom.

Blinky decided to visit him. It took 30 years, but the man had come to his senses and asked to be forgiven. Blinky had a chance to choose between good and not good, between what creates and sustains life and what destroys it. As long as the fact of choice remains unconscious, I do not have "free will."

Michael Brown, in *The Presence Process*, offers a helpful perspective on love and forgiveness: "Our journey into the great mystery called love starts with being unconditional toward ourselves by feeling what we are authentically feeling without judging the feeling in any way, and without trying to fix, change, understand, heal, or transform it. Being willing to integrate our own discomfort—to see it as valid and even necessary, and behaving toward it accordingly—enables us to experience forgiveness and realize peace."[33]

We all behave in ways that come from emotional imprinting, conscious or unconscious. Freud illustrated this with a metaphor of horse and rider: when sitting on a horse, we have the reins and think we are in control, but when the horse senses she is close to the barn, she takes control and makes a dash to the barn.

According to Brown, emotional imprinting during the last seven months in utero and the first seven years is like that. We depend on our minds, our education, and our conscious value systems to stay in control, i.e., "hold the reins," but ultimately, when emotional imprinting from childhood gets triggered, and we go into fear, grief, or anger, we are "galloping off to the barn" before we know it.

I can still be gripped by fear when I see someone drinking too much; it triggers the childhood memory of family members who harmed others or themselves by losing a job, a marriage, or their health.

Brown adds, "By genuinely forgiving ourselves for behavior that emanates from our imprinted predicament (and I would add, knowing I am forgiven), we automatically forgive the world." We begin to see how others' self-centered behaviors are opposed to the common good and destructive of human life, though they may be a misplaced effort to gain unconditional love. Buying bigger houses, fancy cars, the latest fashion, or drinking or drugging are all efforts to gain acceptance and love. It is easy to judge others even when we know these things unless we acknowledge that we, too, at times act out of the unconscious imprinting of childhood.

Alongside the abiding love of our Creator for humanity and all creation stands the Law written in the Ten Commandments. Jesus said he did not come to abolish the law but to fulfill it. In other words, a moral code is inscribed in the universe and on our hearts, and violating it has

---

[33] Michael Brown, *The Presence Process: A Journey Into Present Moment Awareness* (United States: Namaste Publishing, 2010).

consequences. Yet grace fulfills the law. Everything one has done to violate the law can be and is forgiven because God is Love.

In the biblical parable of the unjust servant in Matthew 18:21-35, one servant begged his master to forgive a huge debt, and his request was granted, yet sometime later, he chose not to forgive the much smaller debt of a servant who worked for him. The scripture says his punishment was eternal imprisonment because he chose not to forgive.

What is eternal imprisonment? Could it be that we are not imprisoned by knowing we have done wrong but are imprisoned by refusing to accept responsibility for it? Our hearts become hardened; we find it impossible to have compassion for others or ourselves, so we cannot ask for or receive the forgiveness and grace readily available to us.

When that self-centered refusal to acknowledge we have done wrong becomes consistent, it isolates us from others and imprisons us. Or perhaps we unconsciously project our pain onto other close relationships and distort them with fear and distrust. We cannot live in denial and hold anger, bitterness, and resentment for long. It has to surface somehow, either unconsciously through physical symptoms of ill health, projection onto another, or constant obsessive thinking about it. Or we can offer it to God, confess it to another human being, face the whole range of emotions that want to be expressed, and wait for the Spirit to move us through to forgiveness.

Over the years, I have had several conversations related to forgiveness that have stayed with me. The first was given as a reason to not forgive and went like this ... "If I forgive her (him) for what she has said and done, it will let her off the hook. I won't forgive her until she apologizes."

On another occasion, I was engaged in a conversation with someone at a reception when we were interrupted by a man who asked my conversation partner how he was doing. His response went like this: "My mother has disowned me because I am gay and cut me off from my inheritance."

After he and I resumed our conversation, I said to him, knowing he was a man who believed in God, "So, are you in the process of forgiving your mother?"

With vehemence, he responded, "No, I don't ever want to forgive her. I hope she burns in hell for what she has done to me." The pain and grief expressed in that response were heartbreaking.

As I reflected on those conversations, I remembered what Anne Lamott said in her book, *Traveling Mercies*, "Not forgiving is like drinking rat poison and then waiting for the rat to die."[34] It does absolutely nothing to hurt the other person; we hurt ourselves instead.

Suspending judgment and letting go of the hurt is a process that can take many years. Where another is in that process is not mine to judge. The ability to forgive and be forgiven is central to maintaining intimacy, healing, and becoming whole.

However, it is frightening to risk confessing the wrong you have done to your partner, family member, or friend, especially if what you have done seems unforgivable. Maybe they won't forgive you. Maybe they'll leave and end the relationship. Maybe you have broken the law and will have to go to jail to pay for the wrong you have done. Or maybe confessing will open up a Pandora's box of childhood abuse, which you had boxed off and justified what happened as their treatment made you more resilient. In my experience, speaking the truth about it will begin the long road to healing from unexplained and displaced rage.

Forgiveness by a person or the legal system is not guaranteed by confession. Nor does it remove the harm that was done. I have been reading and hearing about bullying that is happening in school and the harm it has done. There have been some cases in which a young person who was bullied chose to take his or her life. Even if one confesses their participation in bullying and asks for forgiveness, the harm is done, and forgiveness by the parents may not follow.

Reconciliation may follow confession as one takes the steps necessary to repair the wrong, but it is not guaranteed. This is true in small things as well as big ones. Someone offered me a line that has been very helpful when Bill and I disagree on a little thing. For example, we are driving somewhere, and I say, "Turn here," and he says, "No,

---

[34] Anne Lamott, *Traveling Mercies: Some Thoughts on Faith* (New York: Anchor Books, 2006).

that's the wrong way." In this instance, in the end, it becomes clear that one is right and the other is wrong. If one of us completes the conversation by saying, "You were right, and I was wrong," the energy invested in disagreement dissipates. I think of it as a little relationship "gnat," tiny but really annoying, that can leave little red bites in one's relationships.

Reconciliation sometimes involves naming the needs that weren't met by our caregivers, even when they have done a pretty good job of raising us, and we love and respect them. In a way, they are the gnats or no-see-ums of our childhood. We can't see them, but they continue to itch and leave marks.

Over the years, I have come to recognize how I can use shopping to ignore something I am unable to face. Or how I might focus on my health to avoid facing my mortality and order another herbal supplement to fix the problem, or soothe my fear by eating a bowl of ice cream or having a glass of wine.

For a little while, these things satisfy the unconscious and unnamed anxiety until I wake up and face what I am anxious about. I have also overworked to prove my worth and seek to receive praise from whomever I am trying to please. When I feel out of control, I try to control others rather than admit that much of life cannot be controlled.

When thoughts keep returning, I have learned that something resides in my unconscious mind and heart that needs to surface and be released. Often, I resist and take the easy way out by blaming the other for what they did and have conversations with them in my head to prove and convince them that they were wrong.

So, the anxiety continues until I face whatever has separated me from the God of love and from a relationship that keeps bothering me. To be free, I must face it and do what I can to reconcile the rupture.

Defining Love

The question, "What is love?" became the topic of conversation at a dinner I attended a while ago. I am not sure how the discussion of such a serious topic came up, but I had been pondering what it means to love your enemy, and it was on my mind.

I had experienced the woman across from me as a thoughtful person who would share her opinions freely, so I am guessing I raised the issue. My dinner partner said that for her, loving your enemy cheapens the whole experience of what it means to love and is not the same as the love we have for our spouse, children, or friends.

I saw her point, and it made sense, yet it didn't answer my question regarding what was meant in holy scriptures when we are told to love our enemies and why we are told to do so.

I went back to my room and looked up the scripture where Jesus teaches his followers to love their enemies. It is found in both Matthew 5:43-48 and Luke 6:27-38:

> But I say to you to listen, love your enemies, do good to those who hate you, bless those who curse you, pray for those who abuse you. If anyone strikes you on the cheek, offer the other also; and from anyone who takes away your coat do not withhold even your shirt. Give to everyone who begs from you; and if anyone takes away your goods, do not ask for them again. Do to others as you would have them do to you.
>
> If you love those who love you, what credit is that to you? For even sinners love those who love them. If you do good to those who do good to you, what credit is that to you? For even sinners do the same. If you lend to those from whom you hope to receive, what credit is that to you? Even sinners lend to sinners, to receive as much again. But love your enemies, do good, and lend, expecting nothing in return. Your reward will be great, and you will be children of the Most High, for he is kind to the ungrateful and the wicked. Be merciful, just as your Father is merciful.
>
> Do not judge, and you will not be judged; do not condemn, and you will not be condemned. Forgive, and you will be forgiven; give, and it will be given to you.

Sitting in church one day with the sun shining through the multi-colored stained glass windows, I looked down at the engagement ring on my finger, lovingly passed on to me by Bill's mother, to see the many facets of colors radiating from the rough cut diamond. It spoke to me of the many kinds of love formed out of the rough cut of life. Writer and theologian C.S. Lewis chooses four facets of love in his book, *Four Loves*, to describe the different kinds of love.[35]

"Storge" is the Greek word for the love we have for our family members. It is related to blood ties or covenantal relationships like marriage and parenthood, or our siblings with whom we share a common history and know their vulnerabilities. Thus, we can grant them and ourselves some grace when we say or do something hurtful. It is the most basic kind of love: steady and sure.

"Philia" includes friends, neighbors, and colleagues with whom we work and share a common perspective and perhaps love of the mission we share in our work, neighborhoods, or church communities. Friendship is the most rare, least jealous, and freely chosen of the loves. I have experienced philia love with several wise friends with whom I can be my true self. I share philia love with several clergy colleagues who were truly partners in serving a congregation, and in an unlikely place, working with a committee to serve our town house community.

"Eros," which Lewis defines as romantic love, is a part of the attraction of lovers. But it can also be seductive and cause chaos when a mutual passion among work colleagues or friends is misunderstood as romantic love and turns inward to focus on each other rather than turning the passion to love outward to serve the community.

Over the years of a long-term marriage, which began with the excitement of physical attraction, investing in additional forms of shared intimacy and personal growth can help mature love grow between two people who are differentiated from each other. Interdependence and an abiding trust can be created, which enables each to be uniquely

---

[35] C S Lewis, *The Four Loves* (Harvest Books, 1971).

themselves and disagree while respecting the other, and work together to serve each other, their families, and their community.

The last is "Agape" love, the unconditional love God has for all of humanity, no matter what is said or done. This is the kind of love I have always thought was unique to God and that we humans could not offer.

In a way that is true, it can not be humanly generated. The first three kinds of love are ways of being in a relationship in which we choose to invest. I have to say that the experience of friendship feels like a gift given to me initially that doesn't involve choice, however, I do need to choose to nurture it if it is going to continue.

Our families are a given, and like friendship, we have a choice about continuing to be in relationship with family members. The passion and temptation of erotic love can appear unexpectedly, and I can decide whether to pursue it. Thus, I do have a choice about nurturing a friendship, continuing to be in relationship with family members, and defining how I will set the boundaries when eros appears in a relationship that is unbidden and inappropriate to pursue.

The fourth kind of love, "Agape," can only come from the Holy Spirit of God coming to us or passing through us. It is not a humanly generated emotion based on attraction, shared experience, or shared political views, and is not in our control.

I, however, can set the intention to open my heart to love everyone, even those who have done me wrong, those who have undercut my plans or embarrassed me and caused me pain—"my enemy," so to speak. The person does not have to be bad or evil to be my "enemy."

Matthew 5:43-45, taken from *The First Nations Version: An Indigenous Translation of the New Testament* chapter on *The Sermon on the Mount*, put together by a group of Native American scholars and theologians to reflect their cultural perspective, has offered me further insight to understand the possible alternative meaning of this scriptural mandate: "You have been told to love your own people and to despise others as your enemy. But I tell you, treat your enemies with love and respect, and send up good prayers for the ones who make trouble for you and bring you pain. This will show that you are mature children of your Father from above, who sends his blessing of rain on the ones who do right and the ones who do wrong."[36]

This kind of love is not transactional. There is no expectation of reciprocity. It can only come from the Holy Spirit through a willing channel.

The Israelites were never told to hate their enemies. Proverbs 25:21-22 offers the wise guidance that if your enemy is hungry, give him food and drink. In doing this, you will heap burning coals on his head.

Paul repeats this in Romans 12:20. Jesus says to his disciples, "You have heard it said, to hate your enemy," but that is not the Way of Jesus. I previously understood this scripture lesson about heaping burning coals upon the head of the person who has done you wrong, "your enemy," as a way to make the person who has hurt you feel guilty or ashamed for what they have done by being extremely kind and generous toward them.

Contemporary scholars have reinterpreted the passage to offer a different point of view. In ancient times, people would carry coal in a basket on their heads if a fire went out in their village to seek fire from a neighboring village because they would not survive without it. So that passage can be reinterpreted to mean that you can stop the conflict by giving the enemy what they need, such as coal to light their fire.

In a relationship, this can mean offering your neighbor kindness, acceptance, or blessing; give them what they need as a way to love your enemy. It takes prayer and discernment to have a sense of how to "relight someone's fire" in a way that communicates love to them.

Jesus goes on to say that loving our "enemies" will show that we are mature men and women created in the image and likeness of a loving God.

For me, central to opening my heart to loving another who has done me wrong or disagrees with me, who feels like my "enemy," it is intricately connected with the ability to forgive.

---

[36] *The First Nations Version: An Indigenous Translation of the New Testament* (Downers Grove, IL: InterVarsity Press, 2021).

Recalling the story called "Magic Eyes," which I have read and heard a number of times related to mature love as it relates to forgiveness, originating from Lewis Smedes in his book, *Forgive and Forget: Healing the Hurts We Don't Deserve*, offers a way to forgive what can feel unforgivable in a marriage betrayal.

The story also reinterprets verse 20 of Romans 12: "If your enemy is hungry, feed him; if he is thirsty, give him something to drink. In doing this, you will heap burning coals on his head." So, rather than pretending to forgive someone but actually continuing to justify self-righteous judgment so they feel guilty, the story offers a way out of the pain of separation, seeking discernment and listening to the wisdom of the Spirit as a guide to move forward. By walking in the shoes of the other and giving them what they need, rather than continuing to judge them silently to make them feel ashamed, both move toward freedom, and the possibility of a renewed love emerges.

Often, marriage partners choose each other because one is hardworking and more cerebral, and the other is more emotional and warm-hearted; opposites do seem to attract. Without the skill of communicating their needs to each other and developing empathy that engenders a willingness to change to meet their partner's needs, people can fall into relationships outside of their marriage covenant. In metaphorical language, one partner comes to the other needing the coals in their basket to be lit, but instead, they are made to feel guilty for expressing their need and are turned away.

Marriage betrayal is hard to forgive. It is a process and involves a willingness to see how each one has contributed to the broken covenant. It takes courage and willingness to see the other person with new eyes. I have worked with couples, some of whom can see the other with "magic eyes" and truly forgive, and others who can't.

Those who can commit to the process of looking at their failures in the marriage relationship, their unmet childhood needs, and develop compassion for the unmet needs of the other are able to see the other with new eyes, grow, and become more loving, kind human beings, capable of doing their part to restore the relationship.

While looking for a particular presentation on YouTube, I happened upon a YouTube presentation by Tanmeet Sethi, MD, author of *My Joy is My Justice,* who spoke about the incurable disease of her young child. She said, "Your pain is not fair or just. You are not broken because you feel it deeply. Yet every footstep you take toward joy, even while still living with fear or rage, is a radical act of justice that defies the oppressive weight of your pain and creates a powerful change in your biochemistry."[37]

Loving inevitably includes pain. It requires that we come to terms with the unfair nature of what sometimes happens to us or someone we love, or the loss of someone we love. We are challenged to hold fear and grief, together with joy and laughter, when we experience life as painful and unfair. Jesus' resurrection points to the possibility of new life in the future. Our challenge is to keep awake to see it germinate and grow. The Spirit of Love inherent in the resurrection draws us forward, where the power to forgive and hope lives.

Many expressions of love are freely given, which we can observe by just going outside for a walk. The other day, walking along the river near our home, I saw a mother talking to her baby facing her in the carriage, pink hydrangeas were bursting from every branch of a bush, and a woman sitting under a tree holding her dog commented to me that she was, "giving him a break from the heat." I stopped to talk with a neighbor I'd never met and marveled at the beauty of her patio garden. She beamed with delight. Love was everywhere. I just had to open my eyes to see it and let it warm my heart with joy.

A Place Called Home

I woke up early this morning thinking about "belonging." Again. Lani was coming to visit for the weekend. She brought a book written by her

---

[37] Kara Wada, MD, *Becoming Immune Confident Podcast,* "Joy Is My Justice: Reclaim What Is Yours," August 9, 2023.

biological grandfather, which she had had for a while but had not shared with us until now.

Saturday evening, we sat down to read a portion of the book. Bill, Lani, and I concluded that his core message was that faith and doubt go together; you can't have one without the other. And that, for him, a meaningful life seemed rooted in hope.

I have met some folks who seem to have the gift of faith; doubt doesn't seem to be a part of their relationship with God, and to some, if you express doubt, you are somehow lacking in faith. I believe there is a kind of doubt rooted in curiosity that can lead to growth and a new understanding, which enriches my faith. I have found that doubt and curiosity help my faith to grow and be more inclusive, multidimensional, and trusting. Doubt keeps me from putting faith, or my belief system, in a box and tying a ribbon around it and then having to find ways to defend it and judge others who have a different experience of faith.

However, doubt that calls into question whether you are worthy of love and causes you to question your worth and belonging in this world is not a helpful kind of doubt that leads to hope. Claiming you are loved and valued is foundational to hope for the future. Even if that hasn't been true in your family of origin, it can be slowly healed by a loving community and a relationship with a loving God.

After sampling a number of passages in Dr. Malisoff's book, I said, "Well, Lani, you were quite philosophical when you were a child. Maybe you got that in your DNA from your philosophical grandfather. And you got other things from our family."

She is, as I am, a genetic product of our birth parents. And we are just as truly a product of the family who raised and loved us. But in the end, I am a combination of both and have become the person I am based on my choices with what I was given.

We were both given the tools to fashion our own identity—genetic history and a disposition given at birth, and the love and security we each received during the early months of our lives—but it has been and is up to each of us to choose how we will live our one precious life.

The conversation with Lani reminded me to be brave and claim the courage to stand alone, to belong to myself first and know that I belong wherever I am, while at the same time knowing that I am a part of something bigger. I want to continue to engage in a spiritual practice that connects me to the Transcendent, giving me the courage not to live to fit in or to gain the approval of others but to speak my truth as I see it, believing that it is worth something to someone no matter what criticism comes as a result.

It wasn't until I was preparing for surgery to enable me to hear again at age 80 that I had the experience of fully surrendering to a transcendent reality. That surrender enabled me to decide to trust the surgeon and the process of having a cochlear implant.

I had been losing hearing since the age of 50 when I contracted Lyme disease. By age 80, hearing aids were no longer sufficient to enable me to be a full participant in conversations or to work as a pastoral counselor or priest.

Three days before my surgery, two songs I had learned long ago began running through my head. I was surprised that I remembered most of the words to "What a Friend We Have in Jesus" and "Jesus My Lord Will Love Me Forever."

Oliver Sacks, writer and neurologist, wrote a story about one of his patients who was awakened for several nights hearing old Irish lullabies in a vaguely familiar voice. She thought she was going crazy. Sacks suggested that those songs may have come because she needed comfort from the mother who sang lullabies to her as a child but had died when she was young.

Maybe something similar was happening to me. Who knows why those two hymns were the ones that came to me? I hadn't sung them for years and questioned if I still believed some of what the words conveyed, but they came from a time when a sense of belonging to God and being loved unconditionally had just begun to grow in me. I sang them in Sunday School as a child and in high school in Young Life, when I committed to following Jesus' way.

Over the years, my hearing loss had slowly progressed to the point where I could no longer hear well enough to see couples seeking counseling or preside at the altar at church. The last time I went to have my hearing aids adjusted, the audiologist said, "I am sorry, but there is nothing more we can do with hearing aids. Your issue is understandability, and raising the volume will not help you hear any better. You might want to consider a cochlear implant."

I had no idea what a cochlear implant was. When I researched the process of getting one, it felt scary. I noticed that I had begun to isolate because it was so hard to hear. Bill would ask me to go places with him, and I wanted to go but didn't want to smile and pretend I was hearing what people were saying or say something out of context because I misheard what had been said. Being present in social situations had become exhausting.

Even with the help of hearing aids, it is easy and sometimes embarrassing to mishear! And sometimes, when you don't know someone who doesn't ask for clarification about what you said, it can cause embarrassment, hurt, and misunderstanding.

One hope I had while receiving a cochlear implant was that I might avoid these embarrassing mistakes in the future. I wanted to continue to be engaged in life, so I began the long process of interviewing surgeons and being tested to confirm that I would qualify for the surgery.

Finally, the preparation process was completed, and surgery was scheduled. I began to use all the tools I had to prepare to calm my anxiety. One of the things I did was to begin a journal.

Journal Entry May 6, 2023
(Two Days Before Surgery)

There is no question that my thoughts will affect my surgery. I can decide to completely trust the surgeon and his team and not request that he personally do not only the highly technical, skilled part of inserting the electrodes into my cochlear, but also the cutting and sewing up the incision and drilling into my skull to create a ledge for the internal processor to sit on. Or I could choose to simply trust him to decide what he will do and what his senior resident will do.

A physician friend advised that I should trust the surgical team or not go forward with the surgery. But blanket trust is difficult for me, especially trusting a man in authority to make decisions about my health when I am medicated and asleep. And I don't know the skill level of the others on the team. I am concerned that his desire to teach his residents and give them experience might take precedence at some point over what would give me the best surgical outcome.

My prayer is that I enter this surgery without fear and in complete trust that the Holy Spirit of Wisdom will be with me, having directed my discernment, giving me courage, and guiding the surgeon and his team as well. I have done my research and chosen my surgeon carefully. Now, I need to trust the surgeon's wisdom to decide between what is best for me and what is best for the learning experience of his surgical team enough to let him make the decision.

Journal Entry May 7, 2023
(One Day Before Surgery)

The parting gift from Jesus was the Spirit of the living God—Sophia. I prayed that Sophia would be my companion and bring me peace and comfort. I know from visiting as a hospital chaplain with folks preparing for surgery that it is common to feel nervous. I know I have done my part to research and pray every step of the way. Others are praying with me. I yearn to be able to hear again so I can be a friend to all who come on my path, have time to be present for my children and grandchildren, and continue being Bill's partner at home and on the road. We have a lot of travel ahead to offer our experience and encouragement to Communities in Schools affiliates and Leadership Foundation staff around the country.

I began imagining angels surrounding me during surgery. A wise friend suggested that the doctor and surgical team are God's angels, giving me the opportunity to hear again. That imagery worked for me, though it might not for everyone. I want to be a willing participant in the surgery going well. And I know I am not in total control of the outcome: only my attitude going into it. I pray that I will be strong enough to stay the course, no matter the outcome. I can trust that a loving God wants what is good for me. I again use my imagination to picture God's healing energy flowing from above to me and out to the surgical team, who I picture having angel wings on their backs. Jesus walks beside me, holding my hand. I also know that everyone does not get the answer to prayer that they seek.

Three Days Post-Surgery

"What was I thinking?" Waking up with a start in the middle of the night three days after surgery, I had been on opioids the first two days, experiencing no pain, and had decided that I no longer needed to continue the pain medication. The pain that woke me up was not extreme; it was bearable. However, I now know why people who are in extreme physical or emotional pain don't want to stop the pills that mask the pain. I have one more pill left; should I take it now or save it just in case?

Email Sent to Family and Friends Three Weeks Post-Surgery

I thought the audiologist would check my residual hearing this week, which he did. He also put the external cochlear implant magnet and processor on. The implant automatically connected with the hearing aid in my other ear. It was a medical miracle; immediately, I could hear. I had expected to hear just static at first, but I can understand speech pretty clearly already. Bill and I ate out tonight, and I could hear him and the waiter even with background noise.

The most striking sound I heard once the processor was attached was the turn signal driving home. It has been years since I have heard that sound. I have begun some exercises online and am mishearing some words and singing off-tune; I can see there is work to do regarding word recognition. It is challenging to get the processor magnet in my hair in the right place so it connects with the one implanted, but I assume it will become easier to place it with daily practice.

Thank you for your love and prayers,
Jean

Continued Reflections

I resisted writing about my experience of the healing presence of Jesus prior to, during, and post-surgery because I feared it would communicate that I thought I was somehow special; that Jesus healed me but not others who prayed faithfully for healing.

And I was concerned that it might trigger painful memories in those who have been abused by "Christians" who have used the name of Jesus to do violence or exclude others from being free to practice their faith or no faith. Many have been abused as children by clergy who preached about the love of Jesus. I think of our Jewish friends who lost loved ones in the death camps in Germany during the Holocaust and the Christians who supported Hitler.

Clearly, not everyone experiences Jesus as a friend or has their prayers answered in the way they would like. There are dishonest business people, too, who tell stories to engender trust and positive transference by using religious language and present themselves as Christians.

I learned that firsthand when I was in seminary doing doctoral work. A money manager presented to the seminarians and gained our trust by telling us about his minister father, who wasn't good with finances. Growing up seeing his father's struggle with money caused him to go into money management. Many of us could identify with not being good with finances; neither Bill nor I were talented or skilled in that way, and both of us were exceptionally busy. I was one of several who hired him. It turned out he mismanaged our money. It's the character and actions, not the words, that make one a follower of the way of love and justice.

As I said in my email to family and friends, my prayers and meditations before surgery brought me to a place of surrender and allowed me to give up control, put my life and hearing in the hands of the surgeon and his team, and invite Jesus to walk with me. I took a huge step forward by trusting that there is a loving energy in the universe and moving into the Spirit's life-giving flow.

I am reminded of the story in Luke 8:43-48 and Mark 5:24-34 of the woman with an issue of blood who had exhausted other sources of healing and reached out to touch Jesus' robe, believing she would be healed. Why was she healed when many others were there seeking healing as well who weren't healed? Why was she healed after 12 years of suffering and not before? It is a mystery to know why, when, or where the healing Spirit of Jesus will heal our suffering and shame.

My friend Gerry, a Reiki master, was sending me the healing energy of Reiki as I prepared for and recovered from surgery. Because she believes in and has experienced the healing power of Jesus, she has added the healing power of Jesus to her Reiki practice and training.

When I told her about the songs about Jesus that were constantly running through my mind, she wasn't surprised. As a child, in my Sunday school class, we sang, "What a Friend We Have in Jesus." The message of the song is that Jesus bears our sins and griefs, and it is a privilege to take it all to Jesus in prayer. The idea that we can take our pain, fear, and sorrow to Jesus/God has struck me in the past as Pollyannaish and childlike, but now the song is constantly playing in my ears and ringing true to me as an adult, inviting me to do just that.

I have sung this song many times, but didn't experience the reality of removing fear from my mind and heart. I have heard about the practice of tapping on acupuncture points to resolve fear. There are many ways to engage with the emotions of fear, sorrow, and pain, attempting to release them.

I know that when I take the time to be in silence and open to the Spirit of Wisdom, I can see my fears more clearly and discern whether there is anything I can do to resolve the problem. If not, I can choose to let it go. I can tap on acupuncture points, journal about it, and/or take it to Jesus in prayer and ask the Spirit of Love to guide me through it.

The second song, which we sang regularly in our Young Life Club meetings, "Jesus My Lord Will Love Me Forever," spoke to the promise that I not only belong to Jesus now but into eternity, which penetrated deeply into my heart and psyche.

The questions regarding belonging resurfaced. Now I know I belong to Love incarnated in the life of Jesus, the Cosmic Christ, without identifying with any tribe or cult or fully with any denomination despite my strong attachment to and love for the Episcopal Church, which has given me space to be myself, peace, freedom to grow in faith, and belonging. Now I know that everyone belongs, including me.

The last line of the song, which followed my surrendering to the surgical process, promises joy. Unfaithfulness was rooted in my family generations ago, and the sorrow and shame have been passed on. My mother's sadness, sorrow, and shame about being divorced and her parents' divorce are part of what caused her to hang onto a marriage that was no longer viable.

I, too, felt sadness and shame when classmates came to visit and learned I had no father. Later, when my mother remarried, my last name was different from theirs. My peers and their parents often expressed embarrassment when they learned that they had greeted my mother as Ms. Moore when her name was now Kondas.

All of that is not to say that I, myself, haven't done things that have caused me and others sorrow and shame. I have. But finally, I have been able to face my human frailty and "sinfulness," if you will, being self-centered and controlling, feeding my ego needs at the expense of the needs of others, which resulted in my guilt separating me from a relationship with God and others.

I have mostly let go of a desire to be perfect, and upon realizing that I have done wrong, I confess it, set the intention to do better next time, hopefully learn from my mistakes, and make reparation when possible. The "sin" is not the behavior itself, which some churches have taught and still teach, which requires God's judgment and punishment. Rather, we suffer the consequences of what we have done and lack the freedom to live with integrity and be ourselves, resulting in separation and disconnection from the infinite, eternal loving energy of the universe and our human relationships.

When worry begins to occupy my mind, I find myself singing one of my two songs or the song I was given on my Vision Quest, "Dances in

Light." I look for time to sit in silence, asking for infinite Eternal Love to discern the basis of my worry and how to move forward to embrace the goodness of life and let go of worry.

The church and other faith communities, at their best, are places where we can find meaning and purpose to fulfill our dreams and use our gifts in community service. These sacred places can also be places where we can experience the guidance of the Holy Spirit to confess our wrong-doing and feelings of separation. Whether by choosing to violate the laws written in the Ten Commandments or by setting our intention so that our heart's desires for money, power, and/or control lead us astray, we can face what we have done and turn around to head in a new direction.

In the end, faith and hope sustain us and give us a vision for our lives. My husband has said, "Hope is love in action; without hope, people tend to do one of two things: either hurt themselves or hurt others." Anger is often the outward expression of hopelessness, fear, or grief and can keep us from uncovering the emotion that can lead us to healing and finding hope.

In his book, *The Irony of American History*, Reinhold Niebuhr says, "Nothing that is worth doing can be achieved in our lifetime; therefore, we must be saved by hope. Nothing which is true or beautiful or good makes complete sense in any immediate context of history; therefore, we must be saved by faith. Nothing we do, however virtuous, can be accomplished alone; therefore, we are saved by love. No virtuous act is quite as virtuous from the standpoint of our friend or foe as it is from our standpoint. Therefore, we must be saved by the final form of love, which is forgiveness."[38]

As I age, I have faith that I will find new purpose and discover ways to contribute my gifts to the common good. I belong to God, to myself, and the web of life and loving human relationships.

I sense the honey bee of the Spirit is alive everywhere; it appears where it will and to whoever is ready to receive it. My intention is to do my best to stay open to the process of pollination, receiving and being a conduit of love, the energy at the core of the universe.

---

[38] Reinhold Niebuhr, *The Irony of American History* (The University of Chicago Press, 2010).

APPENDIX

Chapel Sermon

Embracing Life's Seasons
50th Reunion—Westminster College, New Wilmington, PA
October 3, 2015, Scripture: Ecclesiastes 3:1-14a

It has been fun during informal conversations this weekend to listen to the stories each of us remembers from our four years here 50 years ago. Often, they are different versions of the same experience. It reminds me of when I am asked how long my husband, Bill, and I have been married, I say, "100 years—the 50 he remembers and the 50 I remember."

I have also become aware of the physical challenges that some of us are facing. For example, I wear hearing aids and often either can't hear or mis-hear what someone is saying to me.

The other day, I was participating in a group Bible study and Sandy, another woman in the group who wears hearing aids, shared the following experience she had had in a small group that she was leading.

"Larry had attended the group weekly for some months but sat slumped down in his seat and said very little. Then, he was gone from the group for about six months.

One day, he returned, and I said to him before the group convened, "You look and act like a different person: so bright and animated."

He replied, "I have been in Mississippi with a favorite uncle and found rice. (At this point in the story, I am thinking, *Well, I know there is red rice that comes in a capsule, which is supposed to be good for your heart, but does it produce a personality change?*)

The group reconvened, and Sandy continued her story. "We are so glad to have Larry back with us. He was in Mississippi with his uncle and found rice."

Larry piped up and said, "No! Not rice! I found Christ!" Even with the help of hearing aids, it is easy and sometimes embarrassing to mishear!

When Terry called me to ask if I was planning to come to the reunion, I hadn't seriously considered it. After he invited me to participate in this service, he told me about the class projects. The "Pay it Forward" opportunity caught my attention because it reminded me of those who made it possible for me to be a student here for four years when my dad was starting his own business, and the money for school was in short supply. Working in the dining hall and as a dorm counselor paid for my room and board, and then, having been given an anonymous scholarship to pay my tuition my senior year, I was able to finish without debt. I am grateful for those opportunities given to me by others who paid it forward, and I decided I wanted to be present to express my gratitude and do the same.

Now I want to tell you about Rose. I haven't met her; I just read about her a while ago, and her story captured my imagination. At age 87, Rose began college. She had always wanted to go, so at age 87, she enrolled. In a few months, she had made a lot of young friends among her fellow students who enjoyed her company and her stories, so they invited her to speak at their sports banquet.

Her speech was written on 3x5 cards, and when she rose to speak, she dropped the cards, and they scattered everywhere. She approached the mic and said, "I am so sorry. I gave up beer for Lent, and this whiskey is killing me." After the laughter in the audience quieted down, she continued, "I will never get these cards back in order, so I am just going to tell you what I know."

Rose shared three important life lessons:

Number 1. Don't drink whiskey or beer (even if it isn't Lent) before you are getting ready to give a public speech.

Number 2. It is important to have a dream, no matter how old you are, and act on it if you can.

Number 3. Speak about what you know.

Companioning folks as a pastoral counselor and priest on their spiritual journeys, I have learned a lot about attempting to avoid uncomfortable feelings by using drugs and alcohol, overworking, overinvolvement with our children, and watching TV or playing video games late into the night. Those behaviors can make the feelings of fear and anxiety go away temporarily, but they will come back. I know that we can learn to experience painful feelings and enrich our lives and relationships by naming our fears and anxieties and facing them.

Now, moving on to the second lesson from Rose's life. It is important to have a dream, no matter how old you are. Not too long ago, I was at a meeting of the retired Episcopal clergy. We meet in the private dining room of a retirement home, and several of those who attend the monthly gatherings live there. At the conclusion of a very lively discussion about the resources we each draw on to meet the challenges of aging, John, one of the clergymen who lives at the retirement home, blurted out, "Well, I wouldn't say this to many people, but let's face it, we have all come here to die." After a prolonged silence, another one of the clergymen who also resides there said, "Well, John, I really see it differently. I have come here to live each day to the fullest." This exchange confirmed to me that although we all have eyes to see, we see through them differently. Our perspective and intention matter, no matter how old we are.

As we age, our dreams change, and usually, our lives slow down a little, so each day offers an opportunity to reflect on our lives, choices, and maybe on unfulfilled dreams we can now either let go of or seek to fulfill as Rose did. Rose died soon after graduating, so she didn't use her education in the traditional sense. The value was in taking the risk to fulfill a dream and live each day to the fullest with humor and hope.

In his book *Falling Upward,* Richard Rohr points out that in the first half of life, we are building our egos. We are choosing our mate or choosing to remain single and investing in other significant relationships. We are creating a home. Building a career. In other words, we are working to fulfill our dreams for what we imagine a successful life will look like. In the second half of life, the spiritual journey is about letting go of the need to feed our egos with all of these things by peeling off layers of our identity that are not really us, by letting go of self-judgment and judgment of others to discover how deeply we are loved by God. As we discover how much we are loved, we can open our hearts to more fully love others.

Learning to love God, oneself, and others is a lifelong journey. As a passage from the book of Ecclesiastes says, we do all of these things to gain happiness, and it is good to enjoy the fruits of our labor, but ultimately, what God is doing in us and in the world is a mystery. Jesus has shown us the way of love that gives life, and we do our best to walk His Way. Sometimes we do it well, and sometimes we don't.

And the last lesson from Rose: Speak about what you know. What I have learned over the years is that God's love and forgiveness are unconditional for everyone everywhere. We don't have to do anything or be anything to earn it. And the more we can open our hearts and minds to internalize God's love and forgive ourselves and others, the more love pours out of us like sun and water to heal our relationships, our bodies, and our environment.

Now, some of us have a harder time than others receiving God's love. How we respond to it depends on where we started from—who our parents were, what messages we were given as children from the culture and our teachers, or what harm was done to us when we were vulnerable children. But I know we can help each other become more and more our true selves if we are willing to enter into committed relationships, learn to listen to each other, and risk speaking our truth to those who might see things differently—that is, to be in dialogue without judgment as the Pope during his recent visit to the U.S. encouraged us to do.

For two years, I co-led a communications group with men and women returning from jail or prison. One of the men, who was new to the group and wasn't sure who had served time and who hadn't, responded to a comment I made by saying, "Have you ever been locked up?" I thought for a minute as various situations flashed through my mind, and I answered, "No, I might have been, but I just never got caught." At the same time, I was aware that he was a black man and I was a white woman with the resources to hire a good attorney, so even if I did get caught, chances were I would not serve time. When I entered the group as a volunteer, I was the helper, the "good" person. I started in the "one up" position, and the returning citizens were "one down." At that moment, I realized how alike we were inside in spite of how different we appeared.

We spent two years weekly confronting prejudices and our projections based on race, gender, age, or education and were learning how to be human beings who simply wanted to be known, understood, valued, and accepted. One day, one of the members said, "I try to read the newspaper, but I don't understand half of the words on the page." This was not uncommon among returning citizens. A significant number had learning difficulties and no one to advocate for them in school to find ways to compensate, so they dropped out and got into trouble hanging out on the street.

In response to our group member's honest confession about his inability to read and understand, we came up with an idea. Every week, each member would enter the room and choose a word from the SAT word box. We would write the word on the board up front, including the definition, as our way to learn new words together and share our history with each other as we used the word in a sentence and told a story to give our reason for choosing that particular word. Like gleeful children in the role of teacher, we wrote on the whiteboard using different colored pens. We were learning that one's energy gets all used up in judgment and fear or envy and jealousy, thus limiting our ability to be ourselves and offer our unique gifts to the world. The exercise enabled each of us to stand on equal ground, learning something new and creating a community of care among us.

Jesus showed us the way to meet each person and listen to their story without judgment in the sacred space in between us where the Holy

Spirit of love and acceptance dwells. And healing can happen as hearts soften and human connection takes place. As the great Sufi poet Rumi said in a different way, "There is a field beyond right thinking and wrong thinking; I will meet you there."

Having reached the fourth quarter of life, it has become clearer that, as Thomas Lynch said in his book, *The Undertaking*, "The meaning of life is connected, inextricably to the meaning of death; that mourning is a romance in reverse, and if you love, you grieve, and there are no exceptions. There are only those who do it well and those who don't."[39]

I, personally, have spent too many years hanging on to my childhood fear of loss and avoiding loving deeply in order to avoid the pain of losing someone I loved. What I have learned, and continue to learn, is that just as light needs darkness, so joy is most often born of sadness, loss, and grief. Joy comes in the midst of mourning; however, that is not always the case. It is a choice. Bitterness and isolation can also come from loss and grief. As our scripture reading says, there is a time for giving birth and a time for dying, a time for mourning and a time for dancing, a time for tears, and a time for laughter.

Happiness in human life is elusive and momentary. Even though, at times, I can affirm that "Happiness is wanting what I already have," it is still elusive and short-lived. Things can change in the blink of an eye. I can be happy one moment, living in my spacious home in the suburbs, and then make the quick decision to downsize and move into a town house in the city with a small kitchen and the loss of space to store anything or accommodate guests overnight. I am happy that our children and grandchildren are doing well and that, after almost six decades of marriage, Bill and I are still married and enjoy each other's company.

Yet I know that circumstances can change quickly in the lives of those I love, and those changes are not within my control. When change takes place, I tighten up and feel the need to control what I cannot control, and thus, I often create my own suffering. I had made assumptions

---

[39] Thomas Lynch, *The Undertaking: Life Studies from the Dismal Trade* (London: Vintage Digital, 2011).

about how things should and would be. I can prolong the need to let go of things I no longer need or use, find an empty corner, and buy a storage cabinet to store some extra linens or family heirlooms that I do not want to give away; that is in my control. Ultimately, however, I have to face letting go of my family treasures that hold memories of the past if I want to create space for the new lifestyle and priorities that are emerging in my life and my new community currently.

True wisdom, I have come to know, is to give thanks to God for all things, whether I can change my circumstances or not. Over time, I am finding freedom and joy in having to maintain fewer things, keep only what I need, and be able to find what I need because it is not in a storage box under the eaves in my office, taking up the little storage space I have.

James Finley, a former Trappist Monk, said, "If we are absolutely grounded in the absolute love of God, that protects us from nothing even as it sustains us in all things, then we can face all things with courage and tenderness and touch the hurting places in others and in ourselves with love."[40]

Perhaps this is how opposites can coexist in our lives: a river of joy that flows underneath the suffering. Joy and suffering, weeping and laughter, I am challenged to hold both in my heart. I believe what Finley says with my mind, and yet to be able to know it in my heart is much more challenging.

I still find it hard to believe that anyone could love me unconditionally and not abandon me when I do something offensive to them. If someone I care about is distant, I immediately assume I have done something to offend them. Then I ask myself, "Could they just be tired or preoccupied, and it has nothing to do with me?"

When I fear Bill will leave me for another woman, he says, "Isn't the fact that we have been married all of these years enough proof that I will

---

[40] "James Finley Quote: 'If We Are Absolutely Grounded in the Absolute Love of God That Protects Us from Nothing Even as It Sustains Us in All ...,'" Quotefancy, accessed April 2, 2025, https://quotefancy.com/quote/1647502/James-Finley-If-we-are-absolutely-grounded-in-the-absolute-love-of-God-that-protects-us.

stick around? Sometimes, I feel like you are trying to push me out so that you can confirm your belief that men don't stay in their marriage when something better comes along."

It is these times when I am confronted with the intergenerational patterning that is deeply embedded in my psyche that I will be abandoned. Multigenerational divorce and abandonment can leave a deep hole in one's soul that is hard to heal. Even when the scar has formed over the wound, it can still be painful and sensitive when the fear gets triggered. I know that scar is there now and can understand and find ways to deal with the momentary or sometimes longer-lasting pain that caused the wound that is being pricked by a present event.

It is through prayer, journaling, and conversations with a trusted friend or two that I can stay aware and move through the suffering and fear to dip my toes into the river of joy to stand on the riverbed of gratitude and thanksgiving for my life.

Ultimately, God's care for me and for the world is ineffable and beyond my ability to feel or put into words. My best attempt is to say, "God is love." My best shot at becoming more human is to be willing, with God's help, to peel off the layers of myself that I have created in order to be acceptable and successful by the world's standards to find the self that was created in the image of God: creative, open-hearted, and unique.

My false self wants others to think I am always self-giving, kind, compassionate, and thoughtful, without acknowledging that the opposites of those admirable qualities also live in me. I am sometimes sad, depressed, and selfish, as well as happy and kind.

Through spending time in prayer and meditation and listening to others who speak the truth in love to me about my strengths and weaknesses and getting outside of myself by serving those in need, I am growing in my ability to receive grace and love and live through personal physical and relationship loss or internal loss of a self-image to be admired. The image I have created to build an ego, be successful, and protect myself from loss is melting away slowly. I am being transformed or saved from my fearful, prideful self.

I have lived through the death of my parents and grandparents and the loss of friends and communities of people I had come to love when we moved from Pittsburgh to New York City to Atlanta and then from our community here in Northern Virginia to a new community not so far geographically, but to new neighbors and from suburbia to the city. I know more loss is inevitable, but I have time for my trust in the goodness of life and of God's love to grow to sustain me.

Today, I was telling my spiritual director how easy it is to be diverted from my plans to pray and exercise regularly. She said to me, "Just sit still in God's presence for 20 minutes. Set a timer, and when the 20 minutes are up, know that the Spirit is working in you even if it doesn't seem like anything is different."

It takes a great deal of moral strength and commitment to sustain a life of faith in God in the face of the way the world is at present. A world that often measures success in terms of the accumulation of money and status. There are so many things that intrude on keeping a schedule of prayer and exercise. Faith isn't just a feeling; it takes work and commitment of the will, prayer, and, in my case, years of therapy to love and trust.

So, congratulations to us, the class of '65! We have survived life's challenges thus far, and no matter how many more days each of us has, we can choose to open our eyes and our hearts to gratitude and love today. We can choose to let go of our expectations of what we think life should bring and surrender control to God. Celebrating the life we have been given, embracing our limitations of failing eyesight, hearing, or mobility, for example.

As we honor our classmates who are no longer with us by placing a rose on the altar, remembering each one by name, let's commit ourselves to sprinkling fun and laughter in and among ourselves and experience the joy of being here together in spite of our losses and sorrows.

PHOTO GALLERY

Jean's mother as a young woman and Jean's stepfather, as a young Marine

Jean's maternal grandmother, Louise House, as a young woman

Norbert (Pop) Vogel, Jean's maternal stepfather and Louise House Vogel,
Jean's maternal grandmother

Anna (Dixon) Moore Scott, Jean's paternal grandmother

Jean, age 5 (right), and Aunt Karen, age 6, at Conneaut Lake, Pennsylvania

Jean on her wedding day, November 6, 1965.

Sean and Lani in 1972

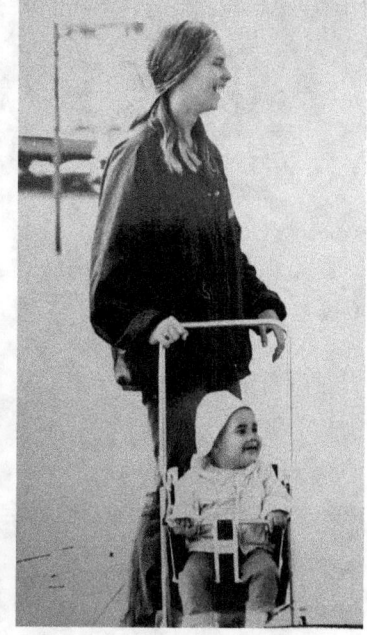

Jean with her son, Sean *Jean with her daughter, Lani*

235

Jean's ordination to the priesthood on December 6, 1980,
at St. Luke's Episcopal Church in Atlanta, Georgia

*Jean, officiant at the weekly healing service
at the Washington National Cathedral, Bethlehem Chapel, in 2005.*

Jean and Bill Milliken

Jean with her brother, Kurt, and sister, Linda

Lois and Andrew Kondas, Jean's mother and stepfather

Lani and Jean

Jean and Sean

*Jean's nuclear family—(back row) Jack, Alex, Sean, and Bill;
Jean, Lani, and Jill (front row)*

Jean and Bill

ABOUT THE AUTHOR

Jean Milliken's passion for a life-long commitment to learning and openness to seek what is universally true, inclusive of faith and doubt, and her curiosity about how one resolves some of life's important questions are explored in this memoir: "Where do I belong?" and "What early imprinting may no longer be helpful to my growth into a healthy human being?"

She explores the questions, "How does multigenerational divorce resulting in the loss of a father's guidance and blessing impact a child?" and "How does alcohol abuse affect the development of one's attitudes and behaviors?"

Jean also confronts the dilemma of how the language of faith currently spoken in religious institutions and the culture-bound translations of scripture limit the growth of our spiritual lives and divide us, creating a tribal mentality that stunts the development of mature faith.

Jean graduated from Westminster College, received her Master of Divinity Degree from Candler School of Theology at Emory University, and her Doctor of Ministry Degree from Wesley Theological Seminary in Washington, DC. She was one of the first women ordained in Atlanta in the Episcopal Church and was named a Canon at the Washington National Cathedral.

At the age of 50, at a time of transition, she journeyed into the wilderness with a group from Animus Valley Institute to seek a vision for herself and "her people." Her vision grew from her training as an Imago Relationship Therapist and her family legacy of broken marriages in her biological family. "Her people," she discovered, were those couples who wanted to explore whether their struggling relationship could be viable and those who wanted to learn how to build life-long partnerships and create a safe family environment for their children.

Dr. Milliken has served as a hospital chaplain, pastoral therapist, and associate in churches in Atlanta, Georgia; Arlington, Virginia; Alexandria, Virginia; and the Washington National Cathedral. She has been married to Bill for 59 years and is the mother of two children, Sean and Lani, mother-in-law to Jill, and grandmother to Alexandra and Jack.

ACKNOWLEDGMENTS

Words can't express my love and appreciation for the more than 60 years of learning and growing shared with my husband, Bill. Our valued friend, the late Burt Bacharach and co-writer Hal David, captured the mutuality of sustained love and commitment to our marriage in their song "The Story of My Life": *I feel that our love affair just may have been the story of my life.*

The birth of my grandchildren, now adults, began another kind of love affair that continues to challenge me as I watch them grow and learn from them. Becoming a grandmother is full of grace and fills my heart with gratitude

As I look back, I have immense gratitude, too, for those who have nurtured and challenged me in my journey of faith:

My Sunday School teachers at Hebron United Presbyterian Church in Penn Hills, Pennsylvania, taught me Bible stories about Jesus. The Young Life Staff in Pittsburgh and New York, the Faith at Work Board and Staff, especially Bruce Larson, Wally Howard, Heidi Frost Heard, Marjory Bankson, and my seminary professors, especially Don Saliers, Charles Gerkin, Carol Sassey, and clinical supervisors, Gerald Jenkins, Don Cabiness, Ed Nash, writer and retreat leader, Carolyn Myss, books written by Barbara Brown Taylor, my fellow student, peer in seminary, and priest colleague; my spiritual directors Sr. Patricia McDermott and Kathleen Curtin, the various church communities in which I have served as priest and counselor in Atlanta, Virginia, and the Washington National Cathedral.

Mentors and friends who have been and continue to be companions on the Way: Marjory and Peter Bankson Cathy Balzarett; Ann and John Gardner;

Marilyn Dimock; Karen Getman; Barbara and Mike Hattwick; Clarke and Edith Jones; Ann and Jeff Cramer and family; Jeanne, Patty Pflum, and Neil Shorthouse and family; Bo and Mary Nixon and family; Ruth and Burt Chamberlain and family; JD and Barbara Borgman and family; Dean and Sandy Borgman and family; the Irwin family; Jurena Hickerson and family; Nickie Shoemaker Rea Haggart; John and Diane McEntyre and family; Doris and Alan Reed; and the many young couples and single people who joined us for a while and enriched our lives during the years living in community in New York and Atlanta. Linda and Phil Lader; Larry and Vivian Houk; The Reverend Jonathan Bryan; and the members of the VIC weekly scripture study.

The women priest colleagues who gathered for our week at the beach: Nancy Baxter, Claiborne Jones, Camille Littleton Hague, Lori Lowe, Rachel Haynes, Eloise Halley, Margaret Rose, and Pat Merchant.

My writing coach, Dawn Montefusco, and my writing support group: Meg Halaska, Sally McGrew, Carol Dover, and Alicia Mundy.

I am grateful for my friends in the Artist Way group in Arlington, The Board and staff of Communities in Schools who have welcomed me into their lives and embraced and valued my role as Bill's companion and partner at home and on the road.

This memoir would never have seen the light of day without the editing and organizing help of Marjory Bankson, Marilyn McEntyre, Allison Gardner Fischer, Rebecca Ruest, and Mary Rembert. Thank you.

www.ingramcontent.com/pod-product-compliance
Lightning Source LLC
Chambersburg PA
CBHW060129130626
46556CB00006B/2281